A WORLD LIT ONLY BY FIRE

William Manchester's previous seventeen books, which have been translated into eighteen languages and Braille, include the bestselling *The Last Lion: Winston Spencer Churchill*, *The Death of a President* and *American Caesar*. He is adjunct professor of history and writer in residence at Wesleyan University, Middletown, Connecticut.

Books by William Manchester

Biography

DISTURBER OF THE PEACE: The Life of H. L. Mencken
A ROCKEFELLER FAMILY PORTRAIT: From John D. to Nelson
PORTRAIT OF A PRESIDENT: John F. Kennedy in Profile
AMERICAN CAESAR: Douglas MacArthur, 1880–1964
THE LAST LION: WINSTON SPENCER CHURCHILL; Visions of Glory:
1874–1932
THE LAST LION: WINSTON SPENCER CHURCHILL; Alone: 1932–1940

History

THE DEATH OF A PRESIDENT: November 20–November 25, 1963
THE ARMS OF KRUPP, 1587–1968
THE GLORY AND THE DREAM:
A Narrative History of America, 1932–1972
A WORLD LIT ONLY BY FIRE. The Medieval Mind and the Renaissance:
Portrait of An Age

Essays

CONTROVERSY: And Other Essays in Journalism, 1950–1975
IN OUR TIME

Fiction

THE CITY OF ANGER
SHADOW OF THE MONSOON
THE LONG GAINER

Diversion

BEARD THE LION

Memoirs

GOODBYE, DARKNESS: A Memoir of the Pacific War
ONE BRIEF SHINING MOMENT: Remembering Kennedy

A WORLD LIT ONLY BY FIRE

THE MEDIEVAL MIND AND THE RENAISSANCE

WILLIAM MANCHESTER

PAPERMAC

TO
TIM JOYNER

ATHLETE COMRADE SCHOLAR FRIEND

Eine Kugel kam geflogen:
Gilt es mir oder gilt es dir?
Ihn hat es weggerissen;
Er liegt mir vor den Füssen,
Als wärs ein Stück von mir.

First published 1992 by Little, Brown & Company, Boston, and simultaneously in Canada
by Little, Brown & Company (Canada) Limited, Toronto

First published in Great Britain 1993 by Macmillan London Limited

This Papermac edition published 1994 by Macmillan London Limited
a division of Pan Macmillan Publishers Limited
Cavaye Place London SW10 9PG
and Basingstoke

Associated companies throughout the world

ISBN 0-333-61347-3

1 3 5 7 9 8 6 4 2

A CIP catalogue record for this book is available from
the British Library

Printed and bound in Great Britain by
Mackays of Chatham PLC, Chatham, Kent

CONTENTS

LIST OF ILLUSTRATIONS

LIST OF MAPS

AUTHOR'S NOTE

COMPLETE AT LAST, this book is a source of pride, which is pleasant, though in this instance somewhat odd. It is, after all, a slight work, with no scholarly pretensions. All the sources are secondary, and few are new; I have not mastered recent scholarship on the early sixteenth century. This being true, I thought it wise to submit my final manuscript to scrutiny by those steeped in the period, or in certain aspects of it. For example, Dr. Timothy Joyner, Magellan's most recent biographer, examined the passages on Magellan. His emendations were many and were gratefully received. My greatest debt, however, is to James Boyden, an authority on the sixteenth century, who was a history professor at Yale when he began his examination of my text and had become a history professor at Tulane when he finished it. I have never known a more scrupulous review than his. His knowledge of the sixteenth century is both encyclopedic and profound. He challenged me — and rightly so — in virtually every passage of the work. Of course, that does not mean that he or anyone else with whom I consulted is in any way responsible for this volume. Indeed, Professor Boyden took exception to several of my interpretations. Obviously I, and I alone, am answerable for the result.

Another oddity of this book is that it was written, so to speak, inside out. Ordinarily a writer does not begin to put words on paper until he knows much he is going to say. Determining how to say it is the last step — the most taxing, to be sure, but one preceded by intricate preparations: conception, research, mastering material, structuring the work. Very rarely are the writing and reading experiences even remotely parallel, and almost never does a narrative unfold for the writer as it will later for those turning his pages. The fact that it happened this time makes the volume unique in my experience.

Actually, at the outset I had no intention of writing it at all. In the late summer of 1989, while toiling over another manuscript — the last volume of a biography of Winston Spencer Churchill — I fell ill. After several months in and out of hospitals, I emerged cured but feeble, too weak to cope with my vast accumulation of Churchill documents. Medical advice was to shelve that work temporarily and head south for a long convalescence. I took it.

The fact that I wasn't strong enough for Winston did not, however, mean I could not work. H. L. Mencken once observed that writing did for him what giving milk does for a cow. So it is for all natural writers. Putting words on paper is essential to their inner stability, even to their peace of mind. And as it happened, I had a small professional commitment to meet — providing an introduction to a friend's biography of Ferdinand Magellan. That manuscript was back in my Connecticut home and I was now in Florida, but the obstacle seemed small; I hadn't intended to write about Magellan anyhow. Instead, I had decided, I would provide the great navigator with context, a portrait of his age. It could be done, I thought, in several pages — a dozen at most.

I actually thought that.

I HAD MISCALCULATED because I had not realized how parochial my previous work had been. Virtually everything in my seventeen earlier books had been contemporaneous. Now, moving back nearly five centuries, I was entering an entirely different world, where there were no clocks, no police, virtually no communications; a time when men believed in magic and sorcery and slew those whose superstitions were different from, and therefore an affront to, their own.

The early sixteenth century was not entirely new to me. Its major figures, their wars, the Renaissance, the religious revolution, the voyages of exploration — with all these I had the general familiarity of an educated man. I could have drawn a reasonably accurate freehand map of Europe as it was then, provided I wasn't expected to get the borders of all the German states exactly right.

But I had no sense of the spirit of the time. Its idioms fell strangely on my ear. I didn't know enough to put myself back there — to see it, hear it, feel it, even smell it — and because I had never pondered the minutiae of that age, I had no grasp of the way the webs of action were spun out, how each event led inexorably to another, then another . . .

Yet I knew from experience that such chains of circumstance are always there, awaiting discovery. To cite a small, relatively recent example: In the first year of John F. Kennedy's presidential administration, four developments appeared to be unrelated — America's humiliation at the Bay of Pigs in April, Kennedy's confrontation with Nikita Khrushchev in Austria six weeks later, the raising of the Berlin Wall in August, and, in December, the first commitment of American ground troops to Indochina. Yet each event had led to the next. Khrushchev saw the Cuban fiasco as evidence that the young president was weak. Therefore he bullied him in Vienna. In the mistaken belief that he had intimidated him there, he built the Wall. Kennedy answered the challenge by sending four hundred Green Berets to Southeast Asia, explaining to those around him that "we have a problem making our power credible, and Vietnam looks like the place."

A subtler, more progressive catena may be found in nineteenth-century social history. In 1847 the old, slow, expensive flatbed press was rendered obsolete by Richard Hoe's high-speed rotary "lightning" press, first installed by the *Philadelphia Public Ledger.* Incorporating lithographic and letter-press features, some of which had been patented in France, Hoe went on to design and build a web press capable of printing — on both sides of a sheet at the same time — eighteen thousand sheets an hour. Vast supplies of cheap paper were required to feed these new presses. Ingenious Germans provided the answer in the 1850s: newsprint made from wood pulp. Now a literate public awaited them. W. E. Forster's Compulsory Education Act, passed by Parliament in 1870, was followed by similar legislation throughout western Europe and the United States. In 1858 only 5 percent of British army recruits could read and write; by the turn of the century the figure had risen to 85.4 percent. The 1880s had brought the institution of free libraries, which was followed by an explosion in journalism and the emergence of the twentieth-century mass culture which has transformed Western civilization.

Though the early 1500s offer a larger, much more chaotic canvas, perspective provides coherence there, too. The power of the Catholic Church was waning, reeling from the failure of the crusades, corruption in the Curia, debauchery in the Vatican, and the breakdown of monastic discipline. Even so, Martin Luther's revolt against Rome seemed hopeless until, abandoning the custom of publishing in Latin, he addressed the German people in their own language. This had two immense but unforeseen consequences. Because of the invention of printing and the increase in literacy throughout Europe, he reached a huge audience. At the same time, the new nationalism which was fueling the rising phenomenon of nation-states — soon to replace the fading Holy Roman Empire — led loyal Germans to support Luther for reasons that had nothing to do with religion. He won a historic victory, which was followed by similar success in England, where loyal Englishmen rallied to Henry VIII.

As each such concatenation came into focus, I came to a dead stop and began major revisions. Sometimes these entailed the shredding of all existing manuscript for a fresh start — an inefficient way to write a book, though I found it exciting. The period became a kind of kaleidoscope for me; every time I shook it, I saw a new picture. Of course, the images I saw, and describe in this work, cannot presume to universal validity. Another writer, peering into another kaleidoscope, would glimpse different views. In fact, that was precisely the experience of Henry Osborn Taylor. Finishing his two-volume work *The Mediaeval Mind* in January 1911, the pietistic Taylor was suffused with admiration for the medieval churches, the pageantry of the age, its romance, its "spiritual passion," and, above all, its interpretation of "Christ's Gospel." He explained candidly: "The present work is not occupied with the brutalities of mediaeval life, nor with all the lower grades of ignorance and superstition abounding in the Middle Ages. . . . Consequently I have not such things very actively in mind when speaking of the mediaeval genius. That phrase, and

the like, in this book, will signify the more informed and con-
structive spirit of the mediaeval time."

No matter how hard I shake my kaleidoscope, I cannot see
what he saw. One reason is that my approach is more catholic
than his. I share his conviction that "a realization of the power
and import of the Christian Faith is needed for an understanding
of the thoughts and feelings moving the men and women of the
Middle Ages, and for a just appreciation of their aspirations and
ideals," but I do not see how that can be achieved without a careful
study of brutality, ignorance, and delusions in the Middle Ages,
not just among the laity, but also at the highest Christian altars.
Christianity survived despite medieval Christians, not because of
them. Fail to grasp that, and you will never understand their
millennium.

Only after one has contemplated the age in its entirety do its
larger patterns emerge. Often these are surprising. For me the
most startling, and the culmination of my work, was a reappraisal
of the extraordinary Magellan, whose biography I had left in New
England. I had foolishly thought that the times in which he lived
would put him in context. Instead, I realized, Magellan was essential to a comprehension of his times — both a key to the period
and, in many ways, its apotheosis. How I reached that conclusion
is the story of this book.

W.M.

Middletown, Connecticut
December 1991

CHRONOLOGY

A.D. 410   Visigoths sack Rome

426   St. Augustine's *De civitate Dei*

476   Fall of Rome, end of Western
        Roman Empire

493   Barbarian Clovis accepts Christ

539   Arthur of Britain slain

800   Charlemagne crowned in St. Peter's

A.D. 1000   Leif Erikson reaches America

1100   200 years of crusades begin

1123   Future priests must be celibates

1215   Medieval papacy reaches culmination

1218–1224   Genghis Khan extends empire in west

1247   Robin Hood dies

1296   Marco Polo dictates memoirs

1347   First Black Death pandemic

1381   Oxford expels Wyclif

A.D. 1400   First stirrings of Renaissance

1414   Jan Hus betrayed

1433   Prince Henry the Navigator flourishes

1453   Constantinople falls

1458   Gutenberg's Bible

1475   Birth of Cesare, Cardinal Borgia's son

1477   *Canterbury Tales*

1478   Pope Sixtus IV conspires to slay
        Medicis during High Mass in
        Florence Cathedral

1480   Birth of Lucrezia, Cesare's sister

1486   Dias rounds the tip of Africa

1484   Pied Piper murders 130 German
        children

1485   *Le morte d'Arthur*

1487   Torquemada named Grand Inquisitor
        Star Chamber in England

1488   King James III of Scotland murdered

1490   Savonarola's first Bonfire of the
        Vanities

1492   Cardinal Borgia buys the papacy,
        becomes Pope Alexander VI
        Columbus discovers the Bahamas

1495   Vatican revels with naked prostitutes
        First syphilis outbreak ravages Naples

1497?   Amerigo Vespucci in the New World

1497   Lucrezia Borgia's triple incest
        The pope's eldest son, Juan,
        is murdered

1498   Manutius's five-volume Aristotle
        published
        Rise of humanism
        Savonarola burned at the stake
        Lucrezia gives birth to the
        Infans Romanus

A.D. 1500   Michelangelo: *Madonna and Child*

1501   Over 1,000 printing shops now in
        Europe
        Pope acknowledges paternity of his
        daughter's child

1502   All books challenging papal authority
        ordered burned

1503   Julius II: the Warrior Pope
        New universities include Wittenberg
        and Frankfurt an der Oder
        Leonardo da Vinci: *Mona Lisa*

1505   Death of Russia's Ivan the Great

1506   First stone of St. Peter's Basilica laid

I

THE MEDIEVAL MIND

THE DENSEST of the medieval centuries — the six hundred years between, roughly, A.D. 400 and A.D. 1000 — are still widely known as the Dark Ages. Modern historians have abandoned that phrase, one of them writes, "because of the unacceptable value judgment it implies." Yet there are no survivors to be offended. Nor is the term necessarily pejorative. Very little is clear about that dim era. Intellectual life had vanished from Europe. Even Charlemagne, the first Holy Roman emperor and the greatest of all medieval rulers, was illiterate. Indeed, throughout the Middle Ages, which lasted some seven centuries after Charlemagne, literacy was scorned; when a cardinal corrected the Latin of the emperor Sigismund, Charlemagne's forty-seventh successor, Sigismund rudely replied, "*Ego sum rex Romanus et super grammatica*" — as "king of Rome," he was "above grammar." Nevertheless, if value judgments are made, it is undeniable that most of what is known about the period is unlovely. After the extant fragments have been fitted together, the portrait which emerges is a mélange of incessant warfare, corruption, lawlessness, obsession with strange myths, and an almost impenetrable mindlessness.

Europe had been troubled since the Roman Empire perished in the fifth century. There were many reasons for Rome's fall, among them apathy and bureaucratic absolutism, but the chain of events leading to its actual end had begun the century before. The defenders of the empire were responsible for a ten-thousand-mile frontier. Ever since the time of the soldier-historian Tacitus, in the first century A.D., the vital sector in the north — where the realm's border rested on the Danube and the Rhine — had been vulnerable. Above these great rivers the forests swarmed with barbaric Germanic tribes, some of them tamer than others but all envious of the empire's prosperity. For centuries they had been intimidated by the imperial legions confronting them on the far banks.

Now they no longer were. They had panicked, stampeded by an even more fearsome enemy in their rear: feral packs of mounted Hsiung-nu, or Huns. Ignorant of agriculture but expert archers, bred to kill and trained from infancy to be pitiless, these dreaded warriors from the plains of Mongolia had turned war into an industry. "Their country," it was said of them, "is the back of a horse." It was Europe's misfortune that early in the fourth century the Huns had met their masters at China's Great Wall. Defeated by the Chinese, they had turned westward, entered Russia about A.D. 355, and crossed the Volga seventeen years later. In 375 they fell upon the Ostrogoths (East Goths) in the Ukraine. After killing the Ostrogoth chieftain, Ermanaric, they pursued his tribesmen across eastern Europe. An army of Visigoths (West Goths) met the advancing Huns on the Dniester, near what is now Romania. The Goths were cut to pieces. The survivors among them — some eighty thousand — fled toward the Danube and crossed it, thereby invading the empire. On instructions from the Emperor Valens, imperial commanders charged with defense of the frontier first disarmed the Gothic refugees, next admitted them subject to various conditions, then tried to enslave them, and finally, in A.D. 378, fought them, not with Roman legions, but using mercenaries recruited from other tribes. Caesar would have wept at the spectacle that followed. In battle the mercenaries were overconfident and slack; according to Ammianus Marcellinus, Tacitus's Greek successor, the result was "the most disastrous defeat encountered by the Romans since Cannae" — six centuries earlier.

Under the weight of relentless attacks by the combined barbaric tribes and the Huns, now Gothic allies, the Danube-Rhine line broke along its entire length and then collapsed. Plunging deeper and deeper into the empire, the invaders prepared to penetrate Italy. In 400 the Visigoth Alaric, a relatively enlightened chieftain and a zealous *religieux,* led forty thousand Goths, Huns, and freed Roman slaves across the Julian Alps. Eight years of fighting followed. Rome's cavalry was no match for the tribal horsemen; two-thirds of the imperial legions were slain. In 410 Alaric's triumphant warriors swept down to Rome itself, and on August 24 they entered it. Thus, for the first time in eight centuries, the Eternal City fell to an enemy army. After three days of pillage it was battered almost beyond recognition. Alaric tried to spare Rome's citizens, but he could not control the Huns or the former slaves. They slaughtered wealthy men, raped women, destroyed priceless pieces of sculpture, and melted down works of art for their precious metals. That was only the beginning; sixty-six years later another Germanic chieftain deposed the last Roman emperor in the west, Romulus Augustulus, and proclaimed himself ruler of the empire. Meantime Gunderic's Vandals, Clovis's Franks, and most of all the Huns under their terrible new chieftain Attila — who had seized power by murdering his brother — ravaged Gaul as far south as Paris, paused, and lunged into Spain. In the years that followed, Goths, Alans, Burgundians, Thuringians, Frisians, Gepidae, Suevi, Alemanni, Angles, Saxons, Jutes, Lombards, Heruli, Quadi, and Magyars joined them in ravaging what was left of civilization. The ethnic tide then settled in its conquered lands and darkness descended upon the devastated, unstable continent. It would not lift until forty medieval generations had suffered, wrought their pathetic destinies, and passed on.

THE DARK AGES were stark in every dimension. Famines and plague, culminating in the Black Death and its recurring pandemics, repeatedly thinned the population. Rickets afflicted the survivors. Extraordinary climatic changes brought storms and floods which turned into major disasters because the empire's drainage system, like most of the imperial infrastructure, was no longer functioning. It says much about the Middle Ages that in the year 1500, after a thousand years of neglect, the roads built by the Romans were still the best on the continent. Most others were in such a state of disrepair that they were unusable; so were all European harbors until the eighth century, when commerce again began to stir. Among the lost arts was bricklaying; in all of Germany, England, Holland, and Scandinavia, virtually no stone buildings, except cathedrals, were raised for ten centuries. The serfs' basic agricultural tools were picks, forks, spades, rakes, scythes, and balanced sickles. Because there was very little iron, there were no wheeled plowshares with moldboards. The lack of plows was not a major problem in the south, where farmers could pulverize light Mediterranean soils, but the heavier earth in northern Europe had to be sliced, moved, and turned by hand. Although horses and oxen were available, they were of limited use. The horse collar, harness, and stirrup did not exist until about A.D. 900. Therefore tandem hitching was impossible. Peasants labored harder, sweated more, and collapsed from exhaustion more often than their animals.

Surrounding them was the vast, menacing, and at places impassable, Hercynian Forest, infested by boars; by bears; by the hulking medieval wolves who lurk so fearsomely in fairy tales handed down from that time; by imaginary demons; and by very real outlaws, who flourished because they were seldom pursued. Although homicides were twice as frequent as deaths by accident, English coroners' records show that only one of every hundred murderers was ever brought to justice. Moreover, abduction for ransom was an acceptable means of livelihood for skilled but landless knights. One consequence of medieval peril was that people huddled closely together in communal homes. They married fellow villagers and were so insular that local dialects were often incomprehensible to men living only a few miles away.

The level of everyday violence — deaths in alehouse brawls, during bouts with staves, or even in playing football or wrestling — was shocking. Tournaments were very different from the romantic descriptions in Malory, Scott, and Conan Doyle. They were vicious sham battles by large bands of armed knights, ostensibly gatherings for enjoyment and exercise but really occasions for abduction and mayhem. As late as the year 1240, in a tourney near Düsseldorf, sixty knights were hacked to death.

Despite their bloodthirstiness — a taste which may have been acquired from the Huns, Goths, Franks, and Saxons — all were devout Christians. It was a paradox: the Church had replaced imperial Rome as the fixer of European frontiers, but missionaries found teaching pagans the lessons of Jesus to be an almost hopeless task. Yet converting them was easy. As quickly as the barbaric tribes had overrun the empire, Catholicism's overrunning of the tribesmen was even quicker. As early as A.D. 493 the Frankish chieftain Clovis accepted the divinity of Christ and was baptized, though a modern priest would have found his manner of championing the Church difficult to understand or even forgive. Fortunately Clovis was accompanied by a contemporary, Bishop Gregory of Tours. The bishop made allowances for the violent streak in the Frankish character. In his writings Gregory portrayed his protégé as a heroic general whose triumphs were attributable to divine guidance. He proudly set down an account of how the chief dealt with a Frankish warrior who, during a division of tribal booty at Soissons, had wantonly swung his ax and smashed a vase. As it happened, the broken pottery had been Church property and much cherished by the bishop. Clovis knew that. Later, picking his moment, he split the warrior's skull with his own ax, yelling, "Thus you treated the vase at Soissons!"

Medieval Christians, knowing the other cheek would be bloodied, did not turn it. Death was the prescribed penalty for hundreds of offenses, particularly those against property. The threat of capital punishment was even used in religious conversions, and medieval threats were never idle. Charlemagne was a just and enlightened ruler — for the times. His loyalty to the Church was absolute, though he sometimes chose peculiar ways to demonstrate it. Conquering Saxon rebels, he gave them a choice between baptism and immediate execution; when they demurred, he had forty-five hundred of them beheaded in one morning.

That was not remarkable. Soldiers of Christ swung their swords freely. And the victims were not always pagans. Every flourishing religion has been intermittently watered by the blood of its own faithful, but none has seen more spectacular internecine butchery than Christianity. In A.D. 330 Constantine I, the first Roman emperor to recognize Jesus as his savior, made Constantinople the empire's second capital. Within a few years, a great many people who shared his faith began to die there for their interpretation of it. The emperor's first Council of Nicaea failed to resolve a doctrinal dispute between Arius of Alexandria and the dominant faction of theologians. Arius rejected the Nicene Creed, taking the unitarian position that although Christ was the son of God, he was not divine. Attempts at compromise foundered; Arius died, condemned as a heresiarch; his Arians rioted and were put to the sword. Over three thousand Christians thus died at the hands of fellow Christians — more than all the victims in three centuries of Roman persecutions. On April 13, 1204, nearly nine centuries later, medieval horror returned to Constantinople when the armies of the Fourth Crusade, embittered by their failure to reach the Holy Land, turned on the city, sacked it, destroyed sacred relics, and massacred the inhabitants.

CHRIST'S missionary commandment had been clearly set forth in Matthew (28:19–20), but in the early centuries after his crucifixion the flame of faith flickered low. Wholesale conversions of Germans, Celts, and Slavs did not begin until about A.D. 500, after Christianity had been firmly established as the state religion of the Roman Empire. Its victories were deceptive; few of its converts understood their new faith. Paganism — Stoicism, Neoplatonism, Cynicism, Mithraism, and local cults — continued to be deeply entrenched, not only in the barbaric tribes, but also among the Sophists, teachers of wisdom in the old imperial cities: Athens, Alexandria, Smyrna, Antioch, and Rome itself, which was the city of Caesar as well as Saint Peter. Constantine had tried to discourage pagan ceremonies and sacrifices, but he had not outlawed them, and they continued to flourish.

This infuriated the followers of Jesus. They were split on countless issues — Arianism, which was one of them, flourished for over half a century — but united in their determination to raze the temples of the pagans, confiscate their property, and subject them to the same official persecutions Christians had endured in the catacombs, including the feeding of martyrs to lions. This vindictiveness seems an incongruity, inconsistent with the Gospels. But medieval Christianity had more in common with paganism than its worshipers would acknowledge. The apostles Paul and John had been profoundly influenced by Neoplatonism. Of the seven cardinal virtues named by Pope Gregory I in the sixth century, only three were Christian — faith, hope, and charity — while the other four — wisdom, justice, courage, and temperance — were adopted from the pagans Plato and Pythagoras. Pagan philosophers argued that the Gospels contradicted each other, which they do, and pointed out that Genesis assumes a

plurality of gods. The devout scorned reason, however. Saint
Bernard of Clairvaux (1090–1153), the most influential Christian
of his time, bore a deep distrust of the intellect and declared that
the pursuit of knowledge, unless sanctified by a holy mission, was
a pagan act and therefore vile.

Ironically, the masterwork of Christianity's most powerful medieval philosopher was inspired by a false report. Alaric's sack of
Rome, it was said, had been the act of a barbaric pagan seeking
vengeance for his idols. (This was inaccurate; actually, Alaric and
a majority of his Visigoths were Arian Christians.) Even so, the
followers of Jesus were widely blamed for bringing about Rome's
fall; men charged that the ancient gods, offended by the empire's
formal adoption of the new faith, had withdrawn their protection
from the Eternal City. One Catholic prelate, the bishop of
Hippo — Aurelius Augustinus, later Saint Augustine — felt challenged. He devoted thirteen years to writing his response, *De
civitate Dei* (*The City of God*), the first great work to shape and
define the medieval mind. Augustine (354–430) began by declaring
that Rome was being punished, not for her new faith, but for her
old, continuing sins: lascivious acts by the populace and corruption
among politicians. The pagan deities, he wrote, had lewdly urged
Romans to yield to sexual passion — "the god Virgineus to loose
the virgin's girdle, Subigus to put her beneath a man's loins, Prema
to hold her down . . . Priapus upon whose huge and beastly member the new bride was commanded by religious order to stir and
receive!"

Here Augustine, by his own account, spoke from personal
experience. In his *Confessions* he had described how, before his
conversion, he had devoted his youth to exploring the outer limits
of carnal depravity. But, he wrote, the original sin, and he now
declared that there was such a thing, had been committed by Adam
when he yielded to Eve's temptations. As children of Adam, he
held, all mankind shared Adam's guilt. Lust polluted every child
in the very act of conception — sexual intercourse was a "mass
of perdition [*exitium*]." However, although most people were
thereby damned in the womb, some could be saved by the blessed
intervention of the Virgin Mary, who possessed that power because she had conceived Christ sinlessly: "Through a woman we

were sent to destruction; through a woman salvation was restored to us." He thus drew a sharp line. The chief distinction between the old faiths and the new were in the sexual arena. Pagans had accepted prostitution as a relief from monogamy. Worshipers of Jesus vehemently rejected it, demanding instead purity, chastity, and absolute fidelity in husbands and wives. Women found this ringing affirmation enormously appealing. Aurelius Augustinus — whose influence on Christianity would be greater than that of any other man except the apostle Paul — was the first to teach medieval men that sex was evil, and that salvation was possible only through the intercession of the Madonna.

But there were subtler registers to Augustine's mind. In his most complex metaphor, he divided all creation into *civitas Dei* and *civitas terrena*. Everyone had to embrace one of them, and a man's choice would determine where he spent eternity. In chapter fifteen he explained: "Mankind [*hominum*] is divided into two sorts: such as live according to man, and such as live according to God. These we mystically call the 'two cities' or societies, the one predestined to reign eternally with God, the other condemned to perpetual torment with Satan." Individuals, he wrote, would slip back and forth between the two cities; their fate would be decided at the Last Judgment. Because he had identified the Church with his *civitas Dei*, Augustine clearly implied the need for a theocracy, a state in which secular power, symbolizing *civitas terrena*, would be subordinate to spiritual powers derived from God. The Church, drawing the inference, thereafter used Augustine's reasoning as an ideological tool and, ultimately, as a weapon in grappling with kings and emperors.

THE HOLY SEE's struggle with Europe's increasingly powerful crowned heads became one of the most protracted in history. When Augustine finished his great work in 426, Celestine I was pope. In 1076 — over a hundred pontiffs later — the issue was still unresolved. Holy Fathers in the Vatican, near Nero's old Circus, were still fighting Holy Roman emperors, trying to end the prerogative of lay rulers to invest prelates with authority. An exasperated Gregory VII, resorting to his ultimate sanction, excommunicated Emperor Henry IV. That literally brought Henry to his knees. He begged for absolution and was granted it only after he had spent three days and nights prostrate in the snows of Canossa, outside the papal castle in northern Italy. Canossa became a symbol of secular submission, but improperly so; the emperor's contrition was short-lived. Changing his mind, he renewed his attack, and, undeterred by a second excommunication, drove Gregory from Rome. Bitterly the pontiff wrote, *"Dilexi justitiam et odi iniquitatem; propterea morior in exilio"* — because he had "loved justice and hated iniquity" he would "die in exile." Another century passed before the papacy wrested independence from the imperial courts in Germany. Even then conflicts remained, and they were not fully resolved until early in the thirteenth century, when Innocent III brought the Church to the height of its prestige and power.

Nevertheless the entire medieval millennium took on the aspect of triumphant Christendom. As aristocracies arose from the barbaric mire, kings and princes owed their legitimacy to divine authority, and squires became knights by praying all night at Christian altars. Sovereigns courting popularity led crusades to the Holy Land. To eat meat during Lent became a capital offense, sacrilege meant imprisonment, the Church became the wealthiest landowner on the Continent, and the life of every European, from baptism through matrimony to burial, was governed by popes, cardinals, prelates, monsignors, archbishops, bishops, and village priests. The clergy, it was believed, would also cast decisive votes in determining where each soul would spend the afterlife.

And yet . . .

The crafty but benevolent pagan gods — whose caprice and intransigence existed only in the imagination of Christian theologians eager to discredit them — survived all this. Imperial Rome having yielded to barbarians, and then barbarism to Christianity, Christianity was in turn infiltrated, and to a considerable extent subverted, by the paganism it was supposed to destroy. Medieval men simply could not bear to part with Thor, Hermes, Zeus, Juno, Cronus, Saturn, and their peers. Idol worship addressed needs the Church could not meet. Its rituals, myths, legends, marvels, and miracles were peculiarly suited to people who, living in the trackless fen and impenetrable forest, were always vulnerable to random disaster. Moreover, its creeds had never held, as the Augustinians did, that procreation was evil; pagans celebrating Aphrodite, Eros, Hymen, Cupid, and Venus could rejoice in lust. Thus the allegiance of converts was divided. Few saw any inconsistency or double-dealing in it. Hedging bets seemed only sensible. After all, it was just possible that Rome *had* fallen because the pagan deities had turned away from the city whose emperors no longer recognized them. What harm could come from paying token tribute to their ancient dignity? If people went to Mass and followed the commandments, there would be no retaliation from new worshipers of the savior, with their commitments to humility, mercy, tenderness, and kindness. The old genies, on the other hand, had never forgiven anyone anything, and as the Greeks had noted, the dice of the gods were always loaded.

So Christian churches were built on the foundations of pagan temples, and the names of biblical saints were given to groves which had been considered sacred centuries before the birth of Jesus. Pagan holidays still enjoyed wide popularity; therefore the Church expropriated them. Pentecost supplanted the Floralia, All Souls' Day replaced a festival for the dead, the feast of the purification of Isis and the Roman Lupercalia were transformed into the Feast of the Nativity. The Saturnalia, when even slaves had enjoyed great liberty, became Christmas; the resurrection of Attis, Easter. There was a lot of legerdemain in this. No one then knew the year Christ was born — it was probably 5 B.C. — let alone the date. Sometime in A.D. 336 Roman Christians first observed his birthday. The Eastern Roman Empire picked January 6 as the day, but later in the same century December 25 was adopted, apparently at random. The date of his resurrection was also unrecorded. The early Christians, believing that their lord's return was imminent, celebrated Easter every Sunday. After three hundred years their descendants became reconciled to a delay. In an attempt to link Easter with the Passion, it was scheduled on Passover, the Jewish feast observing the Exodus from Egypt in the thirteenth century B.C. Finally, in A.D. 325, after long and bitter controversy, the First Council of Nicaea settled on the first Sunday after the full moon following the spring equinox. The decision had no historical validity, but neither did the event, and it comforted those who cherished traditional holidays.

As mass baptisms swelled its congregations, the Church further indulged the converts by condoning ancient rites, or attempting to transform them, in the hope — never realized — that they would die out. Fertility rituals and augury were sanctioned; so was the sacrifice of cattle. After the pagan sacrifice of humans was replaced by Christianity's symbolic Mass, the ceremonial performance of the sacraments became of paramount importance. Christian priests, like the pagan priests before them, also blessed harvests and homes. They even asked omnipotent God to spare communities from fire, plague, and enemy invasions. This was tempting fate, however, and medieval fate never resisted temptation for long. In time the flames, diseases, and invaders came anyway, invariably followed by outbreaks of anticlericalism, or even back-sliding into such extravagant sects as the flagellants, who appeared recurrently in the wake of the Black Death. Nevertheless the traffic in holy relics, to which supernatural powers were attributed, never slackened, and Christian miracle stories continued to attribute pagan qualities to saints.

Neither Jesus nor his disciples had mentioned sainthood. The designation of saints emerged during the second and third centuries after Christ, with the Roman persecution of Christians. The survivors of the catacombs believed those who had been martyred had been received directly into heaven and, being there, could intercede for the living. They revered them as saints, but they never venerated idols of them. All the early Christians had despised idolatry, reserving special scorn for sculptures representing pagan gods. Typically, Clement of Alexandria (A.D. 150?–220?), a theologian and teacher, declared that it was sacrilege to adulate that which is created, rather than the creator. However, as the number of saints grew, so did the medieval yearning to give them identity; worshipers wanted pictures of them, images of the Madonna, and replicas of Christ on the cross. Statues of Horus, the Egyptian sky god, and Isis, the goddess of royalty, were rechristened Jesus and Mary. Craftsmen turned out other images and pictures to meet the demands of Christians who kissed them, prostrated themselves before them, and adorned them with flowers. Incense was introduced in Christian church services around 500, followed by the burning of candles. Each medieval community, in times of crisis, evoked the supposed potency of its patron saint, or of the relics it possessed.

Augustine deplored the adoration of saints, but priests and parishioners alike believed that the devil could be driven away by invoking their powers, or by making the sign of the cross. Medieval astrologers and magicians flourished. Clearly all this met a deep human need, but thoughtful men were troubled. Reaction came in the eighth century. Leo III, the deeply pious Byzantine emperor, believed it his imperial duty to defend true Christianity against all who would desecrate it. To him the adoption of pagan ways was sacrilege, and he was particularly offended by the veneration of relics and religious pictures during the celebration of Mass. After citing Deuteronomy 4:16 — which forbids worship of any "graven image" or "the similitude of any figure, the likeness of male or female" — he issued a draconian edict in 726. On his orders, soldiers were to remove all icons and representations of Jesus and Mary from churches. All murals, frescoes, and mosaics were to be plastered over.

This made Leo history's most celebrated iconoclast. It also enraged his subjects. In the Cyclades Islands they rebelled. In Venice and Ravenna they drove out imperial authorities. In Greece they elected an antiemperor and sent a fleet to capture Leo. He sank the fleet, but when his troops tried to enforce the edict, they were attacked at church doors by outraged mobs. Undeterred, in 730 the emperor proclaimed iconoclasm the official policy of the empire. But then the Church intervened. The lower clergy had opposed image breaking from its outset. They were joined by prelates, then by the patriarch of Constantinople, and, finally, by a council of bishops called by Pope Gregory II. Enforcing Leo's edict proved impossible anyway. At his death in 741 most of the art he had ordered destroyed or covered up was untouched, and forty-six years later, when the Second Council of Nicaea met, the Church formally abandoned his policy. After all, Rome was also the old imperial stronghold of a romantic polytheism whose local deities, now renamed for saints, were cloaked in myth and legend.

Since the fourth century, Christian art there had reflected that heritage. The form, construction, and columnar basilican style of the original St. Peter's basilica, built between 330 and 360, were all in the pagan tradition. And nearby Santa Maria Maggiore, begun by Pope Sixtus III in 432, was actually the site of a former pagan temple.

WAS THE MEDIEVAL WORLD a civilization, comparable to Rome before it or to the modern era which followed? If by civilization one means a society which has reached a relatively high level of cultural and technological development, the answer is no. During the Roman millennium imperial authorities had controlled the destinies of all the lands within the empire — from the Atlantic in the west to the Caspian Sea in the east, from the Antonine Wall in northern Britain to the upper Nile valley in the south. Enlightened Romans had served as teachers, lawgivers, builders, and administrators; Romans had reached towering pinnacles of artistic and intellectual achievement; their city had become the physical and spiritual capital of the Roman Catholic Church.

The age which succeeded it accomplished none of these. Trade on the Mediterranean, once a Roman lake, was perilous; Vandal pirates, and then Muslim pirates, lay athwart the vital sea routes. Agriculture and transport were inefficient; the population was never fed adequately. A barter economy yielded to coinage only because the dominant lords, enriched by plunder and conquest, needed some form of currency to pay for wars, ransoms, their departure on crusades, the knighting of their sons, and their daughters' marriages. Royal treasury officials were so deficient in elementary skills that they were dependent upon arithmetic learned from the Arabs; the name exchequer emerged because they used a checkered cloth as a kind of abacus in doing sums. If their society was diverse and colorful, it was also anarchic, formless, and appallingly unjust.

Nevertheless it possessed its own structure and peculiar institutions, which evolved almost imperceptibly over the centuries. Medievalism was born in the decaying ruins of a senile and impotent empire; it died just as Europe was emerging as a distinctive cultural unit. The interregnum was the worst of times for the imaginative, the cerebral, and the unfortunate, but the strong, the healthy, the shrewd, the handsome, the beautiful — and the lucky — flourished.

Europe was ruled by a new aristocracy: the noble, and, ultimately, the regal. After the barbarian tribes had overwhelmed the Roman Empire, men had established themselves as members of the new privileged classes in various ways. Any leader with a large following of free men was eligible, though some had greater followings, and therefore greater claims, than others. In Italy some were members of Roman senatorial families, survivors who had intermarried with Goths or Huns; as Ovid had observed, a barbarian was suitable if he was rich. Others in the patriciate were landowners whose huge domains (*latifundia*) were worked by slaves and protected by private armies of *bucellaeii*. In England and France the privileged might be descendants of Angle, Saxon, Frank, Vandal, or Ostrogoth chieftains. Many German hierarchs belonged to very old families, revered since time immemorial, and therefore acceptable to the other princes — the *Reichsfürstenstand* — who had to approve each ennoblement. Because this was a time of incessant warfare, however, most noblemen had risen by distinguishing themselves in battle. In the early centuries distinction ended with the death of the man who had won it, but patrilineal descent became increasingly common, creating dynasties.

Titles evolved: duke, from the Latin *dux,* meaning a military commander; earl, from the Anglo-Saxon *eorla* or *cheorl* (as distinguished from *churl*); count or comte, from the Latin *comes,* a companion of a great personage; baron, from the Teutonic *beron,* a warrior; margrave, from the Dutch *markgraaf;* and marquess, marquis, *markis, marques, marqués,* or *marchese,* from the Latin *marca* — literally a frontier, or frontier territory. Serving these, on the lowest rung of the aristocratic ladder, was the knight (French *chevalier,* German *Ritter,* Italian *cavaliere,* Spanish *caballero,* Portuguese *cavalheiro*). Originally the word meant a farm worker of free birth. By the eleventh century knights were cavalrymen living in fortified mansions, each with his noble seal. All were guided, in theory at least, by an idealistic knightly code and bound by oath to serve a

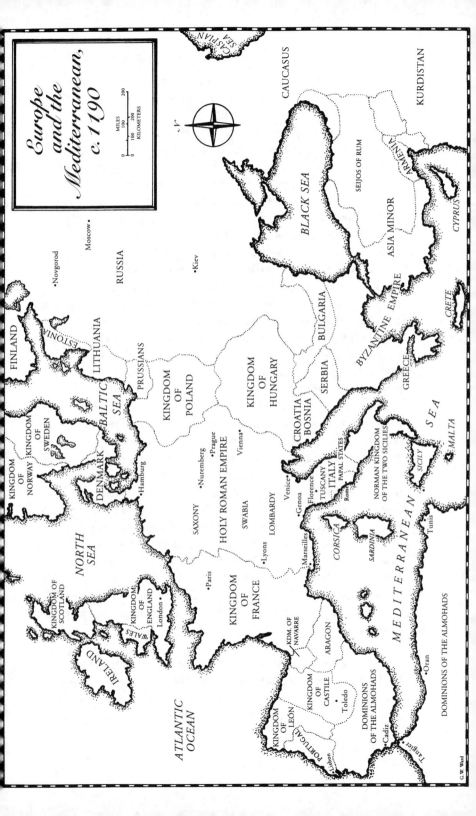

Europe
and the
Mediterranean, c.1190

MILES
0   100   200
0   100   200
KILOMETERS

N

ATLANTIC
OCEAN

IRELAND

KINGDOM
OF
SCOTLAND

KINGDOM
OF
ENGLAND
London •

WALES

KINGDOM OF NORWAY

KINGDOM
OF
SWEDEN

FINLAND

ESTONIA

LITHUANIA

NORTH
SEA

BALTIC
SEA

DENMARK
Hamburg •

SAXONY

Nuremberg •
HOLY ROMAN EMPIRE
SWABIA

Prague •
Vienna •

PRUSSIANS

KINGDOM
OF
POLAND

• Novgorod

Moscow •

RUSSIA

• Kiev

KINGDOM
OF
HUNGARY

CROATIA
BOSNIA

SERBIA

BULGARIA

CAUCASUS

CASPIAN
SEA

KURDISTAN

BLACK SEA

SELJUQS OF RUM

ASIA MINOR

ARMENIA

CYPRUS

BYZANTINE EMPIRE

GREECE

CRETE

KINGDOM
OF
FRANCE

Paris •

LOMBARDY

Lyons •

Marseilles •

Venice •
Genoa •

Florence •
TUSCANY
ITALY
PAPAL STATES
Rome •

CORSICA

SARDINIA

NORMAN KINGDOM
OF THE TWO SICILIES

SICILY

MALTA

MEDITERRANEAN
SEA

Tunis •

KDM. OF NAVARRE

ARAGON

KINGDOM
OF
CASTILE
Toledo •

KINGDOM
OF
LEÓN

PORTUGAL

Lisbon •
Cadiz •

Tangier •

Oran •

DOMINIONS OF THE ALMOHADS

DOMINIONS OF THE ALMOHADS

G. W. Ward

duke, earl, count, baron, or marquis who, in turn, periodically honored him with gifts: horses, falcons, even weapons.

ROYALTY WAS invested with glory, swathed in mystique, and clothed with magical powers. To be a king was to be a lord of men, a host at great feasts for his vassal dukes, earls, counts, barons, and marquises; a giver of rings, of gold, of landed estates. Because the first medieval rulers had been barbarians, most of what followed derived from their customs. Chieftains like Ermanaric, Alaric, Attila, and Clovis rose as successful battlefield leaders whose fighting skills promised still more triumphs to come. Each had been chosen by his warriors, who, after raising him on their shields, had carried him to a pagan temple or a sacred stone and acclaimed him there. In the first century Tacitus had noted that the chiefs' favored lieutenants were the *gasindi* or *comitatus* — future nobles — whose supreme virtue was absolute loyalty to the chief. Lesser tribesmen were grateful to him for the spoils of victory, though his claim on their allegiance also had supernatural roots.

His retinue always included pagan priests — sometimes he himself was one — and he was believed to be either favored by the gods or descended from them. When Christian missionaries converted a chieftain, his men obediently followed him to the baptismal font. Christian priests then enthroned his successors. A bishop's investiture of a Frankish chief was recorded in the fifth century, and by 754, when Pope Stephen II consecrated the new king of the Franks — Pepin the Short, Charlemagne's father — impressive ceremonies and symbols had been designed. The liturgy drew Old Testament precedents from Solomon and Saul; Pepin was crowned and solemnly armed with a royal scepter. The Holy Father exacted promises from him that he would defend the Church, the poor, the weak, and the defenseless; he then proclaimed him anointed of the Lord.

Hereditary monarchy, like hereditary nobility, was largely a medieval innovation. It is true that some barbarian lieutenants had held office by descent rather than deed. But the chieftains had been chosen for merit, and early kings wore crowns only *ad vitam aut culpam* — for life or until removed for fault. Because the papacy opposed primogeniture, secular leaders tried to maintain the fiction that sovereigns were elected — during the Capetian dynasty court etiquette required that all references to the king of France mention that he had been chosen by his subjects, when in fact son succeeded father in unbroken descent for 329 years — but by the end of the Middle Ages, this pretense had been abandoned. In England, France, and Spain the succession rights of royal princes had become absolute. After 1356 only Holy Roman emperors were elected (by seven carefully designated electors), and then only because the Vatican was in a position to insist on it, the office being within the Christian community, or *ecclesia*. Even so, beginning in 1437 the Habsburg family had a stranglehold on the imperial title.

The conspicuous sacerdotal role in the crowning of kings, who then claimed that they ruled by divine right, was characteristic of Christianity's domination of medieval Europe. Proclamations from the Holy See — called bulls because of the *bulla*, a leaden seal which made them official — were recognized in royal courts. So were canon (ecclesiastical) law and the rulings of the Curia, the Church's central bureaucracy in Rome. Strong sovereigns continued to seek freedom from the Vatican, with varying success; in the twelfth century, the quarrels between England's Henry II and the archbishop of Canterbury ended with the archbishop's murder, and the Holy Roman emperor Frederick Barbarossa ("Redbeard"), battling to establish German predominance in western Europe, was in open conflict with a series of popes.

However, the greatest wound to the prestige of the Vatican was self-inflicted. In 1305 Pope Clement V, alarmed by Italian disorders and a campaign to outlaw the Catholic Knights Templars, moved the papacy to Avignon, in what is now southeastern France. There it remained for seven pontificates, despite appeals from such figures as Petrarch and Saint Catherine of Siena. By 1377, when Pope Gregory XI returned the Holy See to Rome, the College of Cardinals was dominated by Frenchmen. After Gregory's death the following year the sacred college was hopelessly split. A majority wanted a French pontiff; a minority, backed by the Roman mob, demanded an Italian. Intimidated, the college capitulated to the rabble and elected Bartolomeo Prignano of Naples. French dissidents fled home and chose one of their own, with

the consequence that for nearly forty years Christendom was ruled
by two Vicars of Christ, a pope in Rome and an antipope in
Avignon.

                              ◈

IN ANOTHER AGE, so shocking a split would have created a crisis
among the faithful, but there was no room in the medieval mind
for doubt; the possibility of skepticism simply did not exist. *Kath-
olikos,* Greek for "universal," had been used by theologians since
the second century to distinguish Christianity from other religions.
In A.D. 340 Saint Cyril of Jerusalem had reasoned that what all
men believe must be true, and ever since then the purity of the
faith had derived from its wholeness, from the conviction, as
expressed by an early Jesuit, that all who worshiped were united
in "one sacramental system under the government of the Roman
Pontiff." Anyone not a member of the Church was to be cast out
of this life, and more important, out of the next. It was consign-
ment to the worst fate imaginable, like being exiled from an ancient
German tribe — "to be given forth," in the pagan Teutonic
phrase, "to be a wolf in holy places." The faithless were doomed;
the Fifth Lateran Council (1512–1517) reaffirmed Saint Cyprian's
third-century dictum: *"Nulla salus extra ecclesiam"* — "Outside the
Church there is no salvation." Any other finding would have been
inconceivable.

Catholicism had thus found its greatest strength in total resistance to change. Saint Jean Baptiste de la Salle, in his *Les devoirs
d'un Chrétien (Duties of a Christian,* 1703), defined Catholicism as
"the society of the faithful collected into one and the same body,
governed by its legitimate pastors, of whom Jesus Christ is the
invisible head — the pope, the successor of Saint Peter, being his
representative on earth." Saint Vincent of Lérins had written in
his *Commonitoria (Memoranda,* c. 430) that the Church had become
"a faithful and ever watchful guardian of the dogmas which have
been committed to her charge. In this secret deposit she changes
nothing, she takes nothing from it, she adds nothing to it."

Subsequent spokesmen for the Holy See enlarged upon this,
assuming, in God's name, the right to prohibit changes by
those who worshiped elsewhere or nowhere. Overstating this
absolutism is impossible. "The Catholic Church holds it better,"

wrote a Roman theologian, "that the entire population of the world should die of starvation in extremest agony . . . than that one soul, I will not say should be lost, but should commit one single venial sin." In the words of one pope, "The Church is independent of any earthly power, not merely in regard to her lawful end and purpose, but also in regard to whatever means she may deem suitable and necessary to attain them." Another pope, agreeing, declared that God had made the Vatican "a sharer in the divine magistracy, and granted her, by special privilege, immunity from error." Even to "appeal from the living voice of the Church" was "a treason," wrote a cardinal, "because that living voice is supreme; and to appeal from that supreme voice is also a heresy, because that voice, by divine assistance, is infallible." A fellow cardinal put it even more clearly: "The Church is not susceptible of being reformed in her doctrines. The Church is the work of an Incarnate God. Like all God's works, it is perfect. It is, therefore, incapable of reform."

THE MOST BAFFLING, elusive, yet in many ways the most significant dimensions of the medieval mind were invisible and silent. One was the medieval man's total lack of ego. Even those with creative powers had no sense of self. Each of the great soaring medieval cathedrals, our most treasured legacy from that age, required three or four centuries to complete. Canterbury was twenty-three generations in the making; Chartres, a former Druidic center, eighteen generations. Yet we know nothing of the architects or builders. They were glorifying God. To them their identity in this life was irrelevant. Noblemen had surnames, but fewer than one percent of the souls in Christendom were wellborn. Typically, the rest — nearly 60 million Europeans — were known as Hans, Jacques, Sal, Carlos, Will, or Will's wife, Will's son, or Will's daughter. If that was inadequate or confusing, a nickname would do. Because most peasants lived and died without leaving their birthplace, there was seldom need for any tag beyond One-Eye, or Roussie (Redhead), or Bionda (Blondie), or the like.

Their villages were frequently innominate for the same reason. If war took a man even a short distance from a nameless hamlet, the chances of his returning to it were slight; he could not identify it, and finding his way back alone was virtually impossible. Each hamlet was inbred, isolated, unaware of the world beyond the most familiar local landmark: a creek, or mill, or tall tree scarred by lightning. There were no newspapers or magazines to inform the common people of great events; occasional pamphlets might reach them, but they were usually theological and, like the Bible, were always published in Latin, a language they no longer understood. Between 1378 and 1417, Popes Clement VII and Benedict XIII reigned in Avignon, excommunicating Rome's Urban VI, Boniface IX, Innocent VII, and Gregory XII, who excommunicated them right back. Yet the toiling peasantry was unaware of the estrangement in the Church. Who would have told them? The village priest knew nothing himself; his archbishop had every reason to keep it quiet. The folk (*Leute, popolo, pueblo, gens, gente*) were baptized, shriven, attended mass, received the host at communion, married, and received the last rites never dreaming that they should be informed about great events, let alone have any voice in them. Their anonymity approached the absolute. So did their mute acceptance of it.

In later ages, when identities became necessary, their descendants would either adopt the surname of the local lord — a custom later followed by American slaves after their emancipation — or take the name of an honest occupation (Miller, Taylor, Smith). Even then they were casual in spelling it; in the 1580s the founder of Germany's great munitions dynasty variously spelled his name as Krupp, Krupe, Kripp, Kripe, and Krapp. Among the implications of this lack of selfhood was an almost total indifference to privacy. In summertime peasants went about naked.

In the medieval mind there was also no awareness of time, which is even more difficult to grasp. Inhabitants of the twentieth century are instinctively aware of past, present, and future. At any given moment most can quickly identify where they are on this temporal scale — the year, usually the date or day of the week, and frequently, by glancing at their wrists, the time of day. Medieval men were rarely aware of which century they were living in. There was no reason they should have been. There are great differences between everyday life in 1791 and 1991, but there were very few between 791 and 991. Life then revolved around the passing of the seasons and such cyclical events as religious holidays, harvest time, and local fetes. In all Christendom there was no such thing as a watch, a clock, or, apart from a copy of the Easter tables in the nearest church or monastery, anything resembling a calendar.* Generations succeeded one another in a meaningless, timeless blur. In the whole of Europe, which was the world as they knew it, very little happened. Popes, emperors, and kings died and were succeeded by new popes, emperors, and kings; wars were fought, spoils divided; communities suffered, then recovered from, natural disasters. But the impact on the masses was negligible. This lockstep continued for a period of time roughly corresponding in length to the time between the Norman conquest of England, in 1066, and the end of the twentieth century. Inertia reinforced the immobility. Any innovation was inconceivable; to suggest the possibility of one would have invited suspicion, and because the accused were guilty until they had proved themselves innocent by surviving impossible ordeals — by fire, water, or combat — to be suspect was to be doomed.

EVEN DURING the Great Schism, as the interstice of the rival popes came to be known, the Holy See remained formidable. In 1215 the medieval papacy had reached its culmination at the Fourth Lateran Council, held in a Roman palace which, before Nero confiscated it, had been the home of the ancient Laterani family. The council, representing the entire Church, was brilliantly attended. Its decrees were of supreme importance, covering confession, Easter rites, clerical and lay reform, and the doctrine of transubstantiation, an affirmation that at holy communion bread and wine are transformed into the body and blood of Christ. The council glorified Vicars of Christ in language of unprecedented majesty and splendor; pontiffs were explicitly permitted to exert authority not only in theological matters, but also in all vital political issues which might arise. Later in the thirteenth century Saint Thomas Aquinas celebrated the accord of reason and

*Because of the complex method used to determine when Easter would fall each year, Easter tables reckoned the future dates of the celebration. Easter in turn determines the dates of all other movable feasts in the Christian calendar.

revelation, and in 1302 *Unam Sanctam* — a bull affirming papal supremacy — was proclaimed. Even during its Avignon exile the Church progressed, centralizing its government and creating an elaborate administrative structure. Medieval institutions seemed stronger than ever.

And yet, and yet . . .

Rising gusts of wind, disregarded at the time, signaled the coming storm. The first gales affected the laity. Knighthood, a pivotal medieval institution, was dying. At a time when its ceremonies had finally reached their fullest development, chivalry was obsolescent and would soon be obsolete. The knightly way of life was no longer practical. Chain mail had been replaced by plate, which, though more effective, was also much heavier; horses which were capable of carrying that much weight were hard to come by, and their expense, added to that of the costly new mail, was almost prohibitive. Worse still, the mounted knight no longer dominated the battlefield; he could be outmaneuvered and unhorsed by English bowmen, Genoese crossbowmen, and pikemen led by lightly armed men-at-arms, or sergeants. Europe's new armies were composed of highly trained, well-armed professional infantrymen who could remain in the field, ready for battle, through an entire season of campaigning. Since only great nation-states could afford them, the future would belong to powerful absolute monarchs.

By A.D. 1500 most of these sovereign dynasties were in place, represented by England's Henry VII, France's Louis XII, Russia's Ivan III, Scandinavia's John I, Hungary's Ladislas II, Poland's John Albert, and Portugal's Manuel I. Another major player was on the way: in 1492, when the fall of Granada destroyed the last vestiges of Moorish power on the Iberian peninsula, Spaniards completed the long reconquest of their territory. The union of their two chief crowns with the marriage of Ferdinand of Aragon and Isabella of Castile laid the foundations for modern Spain; together they began suppressing their fractious vassals. Germany and Italy, however, were going to be late in joining the new Europe. On both sides of the Alps prolonged disputes over succession delayed the coalescence of central authority. As a result, in the immediate future Italians would continue to live in city-states or papal states and Germans would still be ruled by petty princes. But this fragmentation could not last. A kind of centripetal force, strengthened by emerging feelings of national identity among the masses, was reshaping Europe. And that was a threat to monolithic Christendom.

The papacy was vexed otherwise as the fifteenth century drew to a close. European cities were witnessing the emergence of educated classes inflamed by anticlericalism. Their feelings were understandable, if, in papal eyes, unpardonable. The Lateran reforms of 1215 had been inadequate; reliable reports of misconduct by priests, nuns, and prelates, much of it squalid, were rising. And the harmony achieved by theologians over the last century had been shattered. Bernard of Clairvaux, the anti–intellectual saint, would have found his worst suspicions confirmed by the new philosophy of nominalism. Denying the existence of universals, nominalists declared that the gulf between reason and revelation was unbridgeable — that to believe in virgin birth and the resurrection was completely unreasonable. Men of faith who might have challenged them, such as Thomas à Kempis, seemed lost in a dream of mysticism.

At the same time, a subtle but powerful new spirit was rising in Europe. It was virulently subversive of all medieval society, especially the Church, though no one recognized it as such, partly because its greatest figures were devout Catholics. During the pontificate of Innocent III (1198–1216) the rediscovery of Aristotelian learning — in dialectic, logic, natural science, and metaphysics — had been readily synthesized with traditional Church doctrine. Now, as the full cultural heritage of Greece and Rome began to reappear, the problems of synthesis were escalating, and they defied solution. In Italy the movement was known as the Rinascimento. The French combined the verb *renaître*, "revive," with the feminine noun *naissance*, "birth," to form Renaissance — rebirth.

FIXING A DATE for the beginning of the Renaissance is impossible, but most scholars believe its stirrings had begun by the early 1400s. Although Dante, Petrarch, Boccaccio, Saint Francis of Assisi, and the painter Giotto de Bondone — all of whom seem to have been

infused with the new spirit — were dead by then, they are seen
as forerunners of the reawakening. In the long reach of history,
the most influential Renaissance men were the writers, scholars,
philosophers, educators, statesmen, and independent theologians.
However, their impact upon events, tremendous as it was, would
not be felt until later. The artists began to arrive first, led by the
greatest galaxy of painters, sculptors, and architects ever known.
They were spectacular, they were most memorably Italian, notably Florentine, and because their works were so dazzling — and
so pious — they had the enthusiastic blessing and sponsorship of
the papacy. Among their immortal figures were Botticelli, Fra
Filippo Lippi, Piero della Francesca, the Bellinis, Giorgione, Della
Robbia, Titian, Michelangelo, Raphael, and, elsewhere in Europe,
Rubens, the Brueghels, Dürer, and Holbein. The supreme figure
was Leonardo da Vinci, but Leonardo was more than an artist,
and will appear later in this volume, trailing clouds of glory.

When we look back across five centuries, the implications of
the Renaissance appear to be obvious. It seems astonishing that
no one saw where it was leading, anticipating what lay round the
next bend in the road and then over the horizon. But they lacked
our perspective; they could not hold a mirror up to the future.
Like all people at all times, they were confronted each day by the
present, which always arrives in a promiscuous rush, with the
significant, the trivial, the profound, and the fatuous all tangled
together. The popes, emperors, cardinals, kings, prelates, and nobles of the time sorted through the snarl and, being typical men
in power, chose to believe what they wanted to believe, accepting
whatever justified their policies and convictions and ignoring the
rest. Even the wisest of them were at a hopeless disadvantage, for
their only guide in sorting it all out — the only guide anyone ever
has — was the past, and precedents are worse than useless when
facing something entirely new. They suffered another handicap.
As medieval men, crippled by ten centuries of immobility, they
viewed the world through distorted prisms peculiar to their age.

In all that time nothing of real consequence had either improved
or declined. Except for the introduction of waterwheels in the 800s
and windmills in the late 1100s, there had been no inventions of
significance. No startling new ideas had appeared, no new terri-

tories outside Europe had been explored. Everything was as it had been for as long as the oldest European could remember. The center of the Ptolemaic universe was the known world — Europe, with the Holy Land and North Africa on its fringes. The sun moved round it every day. Heaven was above the immovable earth, somewhere in the overarching sky; hell seethed far beneath their feet. Kings ruled at the pleasure of the Almighty; all others did what they were told to do. Jesus, the son of God, had been crucified and resurrected, and his reappearance was imminent, or at any rate inevitable. Every human being adored him (the Jews and the Muslims being invisible). During the 1,436 years since the death of Saint Peter the Apostle, 211 popes had succeeded him, all chosen by God and all infallible. The Church was indivisible, the afterlife a certainty; all knowledge was already known. *And nothing would ever change.*

The mighty storm was swiftly approaching, but Europeans were not only unaware of it; they were convinced that such a phenomenon could not exist. Shackled in ignorance, disciplined by fear, and sheathed in superstition, they trudged into the sixteenth century in the clumsy, hunched, pigeon-toed gait of rickets victims, their vacant faces, pocked by smallpox, turned blindly toward the future they thought they knew — gullible, pitiful innocents who were about to be swept up in the most powerful, incomprehensible, irresistible vortex since Alaric had led his Visigoths and Huns across the Alps, fallen on Rome, and extinguished the lamps of learning a thousand years before.

WHEN THE CARTOGRAPHERS of the Middle Ages came to the end of the world as they knew it, they wrote: *Beware: Dragons Lurk Beyond Here.* They were right, though the menacing dimension was not on maps, but on the calendar. It was time, not space. There the fiercest threats to their medieval mind-set waited in ambush. A few of the perils had already infiltrated society, though their presence was unsuspected and the havoc they would wreak was yet to come. Some of the dragons were benign, even saintly; others were wicked. All, however, would seem monstrous to those who cherished the status quo, and their names included Johannes Gutenberg, Cesare Borgia, Johann Tetzel, Desiderius

Erasmus, Martin Luther, Jakob Fugger, François Rabelais, Giro-
lamo Savonarola, Nicolaus Copernicus, Giordano Bruno, Niccolò
Machiavelli, William Tyndale, John Calvin, Vasco Núñez de Bal-
boa, Emperor Charles V, King Henry VIII, Tomás de Torque-
mada, Lucrezia Borgia, William Caxton, Gerardus Mercator,
Girolamo Aleandro, Ulrich von Hutten, Martin Waldseemüller,
Thomas More, Catherine of Aragon, Christopher Columbus,
Vasco da Gama, and — most fearsome of all, the man who would
destroy the very world the cartographers had drawn — Ferdinand
Magellan.

II

THE SHATTERING

HIS NAME RICOCHETS down the canyons of nearly five centuries — ricochets, because the trajectory of his zigzagging life, never direct, dodged this way and that, ever elusive and often devious. We cannot even be certain what to call him. In Portuguese documents his name appears alternately as Fernão de Magalhães and Fernão de Magalhais. Born the son of a fourth-grade nobleman, in middle age he renounced his native land and, as an immigrant in Seville, took the nom de guerre Fernando de Magallanes. Sometimes he spelled it that way, sometimes as Maghellanes. In Sanlúcar de Barrameda, before embarking for immortality on September 20, 1519, he signed his last will and testament as Hernando de Magallanes. Cartographers Latinized this to Magellanus — a German pamphleteer printed it as "Wagellanus" — and we have anglicized it to Magellan. But what was his real nationality? On his historic voyage he sailed under the colors of Castile and Aragon. Today Lisbon proudly acclaims him: "*Êle é nosso!*" — "He is ours!" — but that is chutzpah. In his lifetime his countrymen treated him as a renegade, calling him *traidor* and *transfuga* — turncoat.

One would expect the mightiest explorer in history to have been sensitive and proud, easily stung by such slurs. In fact he was unoffended. By our lights, his character was knotted and intricate. It was more comprehensible to his contemporaries, however, because the *capitán-general* of 1519–1521 was, to an exceptional degree, a creature of his time. His modesty arose from his faith. In the early sixteenth century, pride in achievement was reserved for sovereigns, who were believed to be sheathed in divine glory. Being a lesser mortal, and a pious one, Magellan assumed that the Madonna was responsible for his accomplishments.

At the time he may have underrated them. That is more

understandable. He was an explorer, a man whose destiny it was to venture into the unknown; what he found, therefore, was new. He had some idea of its worth but lacked accurate standards by which to measure it. Indeed, he couldn't even be certain of what he was looking for until he had found it, and the fact that he had no clear view of his target makes the fact that he hit it squarely all the more remarkable.

His Spanish sponsors did not share his sense of mission. They sought profit, not adventure. His way around that obstacle seems to have been to ignore it and mislead them. Sailing around the world was unmentioned during his royal audience with Carlos I, sovereign of Spain, who, as the elected Holy Roman emperor Charles V, was to play a key (if largely unwitting) role in the great religious revolution which split Christendom and signaled the end of the medieval world. Carlos's commission to Magellan was to journey westward, there to claim Spanish possession of an archipelago then in the hands of his Iberian rival, Manuel I of Portugal. These were the Spice Islands — the Moluccas, lying between Celebes and New Guinea. Now an obscure part of Indonesia, they are unshown on most maps, but then the isles were considered priceless. Officially, the capitán-general's incentive lay in the king's pledge to him. Two of the islands would become Magellan's personal fief and he would receive 5 percent of all profits from the archipelago, thus making his fortune.

But as Timothy Joyner points out in his life of Magellan, this Moluccan plan was a disaster. Indeed, as the leader of the expedition, Magellan was killed before he could even reach there. He had, however, landed in the Philippines. This was of momentous importance, for eastbound Portuguese had reconnoitered the Spice Islands nine years earlier. Therefore, in overlapping them, he had closed the nexus between the 123rd and 124th degrees of east longitude and thus completed the encirclement of the earth.

Yet his achievements were slighted. Death is always a misfortune, at least to the man who has to do the dying. In Magellan's case it was exceptionally so, however, for as a dead discoverer he was unhonored in his own time. Even Magellan's discovery of the strait which bears his name was belittled. Only a superb mariner, which he was, could have negotiated the foggy, treacherous,

350-mile-long Estrecho de Magallanes. In the years after his death, expedition after expedition tried to follow his lead. They failed; all but one ended in shipwreck or turned homeward, and the exception met disaster in the Pacific. Frustrated and defeated, skippers decided that Magellan's exploit was impossible and declared it a myth. Nearly sixty years passed before another great sailor, Sir Francis Drake, successfully guided *The Golden Hind* through the tortuous passage and survived to tell the tale.

Had fortune and a viceregal role in the Moluccas been Magellan's real inducement, he would have been a failure by his own lights. But his original motives remain obscure. Desperately searching for sponsorship of his voyage, he may have feigned interest in the Spice Islands. There is no proof of that, but it would have been in character. And were that the case, he would have confided in no one; he was always the most secretive of men. Moreover, the true drives of men are often hidden from them. Magellan's vision may or may not have been cloudy, but clearly his real inspiration was nobler than profits. And in the end he proved that the world was round.

In so doing, he did much more. He provided a linchpin for the men of the Renaissance. Philosophers, scholars, and even learned men in the Church had begun to challenge stolid medieval assumptions, among them pontifical dogma on the shape of the earth, its size, and its position and movement in the universe. Magellan gave men a realistic perception of the globe's dimensions, of its enormous seas, of how its landmasses were distributed. Others had raised questions. He provided answers, which now, inevitably, would lead to further questions — to challenges which continue on the eve of the twenty-first century.

The Spanish court was less than ecstatic. It had wanted Magellan to hoist its flag over the Moluccas, thereby breaking Portugal's monopoly of the Oriental spice trade: cloves, nutmeg, cinnamon, and pepper. Spices made valuable preservatives, but trafficking in them had other, sinister implications. They were also used, and used more often, to disguise the odors and the ugly taste of spoiled meat. The regimes that encouraged and supported the spice trade were, in effect, accomplices in the poisoning of their own people. Moreover, medieval Europeans were extremely vulnerable to disease. This was the down side of exploration. The discoverers and their crews had carried European germs to distant lands, infecting native populations. Then, when they returned, they bore exotic diseases which could spread across the continent unchecked. Sometimes the source of an epidemic could be quickly traced. Typhus, never before known in Europe, swept Aragon immediately after Spanish troops returned from their Cyprian triumph over the Moors. More often the origin was never identified. No one knows why Europe's first outbreak of syphilis ravaged Naples in 1495, or why the "sweating sickness" devastated England later the same year — "Scarce one among a hundred that sickened did escape with life," wrote the sixteenth-century chronicler Raphael Holinshed — or the specific origins of the pandemic Black Death, which had been revisiting Europe at least once a generation since October 1347, when a Genoese fleet returning from the Orient staggered into Messina harbor, all members of its crews dead or dying from a combination of bubonic, pneumonic, and septicemic plague strains. All that can be said with certainty is that the late 1400s and early 1500s were haunted by dark reigns of pestilence, that life became very cheap, and that this wretched situation can scarcely have discouraged explorers eager to investigate what lay over the horizon.

The mounting toll of disease — each night gravediggers' carts creaked down streets as drivers cried, "Bring out your dead!" and in Germany entire towns, a chronicler of the time wrote, had become like cemeteries *"in ihrer betru benden Einsamkeit"* ("in their sad desertion") — was far from the only sign that society seemed to have lost its way. In some ways the period seems to have been the worst of times — an age of treachery, abduction, fratricide, depravity, barbarism, and sadism. In England, by royal decree, the Star Chamber sent innocent men to the gallows ignorant of both their accusers and the charges against them. In Florence, the fief of Lorenzo de' Medici, local merchants were licensed to organize the African slave trade, after which the first "blackbirders" arrived in Italian ports with their wretched human cargoes. Tomás de Torquemada, a Dominican monk, presided over the Spanish Inquisition — actually conceived by Isabella of Castile — which tortured accused heretics until they confessed.

Torquemada's methods reveal much about one of the age's most unpleasant characteristics: man's inhumanity to man. Sharp iron frames prevented victims from sleeping, lying, or even sitting. Braziers scorched the soles of their feet, racks stretched their limbs, suspects were crushed to death beneath chests filled with stones, and in Germany the very mention of *die verfüchte Jungfer* — the dreaded old iron maid — inspired terror. The *Jungfer* embraced the condemned with metal arms, crushed him in a spiked hug, and then opened, letting him fall, a mass of gore, bleeding from a hundred stab wounds, all bones broken, to die slowly in an underground hole of revolving knives and sharp spears.

Jewry was luckier — slightly luckier — than blacks. If the pogroms of the time are less infamous than the Holocaust, it is only because anti-Semites then lacked twentieth-century technology. Certainly they possessed the evil will. In 1492, the year of Columbus, Spain's Jews were given three months to accept Christian baptism or be banished from the country. Even those who had been baptized were distrusted; Isabella had fixed her dark eye on converted Jews suspected of recidivism — *Marranos,* she called them; "pigs" — and marked them for resettlement as early as 1478. Eventually between thirty thousand and sixty thousand were expelled. Meantime the king of Portugal, finding merit in the Spanish decree, ordered the expulsion of *all* Portuguese Jews. His soldiers were instructed to massacre those who were slow to leave. During a single night in 1506 nearly four thousand Lisbon Jews were put to the sword. Three years later the systematic persecution of the German Jews began.

Blacks and Jews suffered most, but any minority was considered fair game for tyrants. In Moscovy, Ivan III Vasilyevich, the grand duke of Moscow, proclaimed himself the first czar of Russia and then drove all Germans from Novgorod and enslaved Lithuania. Fevered Turks swung their long curved swords in Egypt, leaving the gutters of Cairo awash in Arab blood, and then pillaged Mecca. At the turn of the sixteenth century, Francisco Jiménez de Cisneros — who would become Spain's new inquisitor general — provided Europe with an extraordinary example of medieval genocide. He ordered all Grenadine Moors to accept baptism. Cisneros wasn't really seeking converts. He hoped to goad them to revolt, and when they did rise he annihilated them. Any nonconformity, any weakness, was despised; the handicapped were given not compassion, but terror and pain, as prescribed in *Malleus maleficarum* (*The Witches' Hammer*), a handbook by the inquisitors Johann Sprenger and Heinrich Kraemer, which justified the shackling and burning of, among others, the mentally ill.

These victims were helpless and oppressed, but no one was really safe. In 1500 the eminent Alfonso of Aragon, son-in-law of a pope, was slain by his wife's brother; seven years later Alfonso's killer, who had become brother-in-law of the king of Navarre, was himself murdered by assassins in the employ of the Count of Lerin. Intrigue thickened in every princely court, liquidation of enemies was tolerated among all social classes, and because the technology of homicide was in its infancy — August Kotter, the German gunsmith, did not invent the rifle until 1520 — their deaths were often macabre. Perhaps the most celebrated crime of the Middle Ages had been committed in the Tower of London: the disappearance and, it was thought, the murder of two young heirs to the English throne in 1483. This outrage was widely believed to be the work of the Duke of Gloucester, who became King Richard III. But there were other, equally bizarre royal homicides. The reign of King James III of Scotland ended in his thirty-seventh year when an assassin, disguised as a priest, heard his confession and then eviscerated him. And in his first sovereign act, the new Ottoman sultan Bayezid ordered his brother, whom he regarded as a threat to his power, publicly strangled.

Despots, confronted by violence, struck back with equal fury; for every eye lost, they gouged out as many eyes as they could reach. In gentler times, reformers and protesters are given at least the semblance of a fair hearing. There was none of that then. In 1510 two former speakers of the House of Commons found themselves in vehement disagreement with Parliament over taxation. The issues are obscure, but Parliament's solution of them was not; on the hottest day of that August both men were beheaded. Six years later, on May Day, London's street people staged a public demonstration to express exasperation over their plight. On orders from Thomas Cardinal Wolsey, sixty of them were hanged.

AT ANY GIVEN MOMENT the most dangerous enemy in Europe was the reigning pope. It seems odd to think of Holy Fathers in that light, but the five Vicars of Christ who ruled the Holy See during Magellan's lifetime were the least Christian of men: the least devout, least scrupulous, least compassionate, and among the least chaste — lechers, almost without exception. Ruthless in their pursuit of political power and personal gain, they were medieval despots who used their holy office for blackmail and extortion. Under Innocent VIII (r. 1484–1492) simony was institutionalized; a board was set up for the marketing of favors, absolution, forged papal bulls — even the office of Vatican librarian, previously reserved for the eminent — with 150 ducats (about $3,750)* from each transaction going to the pontiff. Selling pardons for murderers raised some eyebrows, but a powerful cardinal explained that "the Lord desireth not the death of a sinner but rather that he live and pay." The fact is that everything in the Holy See was up for auction, including the papacy itself. Innocent's successor, the Spanish cardinal Rodrigo Borgia, became Alexander VI (r. 1492–1503), the second Borgia pope — Callixtus III had been the first — by buying off the other leading candidates. He sent his closest rival, Ascanio Cardinal Sforza, four mules laden with ingots of gold.

The Vatican's permissive attitude toward men convicted of homicide was not entirely illogical. The papal palace itself was often home to killers and their accomplices. Popes and cardinals hired assassins, sanctioned torture, and frequently enjoyed the sight of blood. In his official history, *Storia d'Italia* (1561–1564), Francesco Guicciardini noted the remarkable spectacle of "the High Priest, the Vicar of Christ on earth" — in this instance Julius II — "excited" by a scene in which Christians slaughtered one

---

*This is a rough conversion. Providing modern equivalents of original currencies is extremely difficult. The sort of basic consumption items for which we have figures — e.g., grain, oil, wine — have tended to grow absolutely less expensive with the productivity of modern agriculture. Moreover, there were at least twenty distinct ducats afloat in the sixteenth century, each with a different value, and a similar number of florins, guilders, livres, pounds, et cetera. The florin and the ducat with the largest circulation had the same value. For the purpose of this narrative, that value may be considered analogous to twenty-five dollars today.

another, "retaining nothing of the pontiff but the name and the robes." The Alsatian Johann Burchard was papal *magister ceremoniarum*, or master of ceremonies, from 1483 to 1506. Burchard was one of those rare men historians bless: a diarist. In his *Diarium*, a day-by-day chronicle of pontifical life, he tells how, at one Vatican banquet, another Holy Father "watched with loud laughter and much pleasure" from a balcony while his bastard son slew unarmed criminals, one by one, as they were driven into a small courtyard below.

That was recreational homicide. The strangling of Alfonso Cardinal Petrucci with a red silk noose — the executioner was a Moor; Vatican etiquette enjoined Christians from killing a prince of the Church — was a graver matter. In 1517 Petrucci, who considered himself ill used by Pope Leo X, had led a conspiracy of several cardinals to dispatch the Holy Father by injecting poison into his buttock on the pretext of lancing a boil. A servant betrayed them. Petrucci's accomplices were pardoned after paying huge fines. The highest, 150,000 ducats, was exacted from Raffaele Cardinal Riario, a great-nephew of a previous pope.

Such grisly tales of pontifical mayhem are found in contemporary diaries, but the details of massacres among the lower Roman classes are lost to us, though we know they occurred; diplomats stationed there attest to that. An envoy from Lombardy wrote of "murders innumerable. . . . One hears nothing but moaning and weeping. In all the memory of man the Church has never been in such an evil plight." That plight grew wickeder; a few years later the Venetian ambassador reported that "every night four or five murdered men are discovered, bishops, prelates, and others." If such slaughters were remarkable, so was the alacrity with which the Eternal City forgot them. When the blood on killers' knives had clotted and dried, when the graves had been filled in and cadavers removed from the Tiber, the mood tended to be hedonistic. "God has given us the papacy," Leo X wrote his brother. "Let us enjoy it." The prelates of that age had large appetites for pleasure. Pietro Cardinal Riario held "a saturnalian banquet," according to one account, "featuring a whole roasted bear holding a staff in its jaws, stags reconstructed in their skins,

herons and peacocks in their feathers, and" — there would be
more of this later — "orgiastic behavior by the guests appropriate
to the ancient Roman model."

In previous centuries, when the cause of Christianity had met
with some striking success, their predecessors had opened St. Peter's for Te Deums of thanksgiving. Now prayer had become
unfashionable. Alexander VI caught the spirit of the new age in
the first year of his reign. Told that Castilian Catholics had defeated
the Moors of Granada, this Spanish pontiff scheduled a bullfight
in the Piazza of St. Peter's and cheered as five bulls were slain.
The menu for Riario's feast and the Borgia pope's celebration
reveal a Church hopelessly at odds with the preachings of Jesus,
whose existence was the sole reason for *its* existence. But sitting
in the Piazza of St. Peter's was more comfortable than kneeling
at the altar within, and other diversions were more entertaining
than holy communion. Among them were compulsive spending
on entertainment, gambling (and cheating) at cards, writing dreadful poems and reciting them in public, hiring orchestras to play
while the prelates wallowed in gluttony, applauding elaborate theatrical performances. During the digestive process, the churchmen
emptied great flagons of strong wine, whereupon intoxication
inspired their eminences and even His Holiness to improvise
bawdy exhibitions with female guests selected from the city's
brothels — which kept the papal master of ceremonies scribbling
in his diary — until dawn brightened the papal palace and hang-
overs gave its inhabitants some idea of how merciless God's vengeance could be.

It was Alexander, the Borgia pope, who first suppressed books
critical of the papacy. He was either unaware of Burchard's diary
or indifferent to it, though there is another possibility: he may
have been incapable of appreciating it. Men accept the values of
their time and reject criticisms of them as irrelevant. Moreover,
iniquitous regimes do not perpetuate themselves in disciplined
societies, nor does a strong, pure, holy institution, supported by
centuries of selflessness and integrity, abruptly find itself wallow-
ing in corruption. Vice, no less than virtue, arises from precedents.
Over the thirteen centuries since Christianity's rise to power the

Church had lost its way because the wrong criteria had insinuated themselves into its sanctuaries, turning piety into blasphemy, supplanting worship with scandal, and substituting the pursuit of secular power for eternal grace.

IRONICALLY, the purity of Christ's vision had been contaminated by its very popularity. As Christianity expanded through mass conversions, its evangelists had tempered their exhortations, accommodating their message to those whose souls they sought to save. Philanthropy, one of the Church's most admirable virtues, had become another source of vitiation. Donations poured in from the faithful, and the unspent wealth was passed up to the ecclesiastical hierarchy, where it accumulated and led to dissipation, debauchery, and — because spendthrifts are always running out of funds — demands for still more money. Here a dangerous solution presented itself, one which, when it was adopted, almost guaranteed future abuse. Ancient German custom offered convicted criminals a choice; they could be punished or, if they were wealthy, pay fines (*Wehrgeld*). Buying salvation was new to the Church. It was also sacrilegious. Early Christians had atoned for their sins by confession, absolution, and penance. Now it became possible to erase transgressions by buying indulgences. The papacy, searching for a scriptural precedent, settled on Matthew 16:19, in which Jesus tells Peter: "I will give unto thee the keys of the kingdom of heaven: and whatsoever thou shalt bind on earth shall be bound in heaven; and whatsoever thou shalt loose on earth shall be loosed in heaven."

On this shakiest of foundations the Holy See built a bureaucracy in which Peter's power, appropriated by pontiffs, was delegated to bishops, who passed it on to priests, who sent out friars in pursuit of sinners, empowered to judge the price to be paid for the sin, from which he deducted his commission. In Rome the contributions were welcomed and, in the beginning, used to finance hospitals, cathedrals, and crusades. Then other, less admirable causes appeared. Holy Fathers permitted those who had violated God's commandments to buy release from purgatory, thus encroaching on the sacrament of penance.

At the same time, the lawlessness and disorders of the Dark

Ages — particularly after the papacy had fallen under the dominance of feudal aristocrats in the ninth century — had led churchmen first to collaborate with secular rulers, and then to seek their subjugation. Pontiffs began by regulating the behavior of despots. Then they erected awesome cathedrals as symbols of their secular power, became enmeshed in political manipulations, and, finally, made war on their enemies.

IN THE VERY BEGINNING the first Vicars of Christ had withdrawn from the world and its temptations. Now they became indistinguishable from the nobility. Once they had held the blessings of austerity to be inviolate, even renouncing marriage and cohabitation. Now celibacy yielded to widespread clerical concubinage and, in the convents, to promiscuity and homes for fatherless children born to women who had pledged their virtue as brides of Christ.

The precept that men of God should sleep alone, established by the Lateran Councils of 1123 and 1139 after nine hundred years of hemming and hawing, had begun to fray well before the dawn of the sixteenth century. Now it was a thing of shreds and patches. The last pontiff to take it seriously had died in 1471, and even he, during his youthful days as a bishop of Trieste, had slept with a succession of mistresses. A generation later the occupants of Saint Peter's chair were openly acknowledging their bantlings, endowing their sons with titles and their daughters with dowries.

In the Vatican nepotism ran amok. Sixtus IV (r. 1471–1484), upon donning the miter, appointed two of his nephews — both dissolute youths — to the sacred College of Cardinals. Later he put red hats on three more nephews and a grandnephew. He also named an eight-year-old boy archbishop of Lisbon and an eleven-year-old archbishop of Milan, though, quite apart from the fact that both were children, neither had received any religious instruction. Innocent VIII, who succeeded Sixtus in 1484, doted on Franceschetto Cibò, his son by a nameless courtesan. Innocent couldn't make a cardinal of Franceschetto. Standards had not deteriorated that far — yet — and the youth didn't seem interested. What excited him was roaming city streets each night with a pack of Roman hoodlums, gang-raping young women, some of them nuns; sodomizing them and then leaving them unconscious, bloody, bruised, often with serious injuries, in the streets. The pope's son was not only a guttersnipe; he was also one of history's great spendthrifts. To support his lifestyle Innocent raised simony to new levels. By the time he found a suitable bride for Franceschetto, a Medici, he had to mortgage the papal tiara and treasury to pay for the wedding. Then he appointed his son's new brother-in-law to the sacred college. The new cardinal and future pope — Leo X — was fourteen years old.

Even Leo X (r. 1513–1521), who fathered no children, shared the passion to honor papal relatives. He began in 1513 with his first cousin, Giulio de' Medici, whose mother, all Rome knew, had been a casual partner at a drunken Holy Week frolic. By now there were precedents for conferring red hats on illegitimate sons; Alexander VI had put one on his own teenaged bastard, Cesare Borgia. Leo had big plans for Giulio, so he perjured himself, swearing out an affidavit that the youth's parents had been secretly married. He then appointed five more members of his family, three nephews and two first cousins, to the cardinal's college. Meantime his hopes for Giulio, like Giulio himself, were maturing. The boy cardinal became a man, served his benefactor as chief minister, and, in 1523, became pope himself. However, it is just as well that Leo did not live to see his dream realized. As Clement VII, Giulio was to become the ultimate pontifical disaster.

UNDISCIPLINED BY PIETY, most of these popes are nonetheless remembered for their consummate skills in the brutal politics of the era. Only men with strong power bases of their own, notably leaders of great Italian families — the Sforzas, Medicis, Pazzis, Aragons — dared challenge them. At the turn of the century the most popular critic of Alexander VI, the Borgia pope, was a Florentine, Girolamo Savonarola of San Marco, a charismatic, idealistic Dominican friar with an enormous following in Florence, where he had introduced a democratic government free of corruption. Savonarola (1452–1498) was among those offended by Vatican orgies and Alexander's celebrated collection of pornography. The friar's protests took the form of annual "bonfires of the vanities" — carnivals in Florence's Piazza della Signoria, where he tossed lewd pictures, pornography, personal ornaments, cards, and gaming tables on the flames. To his multitudes he would roar: "Popes and prelates speak against pride and ambition and they are plunged into it up to their ears." The papal palace, he said, had literally become a house of prostitution where harlots "sit upon the throne of Solomon and signal to the passersby. Whoever can pay enters and does what he wishes."

Savonarola also charged the Vicar of Christ with simony and demanded that he be removed. Alexander at first responded warily, merely ordering the friar gagged. But Savonarola continued to defy him. The pontiff, he declared "is no longer a Christian. He is an infidel, a heretic, and as such has ceased to be pope." The

Girolamo Savonarola (1452–1498)

Holy Father tried to buy him off with a cardinal's hat. Savonarola indignantly rejected it — "A red hat?" he cried; "I want a hat of blood!" — and that was the end of him. Alexander excommunicated him; then, when Savonarola again defied him by continuing to celebrate Mass and give communion, the pope condemned him as a heretic, sentenced him to torture, and finally had him hanged and burned in the Piazza della Signoria.

The pontiffs of that time cannot be said to have been fastidious. They even executed their enemies in churches, where victims' bodyguards were likeliest to be caught off guard. Allying himself with the Pazzi family, who were challenging the Florentine power of Lorenzo de' Medici — Lorenzo the Magnificent — Pope Sixtus IV conspired with them to murder Lorenzo and his handsome brother Giuliano. He chose their most defenseless moment, when they were observing High Mass in the Florentine cathedral. The signal for the killers was the bell marking the elevation of the host. Giuliano fell at the altar, mortally wounded, but Lorenzo was not called magnificent for nothing. Drawing his long sword, he escaped into the sacristy and barricaded himself there until help arrived.

If the pope's attack says much about the era, so does Lorenzo's vengeance. On his instructions some of the Pazzi gang were hanged from balconies of the Palace of the Signoria while the rest were emasculated, dragged through the streets, hacked to death, and flung into the Arno. By medieval standards Lorenzo's revenge had not been excessive, though that cannot be said of Denmark's King Christian II, who invaded Sweden early in 1520. In January, Sten Sture, Sweden's leader, was killed in action. Heavy fighting continued throughout the year, however, and it was autumn before Sture's widow, Dame Christina Gyllenstjerna, surrendered. Christian had promised her a general amnesty, but a king's word wasn't worth much then. He immediately broke his, and in spectacular fashion. First two Swedish bishops were beheaded in Stockholm's public square at midnight, November 8, while eighty of their parishioners, who had been summoned to witness the execution, were butchered where they stood. The Danish king then disinterred Sten Sture's remains. After ten months in the grave they were scarcely recognizable. Rotting, crawling with maggots, emitting a nauseous stench, the corpse was nevertheless burned. Next Sture's small son was flung — alive — into the flames. Then Dame Christina, who had been forced to watch all this, was sentenced to live out her days as a common prostitute.

WHAT WAS the world like — and to them it was the *only* world, round which the sun orbited each day — when ruled by such men? Imagination alone can reconstruct it. If a modern European could be transported back five centuries through a kind of time warp, and suspended high above earth in one of those balloons which fascinated Jules Verne, he would scarcely recognize his own continent. Where, he would wonder, looking down, are all the people? Westward from Russia to the Atlantic, Europe was covered by the same trackless forest primeval the Romans had confronted fifteen hundred years earlier, when, according to Tacitus's *De Germania,* Julius Caesar interviewed men who had spent two months walking from Poland to Gaul without once glimpsing sunlight. One reason the lands east of the Rhine and north of the Danube had proved unconquerable to legions commanded by Caesar and over seventy other Roman consuls was that, unlike the other territories he subdued, they lacked roads.

But there *were* people there in A.D. 1500. Beneath the deciduous canopy, most of them toiling from sunup to sundown, dwelt nearly 73 million people, and although that was less than a tenth of the continent's modern population, there were enough Europeans to establish patterns and precedents still viable today. Twenty million of them lived in what was known as the Holy Roman Empire — which, in the hoary classroom witticism, was neither holy, nor Roman, nor an empire. It was in fact central Europe: Germany and her bordering territories.* There were 15 million souls in France, Europe's most populous country. Thirteen

*The Holy Roman Empire of the German Nation, as it was called after the mid-1400s, was also the First Reich, a cultural nation (*Kulturvolk*) of some three hundred different sovereign states. After Prussia's victory in the Franco-Prussian War of 1870–1871, Otto von Bismarck created the Second Reich, a nation-state (*Staatsvolk*) over which the Hohenzollerns reigned until its defeat in 1918. The Third Reich (1933–1945) was, of course, Adolf Hitler's Nazi Germany.

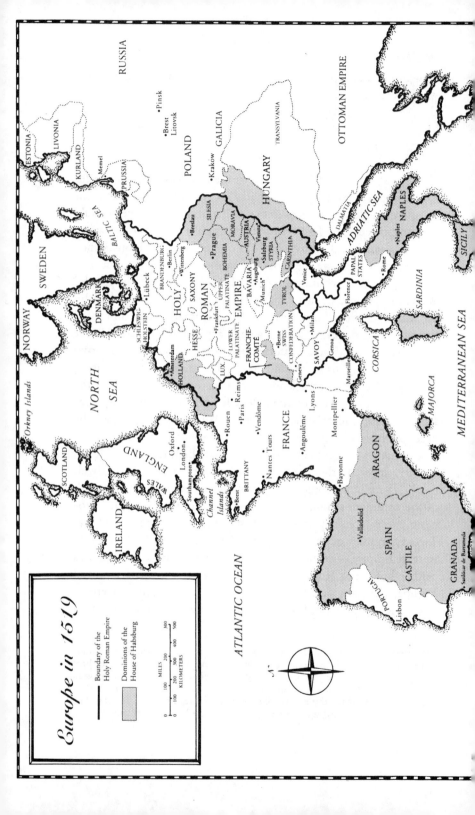

Europe in 1519

Boundary of the
Holy Roman Empire

Dominions of the
House of Habsburg

MILES
0   100   200   300
0   100   200   300   400   500
KILOMETERS

RUSSIA

ESTONIA
LIVONIA
KURLAND
Memel
PRUSSIA
•Brest
Pinsk
Litovsk
POLAND
GALICIA
•Krakow
SILESIA
TRANSYLVANIA
HUNGARY

NORWAY

SWEDEN

BALTIC SEA

DENMARK
SCHLESWIG-
HOLSTEIN
Lübeck•
BRANDENBURG
•Berlin
SAXONY
•Wittenberg
•Breslau
HOLY
ROMAN
•Prague
BOHEMIA
MORAVIA
EMPIRE
AUSTRIA
STYRIA
CARINTHIA
DALMATIA

ADRIATIC SEA

OTTOMAN EMPIRE

HESSE
•Frankfurt
UPPER
PALATINATE
•Augsburg
•Salzburg
•Munich
BAVARIA
TYROL
Venice•
NAPLES
•Naples

NORTH
SEA

Okney Islands

AMSTERDAM
HOLLAND
LOWER
PALATINATE
LUX.
FRANCHE-
COMTÉ
•Berne
SWISS
CONFEDERATION
Geneva•
•Milan
SAVOY
Genoa•
Florence•
PAPAL
STATES
•Rome
SARDINIA

CORSICA

SICILY

MEDITERRANEAN SEA

SCOTLAND
IRELAND
WALES
ENGLAND
Oxford•
London•
Southampton•
Channel
Islands
•Brest
BRITTANY
Nantes•
Tours•
Rouen•
Reims•
•Paris
•Vendôme
FRANCE
•Angoulême
Lyons•
Montpellier•
Marseilles•
•Bayonne
ARAGON
MAJORCA

ATLANTIC OCEAN

SPAIN
•Valladolid
CASTILE
PORTUGAL
Lisbon•
GRANADA
Sanlúcar de Barrameda

million lived in Italy, where the population was densest, 8 millon in Spain, and a mere 4.5 million — the number of Philadelphians in 1990 — in England and Wales.

A voyager into the past would search in vain for the sprawling urban complexes which have dominated the continent since the Industrial Revolution transformed it some two hundred years ago. In 1500 the three largest cities in Europe were Paris, Naples, and Venice, with about 150,000 each. The only other communities with more than 100,000 inhabitants were situated by the sea, rivers, or trading centers: Seville, Genoa, and Milan, each of them about the size of Reno, Nevada; Eugene, Oregon; or Beaumont, Texas. Even among the celebrated *Reichsstädte* of the empire, only Cologne housed over 40,000 people. Other cities were about the same: Pisa had 40,000 citizens; Montpellier, the largest municipality in southern France, 40,000; Florence 70,000; Barcelona 50,000; Valencia 30,000; Augsburg 20,000; Nuremberg 15,000; Antwerp and Brussels 20,000. London was by far England's largest town, with 50,000 Londoners; only 10,000 Englishmen lived in Bristol, the second-largest.

Twentieth-century urban areas are approached by superhighways, with skylines looming in the background. Municipalities were far humbler then. Emerging from the forest and following a dirt path, a stranger would confront the grim walls and turrets of a town's defenses. Visible beyond them would be the gabled roofs of the well-to-do, the huge square tower of the donjon, the spires of parish churches, and, dwarfing them all, the soaring mass of the local cathedral.

If the bishop's seat was the spiritual heart of the community, the donjon, overshadowing the public square, was its secular nucleus. On its roofs, twenty-four hours a day, stood watchmen, ready to strike the alarm bells at the first sign of attack or fire. Below them lay the council chamber, where elders gathered to confer and vote; beneath that, the city archives; and, in the cellar, the dungeon and the living quarters of the hangman, who was kept far busier than any executioner today. Sixteenth-century men did not believe that criminal characters could be reformed or corrected, and so there were no reformatories or correctional institutions. Indeed, prisons as we know them did not exist. Maiming and the lash were common punishments; for convicted felons the rope was commoner still.

The donjon was the last line of defense, but it was the wall, the first line of defense, which determined the propinquity inside it. The smaller its circumference, the safer (and cheaper) the wall was. Therefore the land within was invaluable, and not an inch of it could be wasted. The twisting streets were as narrow as the breadth of a man's shoulders, and pedestrians bore bruises from collisions with one another. There was no paving; shops opened directly on the streets, which were filthy; excrement, urine, and offal were simply flung out windows.

And it was easy to get lost. Sunlight rarely reached ground level, because the second story of each building always jutted out over the first, the third over the second, and the fourth and fifth stories over those lower. At the top, at a height approaching that of the great wall, burghers could actually shake hands with neighbors across the way. Rain rarely fell on pedestrians, for which they were grateful, and little air or light, for which they weren't. At night the town was scary. Watchmen patrolled it — once clocks arrived, they would call, "One o'clock and all's well!" — and heavy chains were stretched across street entrances to foil the flight of thieves. Nevertheless rogues lurked in dark corners.

One neighborhood of winding little alleys offered signs, for those who could read them, that the feudal past was receding. Here were found the butcher's lane, the papermaker's street, tanners' row, cobblers' shops, saddlemakers, and even a small bookshop. Their significance lay in their commerce. Europe had developed a new class: the merchants. The hubs of medieval business had been Venice, Naples, and Milan — among only a handful of cities with over 100,000 inhabitants. Then the Medicis of Florence had entered banking. Finally, Germany's century-old Hanseatic League stirred itself and, overtaking the others, for a time dominated trade.

The Hansa, a league of some seventy medieval towns centering around Bremen, Hamburg, and Lübeck, was originally formed in the thirteenth century to combat piracy and overcome foreign trade restrictions. It reached its apogee when a new generation of rich traders and bankers came to power. Foremost among them

was the Fugger family. Having started as peasant weavers in Augsburg, not a Hanseatic town, the Fuggers expanded into the mining
of silver, copper, and mercury. As moneylenders, they became
immensely wealthy, controlling Spanish customs and extending
their power throughout Spain's overseas empire. Their influence
stretched from Rome to Budapest, from Lisbon to Danzig, from

A sixteenth-century town wall

Moscow to Chile. In their banking role, they loaned millions of ducats to kings, cardinals, and the Holy Roman emperor, financing wars, propping up popes, and underwriting new adventures — putting up the money, for example, that King Carlos of Spain gave Magellan in commissioning his voyage around the world. In the early sixteenth century the family patriarch was Jakob Fugger II, who first emerged as a powerful figure in 1505, when he secretly bought the crown jewels of Charles the Bold, duke of Burgundy. Jakob first became a count in Kirchberg and Weisserhorn; then, in 1514 the emperor Maximilian I — *der gross Max* — acknowledged the Fuggers' role as his chief financial supporter for thirty years by making him a hereditary knight of the Holy Roman Empire. In 1516, by negotiating complex loans, Jakob made Henry VIII of England a Fugger ally. It was a tribute to the family's influence, and to the growth of trade everywhere, that a year later the Church's Fifth Lateran Council lifted its age-old prohibition of usury.

Each European town of any size had its miniature Fugger, a merchant whose home in the marketplace typically rose five stories and was built with beams filled in with stucco, mortar, and laths. Storerooms were piled high with expensive Oriental rugs and containers of powdered spices; clerks at high desks pored over accounts; the owner and his wife, though of peasant birth, wore gold lace and even ignored laws forbidding anyone not nobly born to wear furs. In the manner of a grand seigneur the merchant would chat with patrician customers as though he were their equal. Impoverished knights, resenting this, ambushed merchants in the forest and cut off their right hands. It was a cruel and futile gesture; commerce had arrived to stay, and the knights were just leaving. Besides, the adversaries were mismatched. The true rivals of the mercantile class were the clerics. Subtly but inexorably the bourgeois would replace the clergy in the continental power structure.

THE TOWN, HOWEVER, was not typical of Europe. In the early 1500s one could hike through the woods for days without encountering a settlement of any size. Between 80 and 90 percent of the population (the peasantry; serfdom had been abolished everywhere except in remote pockets of Germany) lived in villages of

fewer than a hundred people, fifteen or twenty miles apart, surrounded by endless woodlands. They slept in their small, cramped
hamlets, which afforded little privacy, but they worked — entire
families, including expectant mothers and toddlers — in the fields
and pastures between their huts and the great forest. It was brutish
toil, but absolutely necessary to keep the wolf from the door.
Wheat had to be beaten out by flails, and not everyone owned a
plowshare. Those who didn't borrowed or rented when possible;
when it was impossible, they broke the earth awkwardly with
mattocks.

Knights, of course, experienced none of this. In their castles —
or, now that the cannon had rendered castle defenses obsolete,
their new manor houses — they played backgammon, chess, or
checkers (which was called *cronometrista* in Italy, *dames* in France,
and draughts in England). Hunting, hawking, and falcony were
their outdoor passions. A visitor from the twentieth century would
find their homes uncomfortable: damp, cold, and reeking from
primitive sanitation, for plumbing was unknown. But in other
ways they were attractive and spacious. Ceilings were timbered,

*A medieval fair: customers, cloth merchants, a beggar, a draper's shop, a
money-weigher, mountebanks*

floors tiled (carpets were just beginning to come into fashion);
tapestries covered walls, windows were glass. The great central
hall of the crumbling castles had been replaced by a vestibule at
the entrance, which led to a living room dominated by its massive
hearth, and, beyond that, a "drawto chamber," or "(with)drawing
room" for private talks and a "parler" for general conversations
and meals.

Gluttony wallowed in its nauseous excesses at tables spread in
the halls of the mighty. The everyday dinner of a man of rank
ran from fifteen to twenty dishes; England's earl of Warwick, who
fed as many as five hundred guests at a sitting, used six oxen a
day at the evening meal. The oxen were not as succulent as they
sound; by tradition, the meat was kept salted in vats against the
possibility of a siege, and boiled in a great copper vat. Even so,
enormous quantities of it were ingested and digested. On special
occasions a whole stag might be roasted in the great fireplace,
crisped and larded, then cut up in quarters, doused in a steaming
pepper sauce, and served on outsized plates.

The hearth excepted, the home of a prosperous peasant lacked
these amenities. Lying at the end of a narrow, muddy lane, his

Home of a medieval nobleman

rambling edifice of thatch, wattles, mud, and dirty brown wood was almost obscured by a towering dung heap in what, without it, would have been the front yard. The building was large, for it was more than a dwelling. Beneath its sagging roof were a pigpen, a henhouse, cattle sheds, corncribs, straw and hay, and, last and least, the family's apartment, actually a single room whose walls and timbers were coated with soot. According to Erasmus, who examined such huts, "almost all the floors are of clay and rushes from the marshes, so carelessly renewed that the foundation sometimes remains for twenty years, harboring, there below, spittle and vomit and wine of dogs and men, beer . . . remnants of fishes, and other filth unnameable. Hence, with the change of weather, a vapor exhales which in my judgment is far from wholesome."

The centerpiece of the room was a gigantic bedstead, piled high with straw pallets, all seething with vermin. Everyone slept there, regardless of age or gender — grandparents, parents, children, grandchildren, and hens and pigs — and if a couple chose to enjoy intimacy, the others were aware of every movement. In summer they could even watch. If a stranger was staying the night, hospitality required that he be invited to make "one more" on the familial mattress. This was true even if the head of the household was away, on, say, a pilgrimage. If this led to goings-on, and the husband returned to discover his wife with child, her readiest reply was that during the night, while she was sleeping, she had been penetrated by an incubus. Theologians had confirmed that such monsters existed and that it was their demonic mission to impregnate lonely women lost in slumber. (Priests offered the same explanation for boys' wet dreams.) Even if the infant bore a striking similarity to someone other than the head of the household, and tongues wagged as a result, direct accusations were rare. Cuckolds were figures of fun; a man was reluctant to identify himself as one. Of course, when unmarried girls found themselves with child and told the same tale, they met with more skepticism.

If this familial situation seems primitive, it should be borne in mind that these were *prosperous* peasants. Not all their neighbors were so lucky. Some lived in tiny cabins of crossed laths stuffed with grass or straw, inadequately shielded from rain, snow, and wind. They lacked even a chimney; smoke from the cabin's fire

left through a small hole in the thatched roof — where, unsur-
prisingly, fires frequently broke out. These homes were without
glass windows or shutters; in a storm, or in frigid weather, open-
ings in the walls could only be stuffed with straw, rags — whatever was handy. Such families envied those enjoying greater
comfort, and most of all they coveted their beds. They themselves
slept on thin straw pallets covered by ragged blankets. Some were
without blankets. Some didn't even have pallets.

Typically, three years of harvests could be expected for one
year of famine. The years of hunger were terrible. The peasants
might be forced to sell all they owned, including their pitifully
inadequate clothing, and be reduced to nudity in all seasons. In
the hardest times they devoured bark, roots, grass; even white
clay. Cannibalism was not unknown. Strangers and travelers were
waylaid and killed to be eaten, and there are tales of gallows being
torn down — as many as twenty bodies would hang from a single
scaffold — by men frantic to eat the warm flesh raw.

However, in the good years, when they ate, they *ate*. To avoid
dining in the dark, there were only two meals a day — "dinner"
at 10 A.M. and "supper" at 5 P.M. — but bountiful harvests meant
tables which groaned. Although meat was rare on the Continent,
there were often huge pork sausages, and always enormous rolls
of black bread (white bread was the prerogative of the patriciate)
and endless courses of soup: cabbage, watercress, and cheese soups;
"dried peas and bacon water," "poor man's soup" from odds and
ends, and during Lent, of course, fish soup. Every meal was
washed down by flagons of wine in Italy and France, and, in
Germany or England, ale or beer. "Small beer" was the traditional
drink, though since the crusaders' return from the East many
preferred "spiced beer," seasoned with cinnamon, resin, gentian,
and juniper. Under Henry VII and Henry VIII the per capita
allowance was a gallon of beer a day — even for nuns and eight-
year-old children. Sir John Fortescue observed that the English
"drink no water, unless at certain times upon religious score, or
by way of doing penance."

THIS MUST HAVE LED to an exceptional degree of intoxication, for
people then were small. The average man stood a few inches over

five feet and weighed about 135 pounds. His wife was shorter and lighter. Anyone standing several inches over six feet was considered a giant and inspired legends — Jack the Giant Killer, for example, and Jack and the Beanstalk. Folklore was rich in such violent tales, for death was their constant companion. Life expectancy was brief; half the people in Europe died, usually from disease, before reaching their thirtieth birthday. It was still true, as Richard Rolle had written earlier, that "few men now reach the age of forty, and fewer still the age of fifty." If a man passed that milestone, his chances of reaching his late forties or his early fifties were good, though he looked much older; at forty-five his hair was as white, back as bent, and face as knurled as an octogenarian's today. The same was true of his wife — "Old Gretel," a woman in her thirties might be called. In longevity she was less fortunate than her husband. The toll at childbirth was appalling. A young girl's life expectancy was twenty-four. On her wedding day, traditionally, her mother gave her a piece of fine cloth which could be made into a frock. Six or seven years later it would become her shroud.

Clothing served as a kind of uniform, designating status. Some raiment was stigmatic. Lepers were required to wear gray coats and red hats, the skirts of prostitutes had to be scarlet, public penitents wore white robes, released heretics carried crosses sewn on both sides of their chests — you were expected to pray as you passed them — and the breast of every Jew, as stipulated by law, bore a huge yellow circle. The rest of society belonged to one of the three great classes: the nobility, the clergy, and the commons. Establishing one's social identity was important. Each man knew his place, believed it had been foreordained in heaven, and was aware that what he wore must reflect it.

To be sure, certain fashions were shared by all. Styles had changed since Greece and Rome shimmered in their glory; then garments had been *wrapped* on; now all classes *put* them on and fastened them. Most clothing — except the leather gauntlets and leggings of hunters, and the crude animal skins worn by the very poor — was now woven of wool. (Since few Europeans possessed a change of clothes, the same raiment was worn daily; as a consequence, skin diseases were astonishingly prevalent.) But there was no mistaking the distinctions between the parson in his vestments; the toiler in his dirty cloth tunic, loose trousers, and heavy boots; and the aristocrat with his jewelry, his hairdress, and his extravagant finery. Every knight wore a signet ring, and wearing fur was as much a sign of knighthood as wearing a sword or carrying a falcon. Indeed, in some European states it was illegal for anyone *not* nobly born to adorn himself with fur. "Many a petty noble," wrote historian W. S. Davis, "will cling to his frayed tippet of black lambskin, even in the hottest weather, merely to prove that he is not a villein."

Furred (and feathered) hats were favored by patricians; so were flowered robes and fancy jackets bulging at the sleeves. It was considered appropriate for the nobly born to flaunt the distinguishing marks of their sex. This had not changed since the death of Chaucer a century earlier. Chaucer himself — who as a page had worn a flaming costume with one hose red and one black — nevertheless deplored, in *The Canterbury Tales,* the custom of wearing trousers with codpieces over the genitalia. This flaunting of "shameful privee membres," he wrote, by men with "horrible swollen membres that they shewe thugh disgisynge [disguise]," also made "the buttokes . . . as it were, the hyndre part of a she-ape in the fulle of the moone."

He was even more offended by "the outrageous array of wommen, God wot that the visages of somme of them seem ful chaste and debonaire, yet notifie they" by "the horrible disordinate scantinesse" of their dress their "likerousnesse [lecherousness] and pride." Both sexes were advertising, not flirting, and they were certainly not bluffing; when challenged, by all accounts, they responded eagerly.

❧

It was a time when the social lubricants of civility, and the small but essential trivia of civilized life, were just beginning to reemerge, phoenixlike, from the medieval ashes. Learning, like etiquette, was being rediscovered. For example, the arithmetic symbols $+$ and $-$ did not come back into general use until the late 1400s. Spectacles for the shortsighted were unavailable until around 1520. Lead pencils had appeared at the turn of the century, together with the first postal service (between Vienna and Brussels). However, Peter Henlein's "Nuremberg Egg," the first watch, said to have been invented in 1502, is now regarded as a myth. Small table clocks and watches, telling time to the hour, would not begin to appear in Italy and Germany until the last quarter of the century. Bartolomew Newsam is said to have built the first English standing clock in 1585.

In all classes, table manners were atrocious. Men behaved like boors at meals. They customarily ate with their hats on and frequently beat their wives at table, while chewing a sausage or gnawing at a bone. Their clothes and their bodies were filthy. The story was often told of the peasant in the city who, passing a lane of perfume shops, fainted at the unfamiliar scent and was revived by holding a shovel of excrement under his nose. Pocket handkerchiefs did not appear until the early 1500s, and it was midcentury before they came into general use. Even sovereigns wiped their noses on their sleeves, or, more often, on their footmen's sleeves. Napkins were also unknown; guests were warned not to clean their teeth on the tablecloth. Guests in homes were also reminded that they should blow their noses with the hand that held the knife, not the one holding the food.

There is some dispute about when cutlery was introduced. Apparently knives were first provided by guests, who carried them in sheaths attached to their belts. According to Erasmus, decorum dictated that food be brought to the mouth with one's fingers. The fork is mentioned in the fifteenth century, but was used then only to serve dishes. As tableware it was not laid out in the French court until 1589, though it had appeared at a Venetian ducal banquet in 1520; writing in his diary afterward, Jacques LeSaige, a French silk merchant who had been among the guests, noted with wonder: "These seigneurs, when they want to take the meat up, use a silver fork."

There *was* such a thing as bad form, but it had nothing to do with manners. Any breach of rules established by the Church was a grave offense. Except for the Jews, of whom there were perhaps a million in Europe, every European was expected to venerate, above all others, the Virgin Mary — Queen of the Holy City, Lady of Heaven, *la Beata Vergine, die heilige Jungfrau, la Virgen María, la Dame débonnaire* — followed by her vassals, the Catholic saints, who did her liege homage. Parishioners were required to hear Mass at least once a week (for knights it was daily); to hate the Saracens and, of course, the Jews; to honor holy places and sacred objects; and to keep the major fasts.

Fasts were the greatest challenge faced by the faithful, and not all were equal to it. In one Breton village the devout affirmed their Lenten piety by joining a procession led by a priest. Afterward one marching woman, who had worn a particularly saintly expression during the parade, retired to her kitchen and elatedly broke Lent by heating, and eating, mutton and ham. The aroma drifted out the window. It was identified by passersby. Seized, she was brought before the local bishop, who sentenced her to walk the village streets until Easter, a month away, with the ham slung around her neck and the quarter of mutton, on its spit, over her shoulder. Ineluctably — and another sign of the age — a jeering mob followed her every step.

THAT WAS a relatively minor infraction. Greater crimes provoked awesome rites. A drunken, irreverent baron found himself in deep trouble after stealing the chalice of a parish church. He had been seen galloping away with it. The local bishop ordered the church bell tolled in the mournful cadence usually reserved for major funerals. The church itself was draped in black. The congregation gathered in the nave. Amid a frightful hush the prelate, surrounded by his clergymen, each carrying a lighted candle, appeared in the chancel and pronounced the name of the thief, shouting: "Let him be cursed in the city and cursed in the field; cursed in his granary, his harvest, and his children; as Dathan and Abiram were swallowed up by the gaming earth, so may hell swallow him. And even as today we quench these torches in our hands, so may the light of his life be quenched for all eternity, unless he do repent!"

As the priests flung their candles down and stamped them out, the parishioners trembled for the knight's soul, which, they knew, had very little chance of surviving so awful an imprecation. The wayward baron was now an outlaw; every man's hand was against him; neither lepers nor Jews were so completely isolated. This social exile was a formidable weapon, and it brought the sinner to his knees, for eventually he bought back his salvation — at a formidable price. First he donated his entire fortune to the bishop. Then he appeared at the chancel barefoot, wearing a pilgrim's robe. For twenty-four hours he lay prostrate before the high altar, praying and fasting; then he knelt while sixty monks and priests clubbed him. As each blow fell he yelled, "Just are thy judgments, O Lord!" At last, when he lay bleeding, bones broken and senses impaired, the bishop absolved him and gave him the kiss of peace. The punishment seems excessive. Such a chalice, not fashioned from precious metal, had little monetary value; its theft had merely been an act of petty larceny. But the medieval Church was strong on law and order, and had this felony gone unpunished, the aftermath could have led to laxity, backsliding, even mutiny. Besides, there were greater sinners than the scourged baron, and crueler penances. For them the road to atonement was literally a series of roads, to be covered, over six, ten, or even twelve years in that greatest of penances, the pilgrimage.

In instances in which pilgrims had offended God and man, their journeys were actually a substitute for prison terms. European castles had dungeons — so did the Vatican — but they couldn't begin to hold the miscreant population. The chief legal penalty was execution. There were alternatives in lay courts — ears were cut off, tongues ripped out, eyes gouged from their sockets; the genitalia of wives who had betrayed their husbands were cauterized with white-hot tongs — but these, although extremely unpleasant, offered no hope for salvation. The violator still faced a writhing afterlife in Hades, and obviously everyone who had violated the law did not deserve that. Therefore the Church, which had its own legal system, paralleling secular courts, took over.

Offenders were ordered to shave their heads, abandon their families, fast constantly (meat only once a day), and set out barefoot for a far destination. Journey's end varied from offender to offender. Rome was a popular choice. Some were sent all the way to Jerusalem. The general rule was the longer the distance, the greater the atonement. If of noble birth, the penitent had to wear chains on his neck and wrists forged from his own armor, a sign of how far he had fallen. Frequently the felon carried a passport, signed by a bishop, specifying his crimes in the grimmest possible detail and then asking good Christians to offer him food and

lodging. From the felon's point of view this approach may have
seemed flawed, but his opinion was unsolicited. And ecclesiastical
verdicts could seldom be appealed.

Some men, in their search for absolution, suffered almost unen-
durable ordeals. The notorious Count Fulk the Black of Anjou,
whose crimes were legendary, finally realized that his immortal
soul was in peril and, while miserable in the throes of his conscience, begged for divine mercy. Count Fulk had sinned for
twenty years. Among other things he had murdered his wife,
though this charge had been dropped on the strength of his un-
supported word that he had found her rutting behind a barn with
a goatherd. The court felt helpless here. Decapitation on the spot
was the fate of an adulteress caught in the act; adulterers usually
went free, to be dealt with by the husbands they had wronged.
In this case there had been no witnesses, and the goatherd had
vanished, but counts, even wicked counts, did not lie. However,
quite apart from that, Fulk the Black's catalog of crimes was a
long one. He expected a heavy sentence, and that is what he got.
He is said to have fainted when it was passed. Shackled, he was
condemned to a triple Jerusalem pilgrimage: across most of France
and Savoy, over the Alps, through the Papal States, Carinthia,
Hungary, Bosnia, mountainous Serbia, Bulgaria, Constantinople,
and the length of mountainous Anatolia, then down through modern Syria and Jordan to the holy city. In irons, his fleet bleeding,
he made this round trip three times — 15,300 miles — and the
last time he was dragged through the streets on a hurdle while
two well-muscled men lashed his naked back with bullwhips.

THE COUNT could have asked, though he didn't, what all this
misery had to do with the teachings of Jesus of Nazareth. In fact
it had nothing to do with them. The distinction between devotion
and superstition has always been unclear, but there was little blur-
ring here. Although they called themselves Christians, medieval
Europeans were ignorant of the Gospels. The Bible existed only
in a language they could not read. The mumbled incantations at
Mass were meaningless to them. They believed in sorcery, witchcraft, hobgoblins, werewolves, amulets, and black magic, and
were thus indistinguishable from pagans. If a lady died, the instant

her breath stopped servants ran through the manor house, emp-
tying every container of water to prevent her soul from drowning,
and before her funeral the corpse was carefully watched to prevent
any dog or cat from running across the coffin, thus changing her
remains into a vampire. Meantime her lord, praying for her salvation, was lying prostrate, his head turned eastward and his arms
stretched out, forming a cross. Nothing in the New Testament
supported such delusions and rituals; nevertheless the precautions
were taken — with the blessings of the clergy. In monastic manuscripts one repeatedly finds such entries as: "Common report has
it that Antichrist has been born at Babylon and that the Day of
Judgment is nigh." The alarm was spread so often that the peasants
ignored it; on the Sabbath, after an early Mass, they would gossip,
dance, sing, wrestle, race, and compete in archery contests until
evening shadows deepened. There was hell enough on earth for
them; they were too drained to ponder the risks of another world.

Nevertheless in pensive moments they worried. Should the left
eye of a corpse not close properly, they knew, the departed would
soon have company in purgatory. If a man donned a clean white
shirt on a Friday, or saw a shooting star, or a will-o'-the-wisp in
the marshes, or a vulture hovering over his home, his death was
very near. Similarly, a woman stupid enough to wash clothes
during Holy Week would soon be in her grave. Should thirteen
people be so thoughtless as to sup at one table, one of those present
would not be there for tomorrow morning's meal; if a wolf howled
through the night, one who heard him would disappear before
dawn. Comets and eclipses were sinister. Everyone knew that an
enormous comet had been sighted in July 1198 and Richard the
Lion-Hearted had died "very soon after." (In fact he did not die
until April 6, 1199.)

Everyone also knew — and every child was taught — that the
air all around them was infested with invisible, soulless spirits,
some benign but most of them evil, dangerous, long-lived, and
hard to kill; that among them were the souls of unbaptized infants,
ghouls who snuffled out cadavers in graveyards and chewed their
bones, water nymphs skilled at luring knights to death by drowning, dracs who carried little children off to their caves beneath the
earth, wolfmen — the undead turned into ravenous beasts — and

vampires who rose from their tombs at dusk to suck the blood of men, women, or children who had strayed from home. At any moment, under any circumstances, a person could be removed from the world of the senses to a realm of magic creatures and occult powers. Every natural object possessed supernatural qualities. Books interpreting dreams were highly popular.

The stars were known to be guided by angels, and physicians were constantly consulting astrologers and theologians. Doctors diagnosing illnesses were influenced by the constellation under which the patient had been born or taken sick; thus the eminent surgeon Guy de Chauliac wrote: "If anyone is wounded in the neck when the moon is at Taurus, the affliction will be dangerous." Thousands of pitiful people disfigured by swollen lymph nodes in their necks mobbed the kings of England and France, believing that their scrofula could be cured by the touch of a royal hand. One document from the period is a calendar, published at Mainz, which designates the best astrological times for bloodletting. Epidemics were attributed to unfortunate configurations of the stars. Now and then a quack was unmasked; in London one Roger Clerk, who had pretended to cure ailments with spurious charms, was sentenced to ride through the city with urinals hanging from his neck. But others, equally bogus, lived out their lives unchallenged.

Scholars as eminent as Erasmus and Sir Thomas More accepted the existence of witchcraft. Conspicuous fakes excepted, the Church encouraged superstitions, recommended trust in faith healers, and spread tales of satyrs, incubi, sirens, cyclops, tritons, and giants, explaining that all were manifestations of Satan. The Prince of Darkness, it taught, was as real as the Holy Trinity. Certainly belief in him was useful; prelates agreed that when it came to keeping the masses on the straight and narrow, fear of the devil was a stronger force than the love of God. Great shows were made of exorcisms. The story spread across the continent of how the fiend entered a man's body and croaked blasphemy through his mouth until a priest, following a magic rite, recited an incantation. The devil, foiled, screamed horribly and fled.

The ecclesiastical hierarchy, through its priests and monks, repeatedly affirmed the legitimacy of specific miracles. Unshriven sinners were not the only pilgrims on Europe's roads. In fact, they were a minority. The majority were simple people, identifiable by their brown wool robes, heavy staffs, and sacks slung from their belts. Their motivation was simple devotion, often concern for a recently departed relative now in purgatory. Although filthy and untidy, they were rarely abused; few wanted to lose the scriptural blessing reserved for those who, having shown kindness to a stranger, had "entertained angels unawares."

Pilgrims headed for over a thousand shrines whose miracles had been recognized by Rome. There was Our Lady of Chartres, Our Lady of the Rose at Lucca, Our Guardian Lady in Genoa, and other Our Ladies at Le Puy, Auray, Grenoble, Valenciennes, Liesse, Rocamadour, Ossier. . . . It went on and on. One popular destination was the tomb of Pierre de Luxembourg, a cardinal who had died, aged eighteen, of anorexia; within fifteen months of his death 1,964 miracles were credited to the magic he had left in his bones. Some saints were regarded as medical specialists; victims of cholera headed for a chapel of Saint Vitus, who was believed to be particularly efficacious for that disease.

But nothing could compete with the two star attractions: scenes actually visited by the savior himself and spectacular phenomena confirmed by the Vatican. At Santa Maria Maggiore, people were told, they could see the actual manger where Christ was born, or, at St. John Lateran, the holy steps Jesus ascended while wearing his crown of thorns, or, at St. Peter in Montorio, the place where Peter was martyred by Nero. Englishmen believed that the venerable abbot of St. Germer need only bless a fountain and lo! its waters would heal the sick, restore sight to the blind, and make the dumb speak. Once, according to pilgrims, the abbot had visited a village parched for lack of water. He led the peasants into the church, and, as they watched, smote a stone with his staff. Behold! Water gushed forth, not only to slake thirsts but also possessing miraculous powers to cure all pain and illness.

TRAVEL WAS slow, expensive, uncomfortable — and perilous. It was slowest for those who rode in coaches, faster for walkers, and fastest for horsemen, who were few because of the need to change and stable steeds. The expenses chiefly arose from the countless tolls, the discomfort from a score of irritants. Bridges spanning rivers were shaky (priests recommended that before crossing them travelers commend themselves to God); other streams had to be forded; the roads were deplorable — mostly trails and muddy ruts, impassable, except in summer, by two-wheeled carts — and nights en route had to be spent in Europe's wretched inns. These were unsanitary places, the beds wedged against one another, blankets crawling with roaches, rats, and fleas; whores plied their trade and then slipped away with a man's money, and innkeepers seized guests' baggage on the pretext that they had not paid.

The peril came from highwaymen, whose mythic joys and miseries were celebrated by the Parisian François Villon. In reality there was nothing attractive about these criminals in the woods. They were pitiless thieves, kidnappers, and killers, and they flourished because they were so seldom pursued. Between towns the traveler was on his own. Except in a few places like Castile, where roads were patrolled by the archers of the Santa Hermandad, no policemen were stationed in the open country. Outlaws had always lurked in the woods, but their menace had increased as their ranks were thickened by impoverished knights returning from the ill-starred crusades, demobilized veterans of various foreign campaigns, and, in England, renegades from the recent War of the Roses. Sometimes these brigands traveled in roving gangs, waiting to ambush strangers; sometimes they stood by the road disguised as beggars or pilgrims, knives at the ready. Even gallant seigneurs declined responsibility for travelers passing through their lands at night, and many a less-principled sire was either a bandit himself or an accomplice of outlaws, overlooking their outrages provided they hold important personages harmless and present him with lavish gifts at Christmas.

Therefore honest travelers carried well-honed daggers, knowing they might have to kill and hoping they would have the stomach for it. Wayfarers from different lands usually banded together, seeking collective security, though they often excluded Englishmen, who in that age were distrusted, suspected of petty thefts, regarded by seamen as pirates, and notorious for the false weights and shoddy goods of their merchants. Even Britons like Chaucer, who denounced greed, were themselves greedy. Their women were unwelcome for another reason. They were so foul-mouthed that Joan of Arc always referred to them as "the Goddams." And the English of both sexes were known, even then, for their insolence. In 1500 the Venetian ambassador to London reported to his government that his hosts were "great lovers of themselves, and of everything belonging to them; they think there are no other men than themselves, and no other country but England; and whenever they see a handsome foreigner they say that 'he looks like an Englishman,' and that it is a great pity that he is not one."

Doubtless the same thing could be said, mutatis mutandis, of other people, but Englishmen, aware of their reputation, always went abroad heavily armed — unless they were rich. Surrounded by bands of knights in full armor, wealthy Europeans traveled in painted, gilded, carved, and curtained horse-drawn coaches. They knew they were marks for thieves, and never left their fiefs to visit cities, or attend the great August fairs, unless heavily guarded.

A YORKSHIRE gravestone bears this inscription:

> *Hear underneath dis laihl stean*
> *las Robert earl of Huntingtun*
> *neer arcir yer az hie sa geud*
> *And pipl kauld in Robin Heud*
> *sick utlawz as he an iz men*
> *il england nivr si agen*
> *Obiit 24 kal Decembris 1247*

Robin Hood lived; this marker confirms it, just as the Easter tables attest to the existence of the great Arthur. But that is *all* the tombstone does. Everything we know about that period suggests that Robin was merely another wellborn cutthroat who hid in shrubbery by roadsides, waiting to rob helpless wayfarers. The possibility that he stole from the rich and gave to the poor is, like the tale of that other cold-blooded rogue, Jesse James, highly unlikely. Even unlikelier is the conceit that Robin Hood, aka Heud, was accompanied by a bedmate called Maid Marian, a giant known as Little John, and a lapsed Catholic named Friar Tuck. Almost certainly they were creatures of an ingenious folk imagination, and their contemporary, the sheriff of Nottingham, is probably the most libeled law enforcement officer in this millennium.

The more we study those remote centuries, the unlikelier such legends become. Later mythmakers invested the Middle Ages with a bogus aura of romance. The Pied Piper of Hamelin is an example. He was a real man, but there was nothing enchanting about him. Quite the opposite; he was horrible, a pyschopath and pederast who, on June 20, 1484, spirited away 130 children in the Saxon village of Hammel and used them in unspeakable ways. Accounts of the aftermath vary. According to some, his victims were never seen again; others told of dismembered little bodies found scattered in the forest underbrush or festooning the branches of trees.

The most imaginative cluster of fables appeared in print the year after the Piper's mass murders, when William Caxton published Sir Thomas Malory's *Le morte d'Arthur*. Later, bowdlerized versions of this great work have obscured the fact that Malory, contemplating medieval morality, seldom wore blinders. He had no illusions about his heroine when he wrote: "There syr Launcelot toke the Fayrest Ladie by the hand, and she was naked as a nedel." Some of his characters may actually have existed. For over a thousand years villagers in remote parts of Wales have called an adulteress "a regular Guinevere." But Launcelot du Lac is entirely fictitious, and given the colossal time sprawl of the Middle Ages, it is highly unlikely that Guinevere, if indeed she lived, even shared the same century with Arthur.

WE KNOW LITTLE of the circumstances under which Magellan and his Beatriz were married in 1517, but if they were united by transcendental love, they were an odd couple. It is true that a young archduke in Vienna's imperial court had introduced the diamond ring as a sign of engagement forty years earlier, but its vogue had been confined to the patriciate, and even there it had found little favor. Typically, news of an imminent marriage spread when the pregnancy of the bride-elect began to show. If she had been particularly user-friendly, raising genuine doubts about the child's paternity, those who had enjoyed her favors drew straws. "Virginity," one historian of the period writes, "had to be protected

by every device of custom, morals, law, religion, paternal authority, pedagogy, and 'point of honor'; yet somehow it managed
to get lost."

No one was actually scandalized; the normal, eternal repro-
ductive instincts were merely asserting themselves. But such random matrimony disappointed parents; a girl's wedding was the
pivotal event in her life, and its economic implications — the ceremony was among other things a merging of belongings — con-
cerned both families. The tradition of arranged marriages, sensibly
conceived, was obviously crumbling. Commentators of the time,
believing that the old way was best, were troubled. In his *Colloquia
familiaria* (*Colloquies*) Erasmus recommended that youths let fathers
choose their brides and trust that love would grow as acquaintance
ripened. Even Rabelais agreed in *Le cinquiesme et dernier livre*. Couples who kicked over the traces were reproached in *The Schole-
master* by Roger Ascham, tutor to England's royal family. Ascham
bitterly regretted that "our time is so far gone from the old discipline and obedience as now not only young gentlemen but even
very young girls dare . . . marry themselves in spite of father,
mother, God, good order, and all." At the University of Wittenberg, Martin Luther, dismayed that the son of a faculty colleague
had plighted his troth without consulting his father — and that a
young judge had found the vow legal — thought the reputation
of the institution was being tarnished. He wrote: "Many parents
have ordered their sons home . . . saying that we hang wives
around their necks. . . . The next Sunday I preached a strong sermon, telling men to follow the common road and manner which
had been since the beginning of the world . . . namely, that parents should give their children to each other with prudence and
good will, without their own preliminary arrangement."

Females could marry — legally, with or without parental consent — when they reached their twelfth birthday. The age for
males was fourteen. Even before she had reached her teens, a girl
knew that unless she married before she was twenty-one, society
would consider her useless, fit only for the nunnery, or, in England, the spinning wheel (a "spinster"). Hence the yearning of
female adolescents for the altar. Getting pregnant was one way to
reach it. On Sundays, under watchful parental eyes, girls would

dress modestly and be demure in church, but on weekdays they opened their blouses, hiked their skirts, and romped through the fields in pursuit of phalli.

Another five centuries would pass before young women would be so open in their pursuit of sex. In Wittenberg Luther complained that "the race of girls is getting bold, and run after the fellows into their rooms and chambers and wherever they can and offer them their free love." Later he fumed that young women had become "immodest, shameless. . . . The young people of today are utterly dissolute and disorderly. . . . The women and girls of Wittenberg have begun to go bare before and behind, and there is no one to punish or correct them." If the lover of a soon-to-be unwed mother decided he was not ready for marriage, her cause was not necessarily lost; often an attractive girl with a fatherless child and a long record of indiscretions could find a respectable peasant willing to take her to the altar.

In this lusty age the most a parent could extract from a daughter was her promise not to yield until the banns had been read. Once a couple was engaged, they slept together with society's approval. If a peasant girl was not pregnant, there were only two practical deterrents to her acceptance of a marriage proposal. It was her desire either to enter a convent or, at the far end of the spectrum, to join the world's oldest profession. Harlotry not only paid well; it was frequently prestigious. Because prostitutes had to expose their entire bodies, they were the cleanest people in Europe. The competition was fierce, but it always had been, and once established, these women became what were now being called courtesans (from the Italian *courtigiane*), or female courtiers. Moves to suppress them were rare and unpopular; Luther lost many followers when, though affirming the normality of sexual desire, he proclaimed that the sale of sex was wrong and persuaded several German cities to outlaw it.

GREAT RENAISSANCE ARTISTS flourished while lesser talents actually starved in garrets; but the highly profitable production of erotica, including salacious illustrations, kept many men well fed. Their work was available at every fair and in all large cities, sold by postmen, strolling musicians, and street hawkers. The dissolute

Pietro Aretino's *Sonetti lussuriosi* (*Lewd Sonnets*) was as popular in
Augsburg and Paris — and, when Clement VII became pope, in
the Vatican — as in the poet's own Arezzo. After Aretino's expulsion from Rome he was thought to have explored the outer
limits of propriety. Then François Rabelais, a priest, published his
Gargantua epic, using gutter language which shocked Aretino but
outsold the *Sonetti*. As happens from time to time, permissiveness
was eclipsing faith. Some pornographic books were used as how-
to sex manuals. And sometimes a community would treat the
most wanton behavior as normal. Witch-hunting being a popular
sport of the age, from time to time suspicious nocturnal gatherings
would be reported to the authorities. In each case, chronicles of
the time attest — with obvious relief — those assembled had been
engaging in an even more popular pastime. Their meetings, according to a historian of the period, were "excuses for promiscuous
sexual relations, and for initiating young people in the arts of
debauchery."

Sex among the nobility was complicated by more intricate
property transactions. Looking to future generations and plotting
bluer bloodlines, patricians usually arranged betrothals for their
sons and daughters shortly after their seventh birthdays. There
were instances in which this was done when they were as young
as three. These alliances could later be annulled, provided they
had not been consummated, but unless strong steps were taken,
consummation naturally began shortly after the parties reached
puberty, opportunity and temptation being, as always, the prime
requisites for coitus. Because these couples had not married for
love, triangular entanglements came later. Since divorce was forbidden by the Church, adultery was an obvious solution, usually
with the consent of both spouses.

Bohemian artists scorned monogamy, and the aristocracy
agreed with them. To the ladies in the Nérac court of Marguerite
of Angoulême, queen of the independent medieval kingdom of
Navarre and the sister of France's King Francis I, extramarital sex
was considered almost obligatory. Those wives in the *noblesse
d'épée* who remained faithful to their husbands were mocked by
the others. To abstain from the pleasures of adultery was almost
a breach of etiquette, like failing to curtsy before royalty. Some

of Marguerite's remarks at the baths of Cauterets have survived. At a time when "love" was a synonym for casual sex, one young *madame la vicomtesse* asked her, "You mean to say, then, that all is lawful to those who love, provided no one knows?" The reply was, "Yes, in truth, it is only fools who are found out." Marguerite never mentioned any intrigue of her own. As a patron of humanists and an author in her own right, she was one of the outstanding figures of the French Renaissance, and was far too shrewd to risk weakening her influence. Besides, women who dropped names were not invited back to Nérac; they had compromised their lovers, thereby eliminating them as candidates for future dalliance. However, according to Seigneur de Brantôme's *Les vies des dames galantes,* Marguerite did advise the young comtesses and marquesas around her to take their marriage vows lightly: "Unhappy the lady who does not preserve the treasure which does her so much honor when well kept, and so much dishonor when she continues to keep it." Rabelais, enchanted, set aside his misogyny and dedicated *Gargantua* to her. ·

By the time they had mastered the sophisticated techniques of seduction, mature lords and ladies were unafflicted by pangs of conscience. However, their youthful married children did not lightly break a solemn, unambiguous commandment, even though many a *petit seigneur* must have been aware of his parents' intrigues. The first lapses of the youthful, once one of them had been attracted to a third party, were made easier by the elaborate embroidery of romantic love, now popular. Aware that infidelity was sinful, young men and women who were married, but not to one another, forswore sex. Sublimated courtship followed. The infatuated couple exchanged gifts, lays, madrigals, sonnets, odes, billets-doux, meaningful glances, and met, their hearts pounding, in secluded trysts. Their platonic fiction was encouraged by Baldassare Castiglione's *Il cortegiano,* the arbiter of aristocratic manners during the Renaissance. Castiglione assured them that although they aroused one another's passions, they could remain just friends, scrupulously chaste. Of course, they couldn't. *Il cortegiano* was a fraudulent work, its author a civilized pied piper. The period was not one of restraint; boys were sexually aggressive, and girls liked them so. Both wrote poetry, but their object was mutual possession; in the end he always settled in between her thighs.

LUBRICITY FLOURISHED in all its various forms. "Sodomy was frequent," a chronicler observes; "prostitution was general, and adultery was almost universal." Contemporary records suggest that extramarital sex was most flagrant in France. Although wives were committing a capital offense, "illicit love affairs," a historian writes, "were part of the normal life of French women of good standing." Yet it appears to have been no different in England, where, historian James Froude later wrote, "private life was infected with impurity to which the licentiousness of the Catholic clergy appeared like innocence" — which, as we shall see, was saying a great deal. "There reigned abundantly," Raphael Holinshed noted in his chronicle, "the filthie sin of lechery and fornication, with abominable adulteries, speciallie in the king."

Holinshed probably had Edward VI in mind, but a number of other monarchs could have fallen under the same indictment. One of Edward's predecessors took Jane Shore, a commoner, as his favorite mistress, and in that role she served as a friend at court for many good Englishmen in need of royal favors. Across the Channel Francis I (r. 1515–1547), *le roi grand nez* — a long nose was thought to signify virility, and he had both — seemed bent on outperforming Don Juan. Francis's most memorable royal concubines were Françoise de Foix, comtesse de Chateaubriant, and Anne de Pisselieu, whom he created duchesse d'Étampes. But he always had other irons, so to speak, in the fire. According to one legend, he invested Milan, not to take the city, but to pursue a pair of lovely eyes he had once glimpsed there. In France his exercise of his *droit du seigneur* was not as popular as he assumed it to be. The husband of la belle Ferroniere, a lawyer's wife who had been chosen to share the royal bed, deliberately infected himself with syphilis and gave it to her so that she might pass it along to the king. Still another mistress-in-waiting disfigured herself in the hope that Francis would find her too repulsive to mount. It didn't work. She had been under the impression that the king was interested in her face.

These two, however, were exceptional. Most young French-
women are said to have been delighted when conscripted to receive
the king in all his manly glory, and in their appearances at court
they competed for his attention. Opening their bodices, they displayed swelling bosoms down to, and sometimes below, their
nipples (unless the bosoms were inadequate, in which case padding
had been inserted under the stays). Their backs had been cut down
to the last vertebra, sleeves billowed, gowns were pinched at the
waist and tightened under the breasts, hidden wires spread out the
skirt, and high heels gave each hopeful candidate a prancing, sexy

King Francis I of France (1494–1547)

walk. In his last years Francis moved to Fontainebleau and surrounded himself with what he called his *petite bande* of lovely
maidens, whom he deflowered while watched by those waiting
their turn. On his deathbed, where he finally slept alone, he summoned his sole heir and warned him not to be dominated by a
woman. But the youth, who ascended to the throne as Henry II,
had already established the format of his domestic life. France
would be ruled by a ménage à trois: the king himself; his queen,
Catherine de' Medici, whose parents had died of syphilis three
weeks after her birth; and the king's mistress, Diane de Poitiers.

Various reasons have been advanced to explain why, as medieval shadows receded, European morals declined. This much
seems certain: behavior had become so abandoned that family ties
were loosened; impudicity threatened to overflow the channels
within which the institution of marriage sought to confine it, if
only for the sake of the social order. To be sure, there were laws
against lascivious behavior, but governments lacked both the man-
power and the will. In such times they generally do. Divorce,
which might have brought the problem under control, was rejected by all authorities. The pope, Luther, Henry VIII, and Erasmus agreed that bigamy was preferable to divorce. After the great
split in Christendom, Protestant theologians moved hesitantly toward the acceptance of divorce, but only in the case of adultery.
"Probably the basic cause in the moral loosening in Western Europe," a modern historian argues, "was the growth of wealth."
Nevertheless, the religious revolution played a role. There were
no theological villains here. Martin Luther agreed that depravity
increased in his Protestant congregations after the Reformation,
but lechery and sexual license had also run amok in Catholic Spain
and Catholic Italy, and Francis, whatever his private sympathies,
ruled a Catholic France. Yet the shocking attacks on Rome and
by Rome clearly led to a decline of respect for all vows and inhibitions. "Nobody cares about either heaven or hell," wrote Andreas Musculus, a Lutheran preacher, sadly; "nobody gives a
thought to either God or the Devil." That was true, however,
only during the transition from one Church to many churches.
Then conservatives on all sides restored moral discipline, and patricians were persuaded to set an example. Indeed, in the case of

some sects — Calvinism, for example — reforms became so excessive that ardent spirits of both sexes looked back with secret envy to the exuberant, orgasmic laxity of the past.

BUT THAT CAME later. During the early sixteenth century lust, and particularly noble lust, seethed throughout Europe. In France this was the age of Rabelais, and across the Channel the lords and ladies of Tudor England were establishing a tradition of aristocratic promiscuity which would continue in the centuries ahead. Yet Rome, the capital of Christendom, was the capital of sin, and the sinners included most of the Roman patriciate. Among the holy city's great families, each of which was represented in the sacred College of Cardinals, were the nouveau riche Della Roveres, whose cupidity matched their enthusiasm for illicit public coupling in all its permutations. They occupied the epicenter of Roman society. Two Della Roveres became popes (Sixtus IV and his nephew Julius II), their names were on every guest list, and if an invitation to their satyrical parties was ever refused, the fact is unrecorded.

They had not, however, been pacesetters. That questionable distinction belongs to the notorious Borgias. So many bizarre stories have been handed down about this hot-blooded Spanish family that it is impossible, after five centuries, to know where the line of credibility should be drawn. Much of what we have is simply what was accepted as fact at the time. However, a substantial part of the legend was documented — enough to set it down here with confidence that, however extraordinary it may seem now, what was believed then was, in the main, undoubtedly true. The tale is a long one. The Borgias had been acting scandalously at least two generations before Giuliano Cardinal della Rovere, taking the name Pope Julius II, assumed the chair of Saint Peter in October 1503. He was lucky to have lived that long. Ten years earlier, when the papal tiara had been placed on the brow of his great rival, Alexander VI, the Borgia pope, Alexander had plotted Cardinal della Rovere's assassination. At the last moment Giuliano had eluded the cutthroats by fleeing to France. Then he — himself a future Vicar of Christ — had taken up arms against the papacy.

The Borgia name had become notorious a half-century earlier, when the reigning pontiff was Pius II. Pius was hardly a prig — as Bishop Aeneas Sylvius Piccolomini he had fathered several children by various mistresses — but when elected pontiff he had put all that behind him, telling his court, "Forget Aeneas; look at Pius." In 1460 he himself had been watching twenty-nine-year-old Cardinal Borgia — the future Alexander — in Siena. Troubled by what he saw there, he sent Borgia a sharply worded letter, rebuking him for a wild party the prelate had thrown. During the festivities, Pius dryly observed, "none of the allurements of love was lacking." He further noted that the guest list had been odd.

Pope Julius II (1443–1513)

Siena's most beautiful young women had been invited, but their "husbands, fathers, and brothers" had been excluded.

In the context of that place and time, this was ominous. It could only have been done, as Pius II wrote, "in order that lust be unrestrained." Women were accustomed to doing what men told them to do. Lacking the protection of any males in her family, and intimidated by a formidable cardinal, a girl was unlikely to survive an evening with her maidenhood intact. The mature woman guest would feel free to ignore the proprieties, particularly when that course was being urged upon her by a prince of the Church.

Pius warned that "disgrace" and "contempt" would be the lot of any Christ's vicar who "seems to tolerate these actions." So, eventually, it was, but Pius was in his grave four years after the Siena orgy, and a century would pass before another pontiff agreed with him. All the Holy Fathers of Magellan's time were uninhibited, but the Borgia pope and his remarkable children symbolize a time, a mood, and an obsession which, after five centuries, is still fascinating. The reaction against it contributed to one of those seismic jolts which history rarely notes more than once every thousand years.

RODRIGO LANZOL Y BORGIA, to give him his full name — it was Borja y Doms in Spain — had been elevated to the College of Cardinals by Pope Calixtus III, his uncle. That was in 1456. No sooner had he donned his red hat than he had removed it, together with the rest of his raiment, for a marathon romp with a succession of women whose identity is unknown to us and may well have been unknown to him.

This performance produced a son and two daughters, who were later joined, when he was in his forties, by another daughter and three more sons. We know the putative mother of this second family. She was Rosa Vannozza dei Catanei, the precocious child of one of his favorite mistresses. Roman lore has it that he was coupling with the older woman when he was distracted by the sight of her adolescent daughter lying beside them, naked, thighs yawning wide, matching her mother thrust for pelvic thrust, but with a rhythmic rotation of the hips which so intrigued the cardinal that he switched partners in midstroke.

Borgia's enjoyment of the flesh was enhanced when the woman beneath him was married, particularly if he had presided at her wedding. Breaking any commandment excited him, but he was partial to the seventh. As priest he married Rosa to two men. She may actually have slept with her husbands from time to time — since Borgia always kept a stable of women, she was allowed an occasional night off to indulge her own sexual preferences — but her duties lay in his eminence's bed. Then, at the age of fifty-nine, he yearned for a more nubile partner. His parting with Rosa was affectionate. Later he even gave her a little gift — he made her brother a cardinal. Meantime he had chosen her successor, the

Alexander VI, the Borgia pope (1431–1503)

breathtakingly lovely, nineteen-year-old Giulia Farnese, who in
the words of one contemporary was *"una bella cosa a vedere"* —
"a beautiful thing to see." Again, as priest, he arranged a wedding
in the chapel of one of his family palaces. After he had pronounced
Giulia and a youthful member of the Orsini family man and wife,
Signor Orsini was told his presence was required elsewhere. Then
Signora Orsini, wearing her bridal gown, was led to the sparkling
gilt-and-sky-blue bedchamber of the cardinal, her senior by forty
years. A maid removed the gown and, for some obscure reason,
carefully put it away. She cannot have thought that Giulia would
want to keep it for sentimental reasons, for thenceforth Borgia's

Giulia Farnese (d. 1524)

new bedmate was known throughout Italy as *sposa di Cristo,* the bride of Christ.

Once he became Pope Alexander VI, Vatican parties, already wild, grew wilder. They were costly, but he could afford the lifestyle of a Renaissance prince; as vice chancellor of the Roman Church, he had amassed enormous wealth. As guests approached the papal palace, they were excited by the spectacle of living statues: naked, gilded young men and women in erotic poses. Flags bore the Borgia arms, which, appropriately, portrayed a red bull rampant on a field of gold. Every fete had a theme. One, known to Romans as the Ballet of the Chestnuts, was held on October 30, 1501. The indefatigable Burchard describes it in his *Diarium.* After the banquet dishes had been cleared away, the city's fifty most beautiful whores danced with guests, "first clothed, then naked." The dancing over, the "ballet" began, with the pope and two of his children in the best seats.

Candelabra were set up on the floor; scattered among them were chestnuts, "which," Burchard writes, "the courtesans had to pick up, crawling between the candles." Then the serious sex started. Guests stripped and ran out on the floor, where they mounted, or were mounted by, the prostitutes. "The coupling took place," according to Burchard, "in front of everyone present." Servants kept score of each man's orgasms, for the pope greatly admired virility and measured a man's machismo by his ejaculative capacity. After everyone was exhausted, His Holiness distributed prizes — cloaks, boots, caps, and fine silken tunics. The winners, the diarist wrote, were those "who made love with those courtesans the greatest number of times."

Despite the unquestioned depravity of Alexander, the most intriguing figure in the carnal history of the time was one of the pope's four children by Vannozza dei Catanei. Born in 1480, the Lucrezia Borgia who has come down to us is an admixture of myth, fable, and incontestable fact. It is quite possible that she was, to some degree, a victim of misogynic slander. The medieval Church saw woman as *Eva rediviva,* the temptress responsible for Adam's fall, and the illegitimate daughter of a pope may have been an irresistible target for gossip, particularly when she was physically attractive. To this day her reputation is controversial.

According to the *Cambridge Modern History,* "Nothing could be less like the real Lucrezia than the Lucrezia of the dramatists and romancers." Historians disagree, however, over what the real Lucrezia *was* like. There is certainly evidence that in at least some respects she was what she was thought to have been, but only a few documents are extant. Although these are shocking, we are largely dependent upon what her contemporaries thought of her. It was not flattering. Even Rachel Erlanger, one of her more sympathetic biographers, agrees that she had "a sinister reputation" for "incredible moral laxity."

Yet it was obvious that there was more to Madonna Lucrezia, as the Vatican court called her, than her celebrated sexuality. Fluent in Tuscan, French, and Spanish, she read classical Greek and Latin, had been educated in manners and style, could engage in lengthy learned discussions, and was an accomplished poet. It seems equally clear that she was vulnerable; beginning in her childhood she had been enveloped in her father's love, and she suffered from an almost fatal compulsion to please. By all accounts she was exceptionally comely. A contemporary described her as "a woman of great loveliness." That was women's impression of her. Men thought her ravishing.

Under the supervision of Giulia Farnese, her father's mistress, she devoted herself to what Jakob Burckhardt, the nineteenth-century Swiss historian, called Italy's "national pastime for external display." In her youth she was called *dolce ciera* (sweet face) because of her innocent expression. Bernadino di Betto di Biago (Pinturicchio) captured that artlessness in his portrait of her, painted in her early teens, and the debauchery and lewd excesses which followed do not seem to have altered it. Her most spectacular feature was her long golden hair, which reached to her feet. To enhance its beauty, she washed it using a formula set out in *Esperimenti,* a book compiled by Caterina Sforza. This was a diluted solution of honey, black sulfur, and alum. It was reported to guarantee a shade called *filo d'oro.*

Lucrezia was said to have inherited her father's lustiness at an early age, and her tales of her orgasmic exploits had made her a Roman legend long before she became, at the age of twenty-one, the duchess of Ferrara. By her seventeenth birthday, she was wise beyond her years. This was perhaps inevitable. Her holy and biological father used her beauty and her sexual appetite as pawns. Papal politics made strange bedfellows for Alexander's daughter. He had wed her to her first husband, Giovanni Sforza, lord of Pesaro and a member of a powerful Milanese family, when she was thirteen and he was negotiating against the Aragonese dynasty of Naples. Then, using his powers of annulment, he moved her from one marriage to another, depending upon which alliance he was forming.

Left to her own devices in the palazzo of Santa Maria in Portico, built near the Vatican by Battista Cardinal Zeno, she is reported

Lucrezia Borgia (1480–1519)

to have spent her time between marriages making an obsessive study of dalliance, seeking to expand the outer limits of lewd pleasure. All the situations, positions, and groupings of participants found in pornographic books and films have been attributed to Lucrezia's lustful imagination. But there must have been more to it than that. The men around her were dissolute. Knowing that they regarded her as a sex object, and wanting to be what they wanted her to be, she may have cultivated debasement. To the degree to which that is true, the consequences for the men in her immediate family — her father and two brothers — were to be both profound and sensational.

ONLY CESARE BORGIA (1475–1507) could have been fit, or unfit, to be Lucrezia's most notorious brother — Cesare, the handsome cardinal who became a multiple murderer while wearing the robes of a prince of the Church. His homicidal career began in his youth and continued to the day he himself was slain in a skirmish outside Viana. Yet — and here he was very much a figure of his time — Cesare was no brute. Dapper, eloquent, and even more erudite than his sister, he was a master of the cruel, perfidious politics of his time — was, in fact, the model for Niccolò Machiavelli's *Il principe*. Machiavelli could not approve of Cesare, but he found him fascinating. And so he was, though the qualities that made him so were hardly endearing.

The circumstances surrounding the death of his elder brother, Juan, duke of Gandía, are the murkiest in the annals of his sinister family, and impossible to confirm. If what was believed then is true, they are also the most sordid. The crime began with Alexander himself. In 1497, the pope, manipulating his daughter in his remarkable fashion, decided to divorce her from Sforza. Knowing his father-in-law, Lucrezia's first husand fled Rome, fearing for his life. In Milan, however, he seethed. The pope had publicly called him impotent. That being a grave insult in Italy, Sforza — who later fathered children — shouted out what all Rome suspected but none had dared whisper: that the Borgia pope's real motive was incestuous, that he wanted his captivating daughter, not remarried, but active in his own bed.

Even for those times, this was scandalous. The rejected husband's family was powerful enough to protect him, which made the pontiff's position extremely awkward. If he kept Lucrezia near the Vatican and discouraged suitors, no one in Rome would doubt that he was spending his nights in her bed; that was consistent with both his reputation and hers. Intimations of lecherous desire on his part were accurate. His daughter had just turned seventeen and was at the height of her beauty. We now know that he was, in fact, her lover. Whether or not that was known in Milan is another question. In any event, he didn't brave it out, which would have been in character; instead he hastily prepared to find a new, politically suitable husband for her.

Cesare Borgia (1475–1507)

Here, however, the tale darkens. Romans had scarcely absorbed the news that the father lusted for his daughter when they heard even more shocking gossip. Lucrezia was said to be unavailable to her father because she was already deeply involved in another incestuous relationship, or relationships — a triangular entanglement with both her handsome brothers. The difficulty, it was whispered, was that although she enjoyed coupling with both of them, each, jealous of the other, wanted his sister for himself.

On the morning of June 15, 1497, Juan's corpse was found floating in the Tiber mutilated by nine savage dagger wounds. Cesare's guilt was immediately assumed — he was a killer, and known to be jealous of his brother for other reasons — and the longer the mystery remained unsolved, the more certain his guilt seemed. History may take another view; Juan, like all Borgias, had other enemies. But myth has a significance all its own. At the time, the only Borgia to emerge unscathed was Lucrezia, whose reputation, by then, was beyond redemption.

It touched bottom with the birth of her illegitimate son Giovanni, the so-called *Infans Romanus,* when she was eighteen. She had conceived the child between marriages, during intercourse with either her father or her surviving brother. We know she had caught the seed of one of them because the pope, deciding to legitimatize his daughter's child, issued two extraordinary bulls September 1, 1501. The first, which was made public, identified the three-year-old boy as the offspring of Cesare and an unmarried woman (*"coniugato genitus et soluta"*). Using Cesare's name permitted Alexander to evade canonical law, which would have prevented him from recognizing a bastard child fathered by him during his pontificate. The second, secret bull acknowledged Giovanni to be the son of the pope and the same woman (". . . *non de praefato duce, sed de nobis et de dicta muliere"*).

Alexander had named the boy a duke and awarded him the duchy of Nepi and Camerino. It is possible that he had accepted paternity to prevent Cesare from getting his hands on the duchy lands, though historian Giuseppe Portigliotti has suggested another reason for the two bulls — that Lucrezia herself, engaging in double incest, may not have known which of her two lovers was the child's father. Rome assumed that the Holy Father was. Actually, the Borgias would have preferred that the public be unaware of Giovanni's existence, and while he was still a fetus plans had been made along those lines. Before Lucrezia had begun to show, she had entered the Convent of San Sisto on the Via Appia, expecting to wait out her pregnancy as a nun. It was impossible. Instead of her finding anonymity in the nunnery, the nunnery, with her present, became notorious. She had brought another of her lovers, a young Spanish chamberlain, with her. The other nuns, an Italian historian wrote, showed themselves 'deplorably susceptible" to the example set by their eminent colleague. Indeed, they went so far in "abandoning the old austerity of their regime" that after her departure "sweeping reforms were necessary to bring them back to the sublime joys of self-mortification and to exorcize the atmosphere . . . which had grown up inside those pious walls."

However, it was her father's ambitions which had exposed Lucrezia's pregnancy to the world. He was arranging a politically advantageous new marriage for her. Later it would end tragically when Cesare murdered the groom, but then it seemed worth pursuing. To that end, she had had to appear at the Lateran Palace on December 22, 1497, for a ceremonial annulment of her ties to Sforza, to be justified on the ground their union had never been consummated. The pope had decided that once the infant was born, Lucrezia could pass him off as her baby brother — as indeed she did for the rest of her life. Her third husband, heir to the dukedom of Ferrara, knew better, but didn't care; his family was accustomed to the mingling of its legitimate and illegitimate children. However, in 1497 that lay in the future. As the Lateran ceremony approached, Vatican servants spread stories of Lucrezia's coital bouts with her father and brothers. A curious crowd flocked to the palace, and there they saw that the pontiff's daughter, despite her loose, full skirt, was six months with child. When the canonical judges delivered their judgment, solemnly declaring her *intacta* — a virgin — laughter echoed throughout the old halls. Jacopo Sannazaro, the Neapolitan humanist, wrote an epigram in the form of a Latin epitaph:

Hoc tumulo dormit Lucretia nomine, sed re
Thais, Alexandri filia, sponsa, nurus.*

Here lies Lucrezia, who was really a tart,
The daughter, wife, and daughter-in-law of Alexander.

MEANTIME, as tumult and intrigue marked papacy after papacy,
Italian arts flourished. It is a paradox that painters and sculptors
frequently thrive amid chaos. The deplorable circumstances — the
ferment, the vigor generated by controversy, the lack of moral
restraint or inhibitions of any kind — all seemed to incite creativ-
ity. Yet it should be added that the greatest of the artists were
shielded from the excesses of the time. To be sure, some of the
era's most gifted men, like everyone else, lived precariously, even
dangerously. The great Albrecht Dürer was reduced at various
times to illustrating tarot cards and designing fortifications for
cities. Lorenzo Lotto, near starvation, was forced to paint numbers
on hospital beds. Carlo Crivelli was imprisoned on the charge
(which was quaint, considering the period) of seducing a married
woman. Luca Signorelli, when not painting in the Sistine Chapel,
was moving from city to city, one jump ahead of the police, and
Benvenuto Cellini was in and out of jails, or plotting an escape
from one, for most of his life.

These illustrations are deceptive, however. Dürer prospered
through most of his career; Lotto was approaching the end of his
life and had lost his talent; Crivelli's real crime was that he had
bedded the *wrong* wife, a Venetian noblewoman; Signorelli, as a
political subversive, was asking for trouble; and Cellini was one
of history's great rogues — a thief, a brawler, a forger, an em-
bezzler, and the murderer of a rival goldsmith; the sort of character
who in any century, whatever the outrage, is wanted by the police
to help them with their enquiries.

More to the point, and more revealing of the time, is the fact
that after Crivelli had paid his debt to a hypocritical society in

---

*Thais was an Athenian *hetaira* (courtesan) who, in the fourth century B.C.,
became Alexander the Great's mistress. She is said to have persuaded him to
burn down the Achaemenian capital of Persepolis during a drunken revel. Dry-
den's *Alexander's Feast* is based on the incident, which is probably apocryphal.

which a *nobildonna* might betray her *nobiluomo* nightly, he was
knighted by Ferdinand II of Naples; and that despite Cellini's
criminal record, he enjoyed the patronage of Alessandro de' Medici, Cosimo de' Medici, Cardinal Gonzaga, the bishop of Salamanca, King Francis I of France, Cardinal d'Este of Ferrara, Bindo
Atoviti, Sigmondo Chigi, and Pope Clement VII, whose other
dependents included Raphael and Michelangelo.

That *was* typical of the age. The most powerful men knew
artistic genius when they saw it, and their unstinting support of
it, despite their deplorable private lives and abuse of authority, is
unparalleled. All the wretched popes — beginning with Sixtus,
who in 1480 commissioned Botticelli, Ghirlandajo, Perugino, and
Signorelli to paint the first frescoes in the Sistine Chapel, and
including Julius II, under whom Michelangelo completed the chapel's ceiling thirty-two years later — were committed to that great-
ness. Of course, their motives were not selfless. Immortal artistic
achievements, they believed, would dignify the papacy and tighten
its grip on Christendom. Nevertheless they were responsible for
countless glories, including the paintings in the large papal apartment Stanza della Segnatura (Raphael), the frescoes for the Cathedral Library in Siena (Pinturicchio), and the soaring architecture
of the new St. Peter's (Bramante and Michelangelo). Nor was all
Renaissance art supported by pontiffs. Their fellow patrons and
patronesses included the Borgia siblings, and Isabella d'Este of
Mantua, whose generous funding of the brilliant, handsome Giorgione Barbarelli is unmitigated by the fact that she was sleeping
with him, since most of her friends were, too.

In an ideal world, genius should not require the largess of
wicked pontiffs, venal cardinals, and wanton contessas. But these
men of genius did not live in such a world, and neither has anyone
else. In art the end has to justify the means, because artists, like
beggars, have no choice. Other ages have provided different
sources of support, though with dubious results. Five centuries
after Michelangelo, Raphael, Botticelli, and Titian, nothing
matching their masterpieces can be found in contemporary gal-
leries. No pandering to popular tastelessness, adolescent fads, or
philistine taboos guided the brushes and chisels of the men who
found immortality in the Renaissance. Political statements did not

concern them. Instead they devoted their lives to artistic statements, leaving time to judge their wisdom.

It is incontestable that the Continent's most powerful rulers in the early sixteenth century were responsible for great crimes. It is equally true that had this outraged the painters and sculptors of their time we would have lost a heritage beyond price. Botticelli pocketed thousands of tainted ducats from Lorenzo de' Medici and gave the world *The Birth of Venus*. In both temperament and accomplishments Pope Julius II was closer to Genghis Khan than Saint Peter, but because that troubled neither Raphael nor Michelangelo, they endowed us with the *Transfiguration, David,* the *Pietà,* and *The Last Judgment.* They took their money, ran to their studios, and gave to the world masterpieces which have enriched civilization for five hundred years.

THE VIGOR of the new age was not found everywhere. Music, still lost in the blurry mists of the Dark Ages, was a Renaissance laggard; the motets, psalms, and Masses heard each Sabbath — many of them by Josquin des Prés of Flanders, the most celebrated composer of his day — fall dissonantly on the ears of those familiar with the soaring orchestral works which would captivate Europe in the centuries ahead, a reminder that in some respects one age will forever remain inscrutable to others.

Yet almost everywhere else there was an awareness of both endings and beginnings. Enormous cathedrals, monuments to the great faith which had held the Continent in its spell since the collapse of imperial Rome, now stood complete, awesome and matchless: Chartres, with its exquisite stained-glass windows and its vast Gothic north tower; Canterbury, the work of over four centuries; Munich's Frauenkirche; and, in Rome itself, St. Peter's, begun nearly twelve hundred years earlier and still, it seemed, unfinished, for Pope Julius II laid the first stone of a new basilica in 1506, proclaiming indulgences which required all sovereigns in Christendom to pay for its renewed splendor, thereby demonstrating their royal fealty to a Church still undivided.

But these achievements were culminations of dreams dreamed in other times, familiar and therefore comfortable to those loyal

to the fading Middle Ages. Their day was ending; for every house
of God now there were thousands of new words and thoughts
challenging the bedrock assumptions of the past. Among the
masses, for example, it continued to be an article of faith that the
world was an immovable disk around which the sun revolved,
and that the rest of the cosmos comprised heaven, which lay
dreamily above the skies, inhabited by cherubs, and hell, flaming
deep beneath the European soil. Everyone believed, indeed *knew*,
that.

Everyone, that is, except Mikolaj Kopernik, a Polish physician
and astronomer, whose name had been Latinized, as was the
custom, to Nicolaus Copernicus. After years of observing the
skies and consulting mathematical tables which he had copied at
the University of Kraków, Copernicus had reached the
conclusion — which at first seemed absurd, even to him — that
the earth was actually *moving*. In 1514 he showed friends a short
manuscript, *De hypothesibus motuum coelestium a se constitutis
commentariolus* (*Little Commentary*), challenging the ancient
Ptolemaic assumptions, and this was followed by the fuller *De
revolutionibus orbium coelestium* (*On the Revolutions of the Celestial
Orbs*), in which he concluded that the earth, far from being the
center of the universe, merely rotated on its own axis and orbited
around a stationary sun once a year.

In the sixth volume of his *Story of Civilization,* Will Durant
notes that Pope Leo X, who succeeded Julius, made no summary
judgment of Copernicus. Being a humanist, the pontiff sent Copernicus an encouraging note, and liberal members of the Curia
approved. But the astronomer's work was not widely circulated
until after his death, and his peers then were divided into those
who laughed at him and those who denounced him. The offended
included some of the brightest and most independent men on the
Continent. Martin Luther wrote: "People give ear to an upstart
astrologer who strove to show that the earth revolves, not the
heavens or the firmament, the sun and the moon. . . . This fool
wishes to reverse the entire scheme of astrology; but sacred Scripture tells us that Joshua commanded the sun to stand still, not the
earth." John Calvin quoted the Ninety-third Psalm, "The world

also is stabilized, that it cannot be moved," and asked: "Who will venture to place the authority of Copernicus above that of the Holy Spirit?"

When Copernicus's chief protégé tried to get his mentor's paper printed in Nuremberg, Luther used his influence to suppress it. According to Durant, even Andreas Osiander of Nuremberg, who finally agreed to assist with its publication, insisted on an introduction explaining that the concept of a solar system was being presented solely as a hypothesis, useful for the computation of the movements of heavenly bodies. As long as it was so represented, Rome remained mute, but when the philosopher Giordano Bruno

Nicolaus Copernicus (1473–1543)

published his Italian dialogues, declaring a rotating, orbiting earth to be an unassailable fact — carrying his astronomical speculations far beyond those of Copernicus — the Roman Inquisition brought him to trial. He was convicted of being the worst kind of heretic, a pantheist who held that God was immanent in creation, rather than the external creator. Then they burned him at the stake. Catholics were forbidden to read Copernicus's *De revolutionibus* until the deletion of nine sentences, which had asserted it to be more than a theory. The ban was not lifted until 1828.

LEONARDO DA VINCI (1452–1519), the most versatile creative figure of that age — perhaps of any age — confronted traditional authority with a more awkward problem. His artistic genius guaranteed his immunity from blacklisting heresimachs; for seventeen years Milan's duke, Ludovico Sforza, shielded him by appointing him *ictor et ingeniarius ducalis,* and after Ludovico's fall Leonardo found other sponsors, even serving Cesare Borgia briefly as his military architect. If Cesare's many crimes deserve to be remembered, as they do, so should this generous gesture. Like the patron himself, however, it was short-lived. Miraculously, the Borgia cardinal manqué had survived to the age of thirty, but now killers with long knives were closing in. Cesare had celebrated his last birthday. His great protégé found new sanctuaries in the courts of the powerful, though, they, too, were to prove temporary, because of all the great Renaissance artists, Da Vinci alone was destined to fall from papal grace.

His disgrace was significant. Leonardo's transgressions were graver than Botticelli's or Cellini's. Indeed, in a larger sense he was a graver menace to medieval society than any Borgia. Cesare merely killed men. Da Vinci, like Copernicus, threatened the certitude that knowledge had been forever fixed by God, the rigid mind-set which left no role for curiosity or innovation. Leonardo's cosmology, based on what he called *saper vedere* (knowing how to see) was, in effect, a blunt instrument assaulting the fatuity which had, among other things, permitted a mafia of profane popes to desecrate Christianity.

In the Age of Faith, as Will Durant called the medieval era, one secret of the papacy's hold on the masses was its capacity to inspire absolute terror, a derivative of the universal belief that whoever wore the tiara could, at his pleasure, determine how each individual would spend his afterlife — cosseted in eternal bliss or shrieking in writhing flames below. His decision might be whimsical, his blessings were often sold openly, his motives might be evil, but that was his prerogative. Earthly life being "nasty, brutish, and short," in Thomas Hobbes's memorable phrase, only the deranged would invite the disfavor and retribution of the Holy See.

This accounts for the last extraordinary moments of Girolamo Savonarola's life. For seven years his Florentine followers had

Leonardo da Vinci (1452–1519), a self-portrait

turned out to cheer his indictments of Pope Alexander VI's depravity. Now, on the day of his last public appearance, which was
also his execution, they flocked into the Piazza della Signoria to
taunt and jeer his final agony. He had given Florence the best
government the city had ever had. His only local enemies were
the Arrabbiati, a political party resentful of his reforms. None of
the witnesses to his agony could doubt that every charge he had
laid at the door of the Borgia pontiff's Vatican apartments was
true. The explanation for their switch, otherwise inexplicable, is
that the pope had threatened to excommunicate the city's entire
population if Florentines refused to turn on him. None had paused
to wonder why God should be party to so monstrous an injustice.
As children they had been taught that a pope possessed that terrible
power, and they had never thought to question it.

Leonardo, sui generis, questioned everything. Rather than accept the world God had created, as Christians had always done,
he probed endlessly into what human ingenuity could achieve by
struggling *against* it. So mighty was his intellect and so broad the
spectrum of his gifts — he was, among other things, a master of
engineering, biology, sculpture, linguistics, botany, music, philosophy, architecture, and science — that presenting an adequate
summary of his feats is impossible. However, it is worth noting
that at a time when Europe was mired in ignorance, shackled by
superstition, and lacking solid precedents in every scholarly discipline, this uneducated, illegitimate son of an Anchiano country
girl anticipated Galileo, Newton, and the Wright brothers.

He did it by flouting absolute taboos. Dissecting cadavers, he
set down intricate drawings of the human body — God's sacred
image — and wrote his *Anatomy* in 1510. Meantime he was di-
verting rivers to prevent flooding; establishing the principle of the
turbine by building a horizontal waterwheel; laying the ground-
work for modern cartography; discovering screw threads, trans-
mission gears, hydraulic jacks, and swiveling devices; creating
detailed, practical plans for breech-loading cannons, guided mis-
siles, and armored tanks; building the world's first revolving stage;
developing a canal system whose locks are still in use; and, after
exhaustive research into water currents and the flight of birds,
designing a submarine, then a flying machine, and then — four

centuries before Kitty Hawk — a parachute. Along the way he left an artistic heritage which includes *The Adoration of the Magi,* the *Mona Lisa,* and the *Last Supper.*

Medieval minds retained the orbs and maces of authority, yet they could not cope with men like Copernicus and Leonardo. Of course, that did not prevent them from trying. Leonardo was left-handed; his notes, seven thousand pages of which have been preserved, were written in mirror script. Though quite legible, they can be read only by holding them up to a looking glass. In the sixteenth century that was enough to envelop him in suspicion. The existence of Satan and his extraordinary powers was believed to be irrefutable. Leonardo was capable of marvels, men whispered, but — and here they would nod knowingly — his inspiration was anything but divine. They knew where and how he would spend *his* afterlife; it had been memorably described two centuries earlier in the *Divine Comedy* of Dante Alighieri, which had included hell's terrible warning to immigrants: "*Lasciate ogni speranza, voi ch'entrate.*"

Among the attentive listeners to this rubbish — predicting that upon his death the most gifted man in the pope's realm would be told to abandon all hope before entering what lay beyond — was the new pontiff. In secret audiences Pope Leo X received the whisperers, nodded thoughtfully, and sent them away with expressions of gratitude. These smears came late in 1513, the worst possible time for Da Vinci. He was sixty-one years old and in straits. Encouraged by the Vatican's patronage of Michelangelo and Raphael, and told that he could expect support from Giuliano de' Medici — a brother of Leo — he appeared in Rome to ask the Holy See for support. He didn't get it. The Holy Father not only denied him alms but decreed that his future research — particularly his sacrilegious mutilations of the divine image — would be either restricted or proscribed. Luckily, the French crown, not for the first time, came to the rescue of Italian genius. Francis I invited the great pariah to Paris as "first painter and engineer to the king." He left his native land immediately and forever, spending his last years in a little castle near Amboise, working to the end on architectural blueprints and canal designs.

BEFORE THE DENSE, overarching, suffocating medieval night could be broken, the darkness had to be pierced by the bright shaft of learning — by literature, and people who could read and understand it. Here Durant is informative. Until late in the fifteenth century most books and nearly all education had been controlled by the Church. Volumes had been expensive, and unprofitable for writers, who, unprotected by copyright, lived on pensions or papal grants, in monastic orders, or by teaching. Few reached wide audiences. Scarcely any libraries possessed more than 300 books. The chief exceptions were those of Humphrey, duke of Gloucester, with 600; of the king of France, with 910, and of Christ Church priory, Canterbury, with some 2,000. So valuable were they that each volume was chained to a desk or lectern.

The typographical revolution did not come all at once. The Chinese had designed wooden typography before 1066 and used it to print paper money; block printing in Tabriz dated from 1294, and the Dutch may have experimented with it in 1430. Practical use of it awaited other discoveries — oily ink, for example, and paper. The ink was quickly found. Paper took longer. Muslims had introduced its manufacture to Spain in the 900s, to Sicily in the 1100s, to Italy in the 1200s, and to France in the 1300s. During that same century linen began to replace wool in the wardrobes of the upper classes; discarded linen rags became a cheap source of paper, and its price declined. The stage was set for the main event.

Its star, of course, was Johannes Gutenberg Gensfleisch, who preferred to be known by his mother's maiden name (his father's name, Gensfleisch, being German for "gooseflesh"). In 1448 he had moved from Strasbourg to Mainz, where, with the help of Peter Schöffer, his typesetter, he developed engraved steel signatures for each number, letter, and punctuation mark. Metal matrixes were formed to hold the figures, and a metal mold to keep them in line. Gutenberg then borrowed money to buy a press and, in 1457–1458, published his superb Bible of 1,282 outsized, double-columned pages. It was one of the great moments in the history of Western civilization. He had introduced movable type.

The invention of printing was denounced by, among others, politicians and ecclesiastics who feared it as an instrument which

could spread subversive ideas. But they were a minority. Copies
of the first type-printed book were studied all over Europe; Gutenberg had built a bonfire in Mainz, and printers throughout
Christendom flocked to kindle their torches from it. Presses du-
plicating his — but at no profit to him, since patents, like copy-
rights, did not exist — appeared in Rome (1464), Venice (1469),
Paris (1470), the Netherlands (1471), Switzerland (1472), Hungary
(1473), Spain (1474), England (1476), Denmark (1482), Sweden
(1483), and Constantinople (1490).

Who were the first readers, and how many were there? Historians have reasoned that businessmen needed books for trade
and industry, and middle- and upper-class women wanted them
for romantic escape. The difficulty here is that by the most positive
estimate over half of the Continent's male population was illiterate,
and the rate among women was higher — perhaps 89 percent.
(East of Vienna and north of the Baltic both figures were a great
deal worse.) Exact calculations are impossible, but we know that
reading was taught before writing. An examination of signed de-
positions, wills, applications for marriage certificates, bonds, and
subscribers to declarations and protests permits a rough reckoning
of illiteracy by both class and occupation.

Literacy rates varied from place to place and from time to time,
but some general figures are available. The percentage of those
who could not read at all was 0 percent in the clergy and professions. Among gentry it was 2 percent, yeomen 35 percent, craftsmen 44 percent, peasants 79 percent, and laborers 85 percent. By
trade, 6 percent of the grocers were illiterate, 9 percent of the
haberdashers, 12 percent of all merchants, 27 percent of bakers,
36 percent of innkeepers, 41 percent of brewers, 44 percent of
tailors, 45 percent of blacksmiths, 48 percent of butchers, 59 percent of sailors, 64 percent of carpenters, 73 percent of gardeners,
76 percent of masons, 88 percent of bricklayers, 90 percent of the
shepherds, and 97 percent of all thatchers.

In one important sense these figures, though reasonably accurate, are misleading. They represent comprehension of the vernacular, or colloquial, tongues — Spanish, Portugese, English,
French, Dutch, Flemish, Danish, German, and Tuscan (Italian).
Some grasp of the vernacular was sought by everyone who wished

to raise himself in the world, but in most of Europe Latin was still the language of the elite — the Church, scholars, scientists, governments, and the courts. During 1501, for example, in France eighty volumes were published in Latin and only eight in French; in Aragon, between 1510 and 1540, one hundred and fifteen were printed in Latin and just five in Spanish. Indeed, throughout the sixteenth century Latin dominated works displayed at the annual Frankfurt book fair. Several reasons account for its survival. It was still the language of international communication; if you wanted to address the European public and be universally understood, you had to use it. In countries whose languages were rarely learned by foreigners — Flemish, German, and, yes, English — Latin was the language of choice.

Those who preferred the colloquial were few, and were sometimes resented by their peers; when the great French surgeon Ambroise Paré chose to publish his work on the method of treating gunshot wounds as *La méthode de traicter les playes faites par les arquebuses et aultres bastons à feu,* he was reproached by colleagues on the Faculty of Medicine at Paris. The Church aggressively opposed vernacular languages. Authors hesitated to use their native tongues because they were at the mercy of printers' foremen and compositors. Thus, in an English manuscript, "be" could come out as "bee," "grief" as "greef," "these" as "thease," "sword" as "swoord," "nurse" as "noorse," and "servant" as "servaunt." Yet in the long run native languages were destined to triumph. The victory was not altogether glorious. It meant that the dream of a unified Christendom, with a single Latin tongue, was doomed.

That outcome was not evident in the early 1500s. The curricula at monastic schools were unchanged. All teaching there was in Latin; younger monks and country youth were led through primary instruction in the *trivium* — grammar, rhetoric, and dialectics (the art of reasoning) — and bright students were encouraged to tackle the *quadrivium:* astronomy, arithmetic, geometry, and music. The monks had made some progress in botany and geology, collecting curious minerals, herbs, and dried bird and animal skins, but a monk reincarnated from the eighth century would have found little that was unfamiliar. Boys from the surrounding countryside who attended classes picked up a kind of pidgin Latin, adequate for the comprehension of political and religious pamphlets. Later that would become important.

❧

MEANTIME, outside monastery walls, the reading public was surging, though not by design. No new literacy programs were introduced, the educational process continued to be chaotic, and those who received any degree of systematic teaching had to be either fortunate or unusually persistent. The number of people who were fortunate remained stable. It was persistence, and the number of schools, which rose. As the presses disgorged new printed matter, the yearning for literacy spread like a fever; millions of Europeans led their children to classrooms and remained to learn themselves. Typically, a class would be leavened with women anxious to learn about literature and philosophy, and middle-class adolescents contemplating a career in trade.

Instruction was available in three forms: popular education, apprenticeship, and the courses of study at traditional schools and universities. Only the first was available to the vast majority, and it is impossible to define because it varied so from place to place. Two generalizations hold: popular education was confined to colloquial tongues, and it was unambitious. The teachers themselves knew no Latin; many were barely literate in their native languages. Some gave their services free, beginning with classes teaching little children their letters; others were poor women eager to make a few pennies. Pupils helped each other. The curriculum was limited to reading, writing, simple arithmetic, and the catechism. "That a relatively large number of people knew how to read, write and count," conclude the authors of *The New Cambridge Modern History*, "was due to the casual and ill-organized efforts of thousands of humble individuals. Such were the uncertain foundations not only of the popularity of vernacular literature but also of technical advance and the diffusion of general knowledge."

Apprentices were fewer. The sons of master journeymen were given special consideration; property qualifications were imposed on outsiders, and the children of peasants and laborers were excluded. In the cruder trades instruction was confined to skills which were mechanically imitated. But the better crafts went beyond that, teaching accounting, mathematics, and the writing of commercial letters. This was especially important to merchants — commerce was still regarded as a trade, though dealers were quickly forming the nucleus of the new middle class — and the sons of merchants led the way in learning foreign languages. They were already among the most attentive pupils. The growth of industry gave education a new urgency. Literacy had been an expensive indulgence in an agrarian culture, but in an urban, mercantile world it was mandatory. Higher education, based on Latin, was another world. Schools concentrated on preparing boys for it, using as fundamental texts Donatus's grammar for instruction in Latin and Latin translations of Aristotle.

In 1502 the Holy See had ordered the burning of all books questioning papal authority. It was a futile bull — the velocity of new ideas continued to pick up momentum — and the Church decided to adopt stronger measures. In 1516, two years after Copernicus conceived his heretical solution to the riddle of the skies, the Fifth Lateran Council approved *De impressione liborum,* an uncompromising decree which forbade the printing of *any* new volume without the Vatican's imprimatur.

As a response, that was about as fruitful as the twentieth-century encyclicals of Popes Pius XI and Paul VI rejecting birth control. *De impressione liborum* was, among other things, too late. The literary Renaissance, dating in England from William Caxton's edition of Chaucer's *Canterbury Tales* in 1477, had been under way for a full generation. As the old century merged with the new, the movement pushed forward, fueled by a torrent of creative energy, by the growing cultivation of individuality among the learned, and by the development of distinctive literary styles, emerging in force for the first time since the last works of Tacitus, Suetonius, and Marcus Aurelius had appeared in the second century. The authors, poets, and playwrights of the new era never scaled the heights of Renaissance artists, but they were starting from lower ground. With a few lonely exceptions — Petrarch's *De viris illustribus,* Boccaccio's *Decameron* — medieval Europe's contributions to world literature had been negligible. Japan had been more productive, and the Stygian murk of the Dark Ages is reflected in the dismal fact that Christendom had then published nothing matching the eloquence of the infidel Muhammad in his seventh-century Koran.

In the years bracketing the dawn of the sixteenth century, that began to change. Indeed, considering the high incidence of illiteracy, a remarkable number of works written or published then have survived as classics. *Le morte d'Arthur* (1495) and *Il principe* (1513) are illustrative, though both authors are misunderstood by modern readers. In the popular imagination Sir Thomas Malory has been identified with the fictive chivalry of his tales. Actually he was a most unchivalrous knight who led a spectacular criminal career, which began with attempted murder and moved on to rape, extortion, robbery of churches, theft of deer and cattle, and promiscuous vandalism. He wrote his most persuasive romances behind bars.

Malory has been spared; Niccolò Machiavelli has been slandered. Machiavelli was a principled Florentine and a gifted observer of contemporary Italy; his concise *Il principe* reveals profound insight into human nature and an acute grasp of political reality in the scene he saw. Nevertheless, because of that very book, he has been the victim of a double injustice. Though he was only analyzing his age, later generations have not only interpreted the work as cynical, unscrupulous, and immoral; they have turned his very name to a pejorative. In fact, he was a passionate, devout Christian who was appalled by the morality of his age. In an introspective self-portrait he wrote:

> *Io rido, e rider mio non passa dentro;*
> *Io ardo, e l'arsion mia non par di fore.*

> I laugh, and my laughter is not within me;
> I burn, and the burning is not seen outside.

Among the other memorable works of the time were Sebastian Brandt's *Das Narrenschiff;* Peter Dorland van Diest's *Elckerlijk;* Guicciardini's *Storia d'Italia;* Rabelais's *Pantagruel;* Castiglione's *Il cortegiano;* Sir Thomas More's *Utopia;* Philippe de Commines's *Mémoires;* William Dunbar's *Dance of the Sevin Deidly Sinnes;* Lu-

dovico Ariosto's *Orlando Furioso;* Fernando de Rojas's *La Celestina;*
Machiavelli's *Discorsi sopra la prima deca di Tito Livio,* his penetrating *Dell'arte della guerra,* and his superb comedy, *La Mandragola;*
the plays of John Skelton; the poetry of Sir Thomas Wyatt and
Henry Howard, earl of Surrey; and all the works of Desiderius
Erasmus, who left his native Holland to roam Europe's centers of
learning and turn out a stream of books, including *Enchiridion
militis Christiani,* and *Adagia,* his collection of proverbs.

Scholars — most of whom were theologians — continued to
be fluent in classical tongues, but in the new intellectual climate
that was inadequate. Publishers could no longer assume that their
customers would be fluent in Latin. In past centuries, when each
country had been a closed society, an author who preferred to
write in the vernacular was unknown to those unfamiliar with it.
No more; provincialism had been succeeded by an awareness of

Niccolò Machiavelli (1469–1527)

Europe as a comity of nations, and readers were curious about the work of foreign writers — so much so that translations became profitable. In England, for example, Brandt's book appeared as *The Ship of Fools,* Van Diest's as *Everyman,* Castiglione's as *The Courtier,* and Machiavelli's comedy as *The Mandrake.* In 1503 Thomas à Kempis's *De imitatione Christi* came off London presses as *The Imitation of Christ.* Erasmus's *Institutio principis Christiani* became available as *The Education of a Christian Prince,* and Hartmann Schedel's illustrated world history was published simultaneously in Latin and German.

Learned men became linguists. Ambrogio Calepino brought out *Cornucopiae,* the first polyglot dictionary, and the Collegium Trilingue was founded in Louvain. This was followed by publication, at the University of Alcalá, of a Bible in four tongues: Greek, Latin, Hebrew, and Aramaic. To be sure, none of them was widely understood in western Europe, but at least the Scriptures could, fifteen centuries after the crucifixion, be read in the language of Christ himself.

THE DAYS WHEN the Church's critics could be silenced by intimidating naive peasants, or by putting the torch to defiant apostates, were ending. There were too many of them; they were too resourceful, intelligent, well organized, and powerfully connected, and they were far more strongly entrenched than, say, the infidel host the crusaders had attacked. Their strongholds were Europe's crowded, quarrelsome, thriving, and above all independent new universities.

Before the Renaissance, Christendom's higher education had been in hopeless disarray. Some famous institutions had been established, though their forms and curricula would be almost unrecognizable to members of twentieth-century faculties. Oxford's earliest colleges dated from the 1200s; Cambridge had begun to emerge a century later; and for as long as Parisians could remember, groups of students had been gathering, at one time or another, in this or that *quartier,* on the left bank of the Seine. But they had represented no formidable force in society.

Various chronicles enigmatically note "the beginnings" of universities in scattered medieval communities, among them Bologna, Salamanca, Montpellier, Kraków, Leipzig, Pisa, Prague, Cologne, and Heidelberg. Precisely what this meant varied from one to another. We know from Copernicus that there was learning in Kraków. He was fortunate. In most cities, academic activity had been confined to the issuance of a charter, the drawing up of rough plans, and, where students and professors met at irregular intervals, heavy emphasis on animism and Scholasticism. Animists believed that every material form of reality possessed a soul — not only plants and stones, but even such natural phenomena as earthquakes and thunderstorms. Scholastics sought to replace all forms of philosophy with Catholic theology. Both were shadowy disciplines, but there was worse: the divine right of sovereigns, for example; astrology; even alchemy; and, late in the period, Ramism.

Within universities, there were no colleges as the term later came to be understood. Selected students lived in halls, but 90 percent of the undergraduates boarded elsewhere. They were governed by peculiar rules: athletics were forbidden, and since 1350 scofflaws at Oxford had been subject to flogging. In theory, classes began at 6 A.M. and continued until 5 P.M. In practice most students spent their time elsewhere, often in taverns. As a consequence, hostility between town and gown was often high; at Oxford one clash, which became known as the Great Slaughter, ended in the deaths of several undergraduates and townsmen.

In those centuries students who yearned for genuine learning had to become autodidacts. Medieval universities had exalted three traditional disciplines: theology, law, and medicine, which were but distantly related to what they would later become. Courses were offered in the "arts" — grammar, logic, rhetoric, dialectics — but these were considered inferior, and were chiefly meant for youths planning to enter the lower clergy. Except in Italy, the arts teachers were usually Benedictine, Franciscan, and Dominican monks. They paid lip service to the great leaders of Hellenic and Roman culture but were largely ignorant of their works, except for selections or adaptations by scholars with an imperfect grasp of the ancient tongues. Few knew Greek; they were dependent upon Latin translations of it.

The Latin of arts faculty members was so corrupted by

scholastic and ecclesiastical overlays that it bore little resemblance
to the language of Rome at its peak. They knew Ovid and Virgil,
but, typically, had interpreted the *Ars amatoria,* the Art of Love,
as they had the Song of Solomon — not as a tribute to human
sensuality, but as a mystic embodiment of divine love. That was
fraudulent, and because of its speciosity, the prestige of universities
declined. Attendance at Oxford fell from its thirteenth-century
peak to as low as a thousand in the fifteenth century. Even academic freedom vanished after the expulsion of John Wyclif, master
of Balliol, in 1381. Wyclif had denounced the inordinate arrogance,
wealth, and power of the Catholic clergy. Five separate bulls had
condemned him, and Oxford lectures since then had been subject
to rigorous episcopal control.

The reawakening — the establishing of new ties with the gems
of antiquity — was one of the great triumphs of the Renaissance.
Its first seeds had been sown early in the fourteenth century, with
the rediscovery of Latin classics; then the fall of Constantinople
to the Turks in 1453 gave impetus to the revival of Greek learning.
Confronted with the overwhelming might of the infidels, the religious and political powers of Byzantium appealed to their fellow
Christians in the West for help, even if the price was capitulation
by the eastern Church to Roman orthodoxy. During the negotiations several Byzantine scholars traveled to Rome, some to par-
ticipate in the talks, some merely anxious to escape the Ottoman
peril. With them they brought genuine Hellenic manuscripts. For
over a thousand years Italian professors fluent in Greek had assumed that the original texts of cultural masterpieces had perished.
Discovering that they had survived, specialists and emissaries traveled through Croatia, Serbia, and Bulgaria to Constantinople,
bearing gifts and gold and passionately searching for old manuscripts, statues, and coins, tokens of the glorious past. Thus began
the transfer of priceless documents from East to West, where they
joined the great Latin heritage of Italy.

The implications reached far beyond scholarship, leading to the
redefinition of knowledge itself. The eventual impact on the Continent's hidebound educational establishment was to be devastating, discrediting medieval culture and replacing it with ancient,
resurrected ideals, paideia and *humanitas.* The best minds in the

West began a scrupulous reappraisal of Scholasticism, which, for two centuries, had been degenerating into an artificial sort of dialectics. In the ancient texts Renaissance scholars found an unsuspected reverence for humanity which, without actually dismissing the Bible, certainly overshadowed it. And in the wisdom of antiquity they discovered respect for man in the free expansion of his natural impulses, unfreighted by the corrupting burden of original sin. The Italian scholar Leonardo Bruni declared: "I have the feeling that the days of Cicero and Demosthenes are much closer to me than the sixty years just past." Acclaim for humanity was the theme of *De dignitate et excellentia,* by Giannozzo Manetti, a Florentine philologist, and the *Oratio de hominis dignitate,* by brilliant young Giovanni Pico della Mirandola. The Christian faith was not repudiated, but the new concept of the cultivated man was the Renaissance *homo universale,* the universal man: creator, artist, scholar, and encyclopedic genius in the spirit of the ancient paideia.

In that spirit Scotland and Ireland, despite their poverty, established the universities of St. Andrews, Glasgow, Aberdeen, and Trinity College, Dublin, institutions destined to pour generation after generation of first-rate men into the intellectual life of the British Isles. Between 1496 and 1516 five new colleges were founded at Oxford and Cambridge. Meantime, across the Channel, the great transition had led to the founding of genuine, postmedieval universities at Genoa (1471), Munich (1472), Uppsala and Tübingen (1477), Copenhagen (1479), Valencia and Santiago (1501), Wittenberg (1502), and Frankfurt an der Oder (1506). Here lay the essence of the emerging intellectualism. Students like young Martin Luther, a member of the third class to enter Wittenberg, and François Rabelais, at the older but restructured Montpellier, were taught that Renaissance meant renewal, a recovery of those disciplines lost in the collapse of Roman civilization. The French refined it to *la Renaissance des lettres,* and though its leaders embraced more than literature — they sought the reemergence of all the lost learning of the old world, including the flowering of art, esthetics, mathematics, and the beginnings of modern science — the heaviest emphasis was on reverence for classical letters, the poetical and philosophical Hellenic heritage, scholarly purity, and the meticulous translation of the ancient manuscripts retrieved in Athens and Rome.

THE NEW PROFESSORS, called humanists, declared the humanities to be superior to medicine, law, and theology — especially theology. Der Humanismus, as the movement was known in Germany, its stronghold, coalesced during the last years of the Borgia papacy. In 1497, the Holy Roman emperor Maximilian I served as humanism's midwife by appointing Conradus Celtis, a Latin lyrical poet, to the most prestigious academic chair in Vienna. Celtis used his new post to establish the Sodalitas Danubia, a center for humanistic studies, thereby winning immortality among intellectual historians as Der Erzhumaniste (the Archhumanist).

Within a year his first manuscripts were at hand. Aldus Manutius, the great Italian printer and inventor of italic type (for an edition of Virgil), had been toiling for twenty years on the Aldine Press to produce a series of Greek classics. His *editio princips,* a five-volume folio Aristotle edited by Aldus himself, was in proof and ready for scholars by late 1498. During the next fourteen years it was followed by the works of all the Hellenic giants: Theocritis, Aristophanes, Thucydides, Sophocles, Herodotus, Euripides, Homer, and Plato.

All this ferment led to that rarest of cultural phenomena, an intellectual movement which alters the course of both learning and civilization. Pythagoreans had tried it, four hundred years before the birth of Christ, and failed. So, in the third and fourth centuries A.D., had Manichaeans, Stoics, and Epicureans. But the humanists of the sixteenth century were to succeed spectacularly — so much so that their triumph is unique. They would be followed by other ideologies determined to shape the future — seventeenth-century rationalism, the eighteenth-century Enlightenment, Marxism in the nineteenth century, and, in the twentieth, by pragmatism, determinism, and empiricism. Each would alter the stream of great events, but none would match the achievements of Renaissance humanists.

By the end of the decade following Manutius's accomplishment, humanism had begun to replace the old curricula, dominating both the new universities and the refurbished old. Lecture

halls were crowded, great libraries kept their well-worn works of
humanist scholars in constant circulation, and leaders of Europe's
metropolises — merchants, lawyers, physicians, bankers, ship-
owners, and the bright priests who, in the century's fifth decade,
would join the new Jesuit order — studied and discussed the newly
published humanist treatises, including the denunciation of Scholasticism by England's Thomas More, who wrote that exploring
the subtleties of Scholastic philosophy was "as profitable as milk-
ing a he-goat into a sieve."

We picture the eminent scholars of the time, each in the short
jacket favored by the professional classes then, wearing their distinctive outsized berets, the floppy brims hooding their ears,
bowed over desks tilted toward them, pen and ink at hand. Poring
over manuscripts and proofs in several languages, reliving the
glories of the ancient past, half lost in the life of the mind, they
were exalted by the awareness that they were rekindling flames
extinguished in the glorious past. They cannot have been unaware
of the recognition of their contemporaries. Each was a personage,
admired beyond the borders of his own state, a man of substance
in whom his compatriots took pride and a friend and confidant —
at least in the first fifth of the century — of the Roman Catholic
hierarchy. The peasant, the tradesman, the ordinary townsman,
lacked the feeblest grasp of the source for the scholars' fame, and
wouldn't have understood it if told, but he doffed his cap or
tugged his forelock in the presence of such towering humanists
as Pico della Mirandola of Florence, the Neapolitan Alessandro
Alessandri, Genoa's Julius Caesar Scaliger, the French philologist
Guillaume Budé, the Spaniard Juan Luis Vives, John Colet and
Thomas More in England, and Erasmus of Rotterdam, doyen of
the movement.

THEY CONSTITUTED the Western world's first community of powerful lay intellectuals since Constantine's Ecumenical Council in
the fourth century A.D. Among their strengths was society's traditional respect for learning. Anti-intellectualism as it later evolved
was unknown; even the incomprehensible jabber of the Latin Mass
inspired humility as well as reverence. But beyond that, the humanists were honored as though they were nobility. Since the

beginning of the Renaissance, their status had risen as rulers of states and principalities singled them out, granting them perquisites reserved for the favored, establishing them as a privileged class. Ulrich von Hutten, for example, held an imperial appointment in Maximilian's court, enjoyed the patronage of the elector of Mainz, and dined frequently with Mainz's archbishop. Pico della Mirandola was a protégé of both Lorenzo de' Medici and the philosopher Marsilio Ficino. Huldrych Zwingli, rector of Zurich, was a formidable political and religious leader, and so great was Budé's prestige that Francis I founded a college at his suggestion. Girolamo Aleandro, who taught Greek and held the office of rector at the University of Paris, served as Vatican librarian, papal nuncio to France, Germany, and the Netherlands, and, finally, became a cardinal. The Vatican brought Manutius's son Paulus to Rome as the official Vatican printer; Henry VIII chose Polydore Vergil, an Italian humanist, as his official historiographer and summoned Juan Luis Vives from Spain to tutor his daughter. Erasmus, at Cambridge, and Philipp Melanchthon, at Wittenberg, held their chairs as professors of Greek with royal approval. John Colet's position as dean of St. Paul's Cathedral also had royal sanction. And John Skelton, England's poet laureate, had served as royal tutor to the future King Henry VIII, with the consequence that Henry, when he mounted the throne in 1509, was the product of a thorough humanist education.

No humanist rose higher in public life than Sir Thomas More, who, until his fall from royal grace, was as distinguished a statesman as he was a scholar. During Henry VIII's early reign More had been appointed undersheriff of London, king's councillor, and a judge of the courts of requests. In 1520, when the sovereigns of England and France conferred on the Field of the Cloth of Gold outside Calais, he served as Henry's aide. Knighted, he then rose swiftly through a series of royal appointments — undertreasurer, speaker of the House of Commons, high steward of Oxford and then of Cambridge, chancellor of the Duchy of Lancaster, and, finally, when he succeeded Cardinal Wolsey, lord chancellor, the foremost living Englishman, after the king, of his time.

Erasmus, whose close friend he was, asked: "What did Nature ever create milder, sweeter, and happier than the genius of Thomas

More?" But that says more about Erasmus's generosity than More's character. Unquestionably the Englishman was benevolent for his time, but it was not an age when men of mild and sweet disposition rose to power; a savage streak was almost a prerequisite for achievement. So it was with Sir Thomas More. He had first attracted royal notice — from Henry VII — for his skills as a Star Chamber prosecutor. In argument he was bitter, vituperative, given to streams of invective. And although as a writer he celebrated religious tolerance in his *Utopia,* in practice he was a rigid Catholic, capable of having a servant in his own home flogged for blasphemy. He believed that heretics, atheists, and disbelievers in a hereafter should be executed, and as chancellor he approved such

Sir Thomas More (1478–1535) as lord chancellor of England

sentences. At the same time, he was a loyal subject to Henry VIII.
Presiding over the House of Commons, he cannot have imagined
a time when he would be forced to choose between his king in
Hampton Court and the pope in Rome. But that time was coming.

IN 1502, WHEN King Henry VII's reign had seven years to run,
his mother, Margaret Beaufort, had used her largess to found
professorships of divinity at Oxford and Cambridge. Autocratic,
wealthy, cultivated, and still vigorous in her late fifties, Margaret
lay at the epicenter of England's noble hierarchy. As viscountess
of Richmond and Derby and a great-granddaughter of John of
Gaunt, she was the paradigm of what a sovereign's mother should
be. Despite her conservatism, she welcomed change, particularly
in the arts. Her country home had become a rendezvous for scholars, statesmen, poets, prelates, philosophers, and artists, and her
endowment of the chairs in divinity had been inspired by her
respect for the new learning as epitomized in Europe's rising universities.

At the same time, she remained deeply respectful of tradition.
Like More, she was a staunch Catholic; it was said that she had
never missed a Mass. Therefore she would have been mortified if
she had known that within a generation the theologians holding
her professorships would be blessed, not by the Holy See, but by
her younger grandson, who as sovereign would establish an An-
glican church independent of the Vatican and consecrate himself
as head of it, thus becoming Christ's vicar on the island his grand-
mother and forty generations of ancestors had cherished as a bas-
tion of the only true faith.

Virtually all humanists in the opening years of the new century
shared Margaret's reflexive loyalty to Rome. There had been a
few striking exceptions, but they all had been in Germany. In that
age the bewildering quilt of tiny principalities east of the Rhine
was as remote to Englishmen as the Germania of Tacitus had been
in Caesar's time. Learned though Margaret Beaufort was, it is
doubtful that she had even heard of Conradus Celtis, the Archhumanist, of whom it was written that "wherever he went, he
gathered students about him, and inspired them with his passion
for poetry, classical literature, and antiquities." Yet at about the

time the viscountess established her chairs of divinity, this academic giant abandoned his soul by denying its existence and embraced atheism. His new lectures bore such titles as "Will the soul live after death?" and "Is there a God?" His answer to both was No.

Skepticism, and then sacrilege, became stylish among his colleagues. In 1514 Eoban Hesse, a protégé of Celtis, published *Heroides Christianae,* a volume written in flawless Latin. Actually, as Durant points out, the work was a clever parody of Ovid. Only accomplished Latinists could recognize the style, however. Others, taking it at face value, were appalled. Hesse had forged blasphemous documents profaning the sacred origins of Christianity. Among his apocrypha, which the credulous accepted as genuine, were passionate love letters from Mary Magdalene to Jesus and, even more shocking, from the Virgin Mary (whose virginity was exposed as myth) to God the Father, *Domine Deus.* Subtly exploiting the plural definition of *dominus,* which may mean "lover" as well as "father," Hesse implied that the missives had been sent to a rake who had been cuckolding Joseph of Nazareth, and by whom she had conceived Jesus.

Nowhere was the faith of humanists so fragile as in Celtis's homeland. Elsewhere, his adversaries, the German defenders of Christianity, would not have been considered Christian at all. One of them, Conradus Mutianus Rufus, gave lip service to the Church, arguing that ceremonies and creeds should be judged on their moral effects, not their literal claims; if they encouraged private virtue and a disciplined society, he said solemnly, they should be accepted unquestioningly. Mutianus wrote: "I shall turn my studies to piety, and will learn nothing from poets, philosophers, or historians, save what can promote a Christian life." According to Durant, he was attempting to marry "skepticism with religion." If so, his efforts ended in the divorce courts, and the blame lay with him. His public professions of piety appear to have been mere pap, intended to mollify orthodox congregations resentful of Celtis. He was singing a different song with undergraduates, and it bore no resemblance to a hymn. In Gotha, J. M. Robertson writes, Mutianus taught his students that Masses for the dead were worthless, fasts ineffectual, and confessions both pointless and embarrassing. The Bible, he said, was a book of fables; only a *Dummkopf* could listen to the trials of Job and Jonah without laughing. The crucifixion was absurd. So was baptism, and if paradise really existed, the Romans and Greeks who had lived decent lives were already there. According to Mandell Creighton, a scholar of the Reformation, Mutianus urged under-graduates to "esteem the decrees of philosophers above those of priests," but he advised them to hide their agnosticism from the masses. "By faith," he explained, "we mean not the conformity with fact of what we say, but an opinion about divinity based on credulity and persuasiveness, which leads to profit." Over his door he hung the motto *Beata Tranquillitas,* honoring tranquillity. It should have read *Beata Simulatio,* praising hypocrisy.

BUT GERMANY was unique, Christendom's greatest headache, pre-senting difficulties so vexing that there must have been times when pontiffs wished it had been left unconverted. Elsewhere European *eruditum* — with a few striking exceptions, which would emerge later — was made up of devout men who, like the artists respon-sible for St. Peter's new majesty, reflected glory on the Church. The Vatican had been hospitable to the emerging Renaissance from the outset, and saw no reason for regret.

It would. Humanism, the Holy See would bitterly learn, led to the greatest threat the Church had ever faced. Actually it posed two threats. Martin Luther identified the first when he wrote: "Reason is the greatest enemy that faith has; it struggles against the divine word, treating with contempt all that emanates from God. The Virgin birth was unreasonable; so was the Resurrection; so were the Gospels, the sacraments, the pontifical prerogatives, and the promise of life everlasting." If you were a believer, you never subjected piety to the test of logic. Intellectuals, however, found logic an irresistible attraction, and therein lay their menace.

The second threat was inherent in the medieval Church's preoc-cupation with the afterlife. As early as A.D. 166 Lucian had defined Christians as "men who are persuaded that they will survive death and live forever; in consequence, they despise death and are willing to sacrifice their lives to that faith." Belief in a life everlasting lay at the very center of Christianity. To true Christians, life on earth was almost irrelevant. During it they obeyed the precepts of Catholicism to safeguard their future in paradise, disciplined by the fear that if they didn't, they might lose it. The thought of living for the sheer sake of living, celebrating mortal existence before God took them unto his own, was subversive of the entire structure. Yet that was precisely the prospect humanism offered. The new scholars took their worldly scripture from the first surviving fragment of Plato's Protagoran dialogue: "Man is the measure of all things."

Abandoning the past's preoccupation with eternity, humanists preached enrichment of life in the here and now. Their message, reversing ten centuries of solemnity, was hearty — an expression of confidence that men would learn to understand, and then master, natural forces, that they could grasp the nature of the universe, even shape their individual destinies. Those steeped in the habitude of the Middle Ages should have recognized this as a dangerous heresy, eclipsing the pitiful defiance of a Savonarola, but they didn't. The prestige of the scholars, and the eminence of their supporters, obscured the enormity of the challenge. So did confusion over the relationship between the artists of the Renaissance, who were above controversy, and the militant humanists. Those who translate revolutionary concepts into action are never as acceptable, or even as respectable, as those who express themselves indirectly. Humanism, by its very character, implied a revolt against all religious authority. It still does; the evangelists who denounce "secular humanism" five centuries later recognize the true adversary of fundamentalism.

As the apostasy grew, its character would slowly become clear to those who remained blindly loyal to the old Catholicism — to men like England's Sir John Fortescue, His Majesty's chief justice, who, after paying fulsome tribute to his country's laws, an Englishman's right to trial by jury, and the principle that civilized sovereigns should be law-abiding servants of those over whom they reigned, ended with a baffling non sequitur. All governments, he wrote, must be subject to the pope, *"usque ad pedum oscula,"* — "even to kissing his feet."

Men whose dedication to the papacy extended that far would ultimately come to realize that the humanists were moving in a

very different direction. They had begun as pure scholars dedicated
to the rediscovery of Latin, and then Greek, classics. But their
emphasis on wisdom not derived from religious sources had led
them to turn away from the supernatural. They did not reject it —
not yet, at any rate not outside Germany. Their movement was
still transitional; the change was one of emphasis, toward a new
faith which held that man's happiness and welfare in this lifetime
should come first, taking precedence over what might or might
not follow it, that mankind's highest ethical objective is not the
salvation of his soul but the earthly good of all humanity.

EVEN AFTER it had become obvious that medieval Christianity and
the reawakened reason of the ancient world were on a collision
course, the clash was not abrupt. Critics of the new intellectualism
approached the issue cautiously, beginning, in an early reference
to it, with a straightforward (if restrictive) definition: "The Humanist, I meane him that affects the knowledge of State affairs,
Histories, [et cetera]." True believers began to draw a distinction — it was to be observed for more than a century — between
"secular writers" (humanists) and "divines," or "devines" (themselves). Then a scholar was singled out for oblique censure: "I
might repute him as a good humanist, but not a good devine."

By then the divines were ready to fight, and the first quarrel
they opened — over higher education — was one the humanists,
it seemed, could hardly ignore. Proper university instruction,
wrote one cleric, should consist in "deliuering a direct order of
construction for the releefe of weake Grammacists, not in tempting
by curious deuise and disposition to conte [content] courtly Humanists." But the flung gauntlet was ignored. Another divine
described the spectrum of learning as arching from "the strictest
Roman Catholicism," representing perfection, to "the nakedest
humanism." This too provoked no response. An abusive reference
to "heathen-minded Humanists" was followed by another, to
"their system — usually called *Humanism*," which, the writer explained, sought "to level all family distinctions, all differences of
rank, all nationality, all positive moral obligations, all positive
religion, and to train all mankind to be as . . . the highest accomplishment." These were absurd charges, easily refuted, but no

learned scholar bothered to do it, and the divines, never an intellectual match for those they sought to draw, were reduced to limning the plight of a man bereft of his soul: "With the accession of humanistic ideas, he had lost all belief in the Christian religion."

Although the issue was profound, discussion of it remained a monologue. The humanists were hardly inarticulate; they were merely reserving their concern for immediate issues, such as the gross abuse of authority in the ecclesiastical hierarchy. Here the divines tried to intervene as amicus curiae. One asked sarcastically: "What a Discovery is it . . . that Vice raged at Court? Is it but the Hackney Observation of all Humanists?" In a sense it was exactly that; eminent spokesmen for humanism were discovering vice in parishes, dioceses, monastic orders, and, above all, in the Holy See, and if they sounded hackneyed it was because repetition is unavoidable when the same offenses turn up again and again.

Reflective men make uncomfortable prosecutors. By nature and by training, they tend to see the other side and give it equal weight. Clerical misconduct aroused the anger of some humanists, but others, bred to be devout, found the matter disturbing. They searched for compromises, envying painters and sculptors who could overlook the goings-on in Rome. Not all artists did, however. The shrewdest of them, aware that the papacy was spending fortunes on Vatican art even as famine stalked Europe, suspected the Vatican of exploiting them, tightening its grip on the masses by overawing them with beauty. One surprise rebel was Michelangelo, in his role as coarchitect for the new St. Peter's. Pope Leo ordered exquisite Tuscan marble from the remote Pietrasanta range. The artist balked. Bringing it out, he said, would be too expensive. Unaware of Michelangelo's mutiny, but thinking along the same lines, Martin Luther objected to the vast sums being raised for reconstruction of the great cathedral's basilica. Luther was a man of faith, not reason. Nevertheless Leo's prodigality troubled him. If the pope could see the poverty of the German people, he wrote, "he would rather see St. Peter's lying in ashes than that it should be built out of the blood and hide of his sheep."

Michelangelo had a choice. Luther's conscience denied him one. That was also true of other troubled clerics, scholars, writers, and philosophers. They *had* to speak out. Change was imperative.

Only the informed and the literate could demand it, and in the Europe of that time, they were few. At the outset, their objective was rehabilitation of the system, but this revolution, like Saturn — like all revolutions — was destined to eat its own children.

To them this was tragic. The doctrine that the Church was perfect, that the very idea of change was heretical, deeply disturbed learned Catholics, leaving them torn between faith and reason. In the eyes of Rome, Copernicus had died an apostate who had tried to subvert Ptolemaic theory, endorsed by the Church in the second century, more than two hundred popes earlier. But the solar system would not go away. It was too enormous. Within a century

Michelangelo's cupola of St. Peter's, seen from the rear

Galileo Galilei of Florence would confirm the Copernican system. Summoned to Rome, he, too, was found guilty of heresy. When he persisted in publishing his findings, he was called before the Inquisition, where, in 1633, under threat of torture, he disavowed his belief in a revolving earth. As he left the tribunal, however, he was heard to mutter, *"E pur si muove"* ("And yet it does move"). His recantation therefore was judged inadequate. He died blind and in disgrace. More than two centuries later, Thomas Henry Huxley, eulogizing him, scorned the Church as "the one great spiritual organization which is able to resist, and must, as a matter of life and death, resist, the progress of science and modern civilization."

But there had been little science and no modern civilization in the Dark Ages, when acceptance of papal supremacy by all Christendom had rescued a continent from chaos. Faith had literally held Europe together then, giving hope to men who had been without it. The most callous despots of the time, fearing God's wrath, had yielded to papal commands, permitting the Church to intervene when princes had been devouring one another, forcing them to submit to the argument that temporal rulers must yield to the one authority whose sacraments promised eternal salvation. Eminent Catholics knew that. And their piety was central to their personal lives. Now, though torn by inner conflict, they would shred "the seamless robe of Christ." Jesus, commanding Peter to build his Church, had predicted that "the gates of hell shall not prevail against it." The gates of hell hadn't; instead the terrible task of destroying the inviolability of the one true faith fell upon the devout, who prayed that they be spared it, and whose prayers were to be unanswered.

ERASMUS, THE SON of a priest, was a fastidious insomniac who spent much of his life in monasteries. Throughout the coming turmoil he remained an orthodox Catholic, never losing his love of Christ, the Gospels, and rites that comforted the masses. In his *Colloquia familiaria* he wrote: "If anything is in common use with Christians that is not repugnant to the Holy Scriptures, I observe it for this reason, that I may not offend other people." Public controversy seemed to him an affront; though his doubts about clerical abuses were profound, he kept them to himself until he was well into his forties. "Piety," he wrote in a private letter, "requires that we should sometimes conceal truth, that we should take care not to show it always, as if it did not matter when, where, or to whom we show it. . . . Perhaps we must admit with Plato that lies are useful to the people."

These were reassuring words in the College of Cardinals, where, in 1509, Erasmus, then in his early forties, was a guest. His hosts yearned for serenity; they were weary of the bellicose Pope Julius II, who was forever invading this or that nearby duchy, on one pretext or another, and they had become troubled by the increase in indiscretions of humanists who were more aggressive and more outspoken than Erasmus. Among the first to arouse the Vatican's displeasure had been Giovanni Pico della Mirandola, whose father, the ruler of a minor Italian principality, had hired tutors to give his precocious son a thorough humanist education.

The mature Pico developed a gift for combining the best elements from other philosophies with his own work, and his scholarship had been widely admired until he argued that the Hebrew Cabalistic doctrine, an esoteric Jewish mysticism, supported Christian theology. Greek and Latin scholarship were fashionable in Rome; but the suggestion of an affinity between Jewish thought and the Gospels was unwelcome. Pico drew up nine hundred theological, ethical, mathematical, and philosophical theses which Christianity had drawn from Hebrew, Arabic, Greek, and Latin sources and, in 1486, proposing to defend his position against any opponent, invited humanists from all over the continent to Rome to debate them. No one arrived. They weren't allowed to enter the city. The pope had intervened. A papal commission denounced over a dozen of Pico's theses as heretical, and he was ordered to publish an *Apologia* regretting his forbidden thoughts. Even after he had complied, he was warned of further trouble. Fleeing to France, he was arrested, briefly imprisoned, and, on his release — another sign of the age — was poisoned by his secretary.

Pico's ordeal had been followed by the even more awkward Reuchlin affair. Johannes Reuchlin, a Bavarian humanist, had become fluent in Hebrew and taught it to his Tübingen students.

Then, in 1509, Johannes Pfefferkorn, a Dominican monk who was also a converted rabbi, published *Judenspiegel* (*Mirror of the Jews*), an anti-Semitic book proposing that all works in Hebrew, including the Talmud, be burned. Reuchlin, dismayed by the possibility of such desecration, formally protested to the emperor. Jewish scholarship should not be suppressed, he argued. Rather, two chairs in Hebrew should be established at every German university. Pfefferkorn, he wrote, was an anti-intellectual "ass." Furious, the rabbi who had become a monk struck back with *Handspiegel* (*Hand Mirror*), accusing Reuchlin of being on the payroll of the Jews. Reuchlin's riposte, *Augenspiegel* (*Eyeglass*), so outraged the Dominicans that the order, supported by the obscurantist clergy throughout Europe, lodged a charge of heresy against him with the tribunal of the Inquisition in Cologne. The controversy raged for six years. Five universities in France and Germany burned Reuchlin's books, but in the end he was triumphant. Erasmus and Ulrich von Hutten, Maximilian's new poet laureate, were among those who rallied to his side. An episcopal court acquitted him, Pfefferkorn's fire was canceled, and the teaching of Hebrew spread, using Reuchlin's grammar, *Rudimentia Hebraica,* as the universities' basic text.

Because Erasmus was in Rome when this dispute broke out, his opinion was solicited. His mild reply — that he believed the issue could be solved by quiet compromise — endeared him to his hosts. They first urged him to prolong his stay, then offered him an ecclesiastical sinecure, suggesting that he settle among them permanently. Because of his eminence he had been courted in every other European capital. This seemed the ultimate opportunity, however, and he was at the point of accepting it when word arrived that the king of England had just died. Erasmus had known the new monarch, Henry VIII, since Henry's boyhood. Both were ardent Catholics, and while he was debating his future a personal letter from Henry reached him, proposing that "you abandon all thought of settling elsewhere. Come to England, and assure yourself of a hearty welcome. You shall name your own terms; they shall be as liberal and honourable as you please."

That decided Erasmus; he packed his bags. The offer was irresistible — for private reasons. In Rome, even if he became a

cardinal, his manuscripts would be carefully scrutinized for possible heresy, but in England he would be free, protected by a
powerful sovereign. This was important because there were certain
unorthodox reflections Erasmus wanted to put on paper and then
publish. Had his hosts at the Vatican known of them, it is likely
that he would never have left the city. Given the morality of the
time, it is even possible that his body, like so many thousands
before it, would have been washed up by the waters of the Tiber.

IN REASONING that truth must sometimes be concealed in the name
of piety, Erasmus had been completely sincere. He had, in fact,
done exactly that with the sacred college. Safe in England, he
intended to attack the entire Catholic superstructure. But he was
no hypocrite. Nor, by his lights, was he guilty of treachery; betrayal as we know it was so common in that age that it carried
few moral implications and aroused little resentment, even among
sovereigns, prelates, and the learned. Furthermore, he was moved
by a higher loyalty. He had always assigned absolute priority to
principles and was baffled by those who didn't. "We must not
look to Erasmus for any realistic conception of human nature,"
writes an intellectual historian. Brilliant, an accomplished linguist,
familiar with all the capitals of Europe, he was nevertheless ignorant of, and indifferent to, the secular world.

He never pondered, for example, the dilemma which was troubling Machiavelli in these years: whether a government can remain
in power if it practices the morality it preaches to its people. Nor
had he ever coped with the vulgar tensions of everyday life —
sexual tension (he was a celibate), for example, or the need to earn
a living. Others had always handled money matters for him. It
was no different in England. On his arrival there, the bishop of
Rochester endowed him with $1,300 a year, a Kentish parish
awarded him its annual revenues, and friends and admirers provided him with cash gifts. He was spared any concern about lodg-
ings by Sir Thomas More, who, taking him into his own home,
provided him with a servant. Erasmus scarcely noticed. He said:
"My home is where I have my library."

His, in short, was the peculiar naïveté of the isolated intellectual.
As an ecclesiastic, he had an encyclopedic knowledge of clerical

scandals, including the corruption in Rome. Other humanists had withdrawn from this squalor and found solace in the Scriptures. Not Erasmus; by force of reason, he believed, he could resolve the abuses of Catholicism and keep Christendom intact.

He miscalculated. Because the press as we know it had not even reached an embryonic stage, his knowledge of the world around him, like that of his contemporaries, was confined to what he saw, heard, was told, or read in letters or conversation. And because those around him were all members of the learned elite, he had no grasp of what the masses, the middle class, or most of the nobility knew and thought. His appeal was to his peers. Once he took his stand, they would find him immensely persuasive. But since his message would be incomprehensible to the lower clergy, where it counted, his appeals for reform would be impotent, his triumph literally academic.

Had that been the sum of it, he would have been unheard. But he was a man of many gifts, and one of them altered history. He possessed the extraordinary talent of making men laugh at the outrageous. Medieval men had known laughter — it is hard to see how they could have got through the day without it — but their expression of merriment had been the guffaw, mirth for its own sake; as Rabelais had written in his prologue to *Gargantua,* that kind of laughter is almost a man's birthright (*"Pour ce que rire est le propre de l'homme"*). Erasmus, instead, wrote devastating satire. If the guffaw is a broadsword, satire is a rapier. As such, it always has a point. Erasmus's points were missed by the common people, lay as well as clerical, but the coming religious revolution was not going to be a mass movement. It would be led by the upper and middle classes, which were gaining in literacy every day, and his brilliant thrusts had the unexpected effect of convulsing them and then arousing them.

In the beginning his intentions were very different. He meant to reach a small, elite audience which would be moved to act behind the scenes, within the existing framework of their faith. Instead his works became best-sellers. The first of them, written during his first year in England, was *Encomium moriae* (*The Praise of Folly*). Its Latinized Greek title was partly a pun on his host's name, but *moros* was also Greek for "fool," and *moria* for "folly."

His postulate for the work was that life rewards absurdity at the expense of reason.

COMING FROM A MAN OF GOD, it was an astonishing volume. Some passages might have been written by a radical, atheistic German humanist, and had the author been a man of lesser renown, he would certainly have been condemned by the inquisitors. Being Erasmus, he laughed at them, daring them to "shout 'heretic' . . . the thunderbolt they always keep ready at a moment's notice to terrify anyone to whom they are not favorably inclined."

He opened his argument by declaring that the human race owed its very existence to folly, for without it no man would submit

Desiderius Erasmus (1466? –1536)

to lifelong monogamy and no woman to the trials of motherhood. Bravery was foolish; so were men who pursued learning; and so, he added slyly, were theologians, whom he mocked for defending the absurdity of original sin, for spreading the myth that "our Saviour was conceived in the Virgin's womb," for presuming, during holy communion, to "demonstrate, in the consecrated wafer . . . how one body can be in several places at the same time, and how Christ's body in heaven differs from His body on the cross or in the sacrament."

Next he went after the clergy, his targets running up the ecclesiastical scale from friars, monks, parish priests, inquisitors, to cardinals and popes. To him, curative shrines, miracles, and "such like bugbears of superstition" were "absurdities" which merely served as "a profitable trade, and [to] procure a comfortable income to such priests and friars as by this craft get their gain." He mocked "the cheat of pardons and indulgences." And "what," he asked, "can be said bad enough of others who pretend that by the force of . . . magical charms, or by the fumbling over their beads in the rehearsal of such and such petitions (which some religious impostors invented, either for diversion, or, what is more likely, for advantage), they shall procure riches, honors, pleasure, long life, and lusty old age, nay, after death, a seat at the right hand of the Saviour?" As for the pontiffs, they had lost any resemblance to the Apostles in "their riches, honors, jurisdictions, offices, dispensations, licenses . . . ceremonies and tithes, excommunications and interdicts." Erasmus, the intellectual, could find only one explanation for their success: the stupidity, ignorance, and gullibility of the faithful.

Encomium moriae was translated into a dozen languages. It enraged the priestly hierarchy. "You should know," one of them wrote him, "that your *Moria* has excited a great disturbance even among those who were formerly your most devoted admirers." But few academic writers, having tasted popular success, can turn away from it, and he was no exception. His faith in the wisdom of his cause was now confirmed. Indeed, his next satire, which appeared three years later, turned out to be even more startling. This time he assailed a specific pontiff, "the warrior pope," Julius II.

Julius had been a strong pope and is remembered, deservedly, for his patronage of Michelangelo. But like all the pontiffs in that troubled age, he was more sinner than sinned against. He was also a Della Rovere — hot-tempered, flamboyant, and impetuous; Italians spoke of his *terribilità* (awesomeness). For five years he and his allies fought Venice. This campaign was successful; he recovered Bologna and Perugia, papal cities which the Venetians had seized during the misrule of the Borgia pope. In his second war, an attempt to expel the French from Italy, he was less fortunate, though by all accounts he cut a spectacular figure in combat, taking command at the front, white bearded, wearing helmet and mail, swinging his sword and always on horseback.

In satirizing this formidable pontiff Erasmus neither sought notoriety nor welcomed it; he had tried to deflect personal controversy by presenting his new work anonymously, but that was a doomed hope. He had shown it to too many colleagues. Sir Thomas More stripped his friend's disguise away in a careless moment, and the responsibility was fixed. Within the Catholic hierarchy, resentment against the author was deepened by what, even today, would be considered questionable taste. The year before the presentation of Erasmus's work in Paris — it was a dialogue — Julius had died. Thus the Church was actually in mourning for the victim of *Iulius exclusus.* Yet this did not dampen the hilarity of the Parisian audience, to whom it was first presented as a skit, or the multitude of readers in the months and years to come. In his onslaught on the papacy, Erasmus had struck a nerve; his followers thought the blow long overdue.

Julius is one character in the dialogue; Saint Peter is the other. Both stand at the gates of heaven, where the pope has presented himself for admittance. Peter won't let him in. Beneath the applicant's priestly cassock he notes "bloody armor" and a "body scarred with sins all over, breath loaded with wine, health broken by debauchery." To him the waiting pontiff is "the emperor come back from hell." What, he asks, has Julius "done for Christianity?"

Heatedly the applicant replies that he has "done more for the Church and Christ than any pope before me." He cites examples: "I raised the revenue. I invented new offices and sold them. . . . I set all the princes of Europe by the ears. I tore up treaties, and kept great armies in the field. I covered Rome with palaces, and left five millions in the treasury behind me."

To be sure, he concedes, "I had my misfortunes." Some whore had afflicted him with "the French pox." He had been accused of showing one of his sons favoritism. ("What?" asks Peter, astounded. "Popes with wives and children?" Julius, equally surprised, replies, "No, not wives, but why not children?") Julius acknowledges that he had also been accused of simony and pederasty, but is evasive when asked if his plea is Not guilty, and after Peter, bearing in, inquires, "Is there no way of removing a wicked pope?" Julius snorts: "Absurd! Who can remove the highest authority of all? . . . He cannot be deposed for any crime whatsoever." Peter asks: "Not for murder?" Julius replies: "Not for murder." Under questioning he adds that a pontiff cannot lose his miter even if guilty of fornication, incest, simony, poisoning, parricide, and sacrilege. Peter concludes that a pope may be "the wickedest of men, yet safe from punishment." The audience howled, knowing that was precisely Rome's position.

There is no way Peter is going to let this man into paradise. Julius, apoplectic, tells him that the world has changed since the time "you starved as a pope, with a handful of poor hunted bishops about you." When that line of reasoning is rejected, he threatens to excommunicate Peter, calling him "only a priest . . . a beggarly fisherman . . . a Jew." Peter, unimpressed, replies, "If Satan needed a vicar he could find none fitter than you. . . . Fraud, usury, and cunning made you pope. . . . I brought heathen Rome to acknowledge Christ; you have made it heathen again. . . . With your treaties and your protocols, your armies and your victories, you had no time to read the Gospels." Julius asks, "Then you won't open the gates?" Peter firmly replies, "Sooner to anyone else than to such as you." When the pontiff threatens to "take your place by storm," Peter waves him off, astounded that "such a sink of iniquity can be honored merely because he bears the name of pope."

LIKE ITS PREDECESSOR, *Iulius exclusus* was a *succès fou;* an Antwerp humanist wrote the author that it was "for sale everywhere here. Everyone is buying it, everyone is talking of it." The Curia,

alarmed now, urged Erasmus to lay his pen aside and spend the
rest of his life in repentant piety. It was too late. That same year,
1514, saw the appearance of *Familiarium colloquiorum formulae* in
the first of its several editions. Eventually the *Colloquia familiaria*,
as it came to be called, became the bulkiest and most loosely
organized of his works, and it is the most difficult to characterize.
Essentially it was a miscellaneous collection of random thoughts;
the full title, *Forms of Familiar Conversations, by Erasmus of Rotterdam, Useful Not Only for Polishing a Boy's Speech But for Building
His Character*, suggests his lack of a theme. Written in idiomatic,
chatty Latin, these colloquies included a peculiar blessing to be
bestowed on pregnant women — "Heaven grant that the burden
you carry may have as easy an exit as it had an entry" — together
with encouragement of circumcision, advice on the proper response when someone sneezed, paeans to piety, discouragement
of the burning of heretics, and an endless, tedious colloquy between "The Young Man and the Harlot," at the end of which the
prostitute, perhaps exhausted, agrees to abandon her calling. There
were off-color jokes, droll observations on the irrationality of
human behavior, an endorsement of the institution of marriage,
et cetera, et cetera.

Had that been all, his public, disappointed, would have left the
work unread. But Erasmus had not finished savaging the Church
and her clergy. An eighteenth-century Protestant translator later
wrote that he knew of "no book fitter to read which does, in so
delightful and instructing a manner, utterly overthrow almost all
the Popish Opinions and Superstitions." Certainly that seemed
the author's intent. He attacked priestly greed, the abuse of excommunication, miracles, fasting, relic-mongering, and lechery
in the monasteries. Women were urged to keep a safe distance
from "brawny, swill-bellied monks. . . . Chastity is more endan-
gered in the cloister than out of it."

Once more, however, he leveled his heaviest artillery on the
Vatican. His contempt for Julius's wars was venomous — "as if
the Church had any enemies as pestilential as impious pontiffs
who by their silence allow Christ to be forgotten, enchain [him]
by their mercenary rules . . . and crucify him afresh by their scandalous life!" Depravity and corruption still outraged him: "As to

these Supreme Pontiffs, who take the place of Christ," he wrote, "were wisdom to descend upon them, it would inconvenience them! . . . It would lose them all that wealth and honor, all those possessions, triumphal progresses, offices, dispensations, tributes and indulgences," requiring instead vigils, prayer, meditation, "and a thousand troublesome tasks of that sort." In a private letter he wrote, "The monarchy of Rome, as it is now, is a pestilence to Christendom."

In the first rush after publication, twenty-four thousand copies of the colloquies vanished from bookshops, and between then and midcentury only the Bible outsold it. There was a continuing demand for all his popular works. In 1520 an Oxford bookseller noted that a third of all the volumes he sold were written by Erasmus. Forty editions of *Encomium moriae* were published in the author's lifetime, and as late as 1632 Milton found the book "in everyone's hand" at Cambridge. It was this popularity, not the barbs themselves, which outraged those ecclesiastics who saw themselves as enforcers of the holy faith. Like every writer who has reached a large audience, he was dismissed for pandering to the masses, telling them what they wanted to hear, motivated solely by the base desire to make money. The impact of his successes on Christendom's establishment may be judged by an edict from the Holy Roman emperor. Any teacher found using the *Colloquia* in a classroom, he ordered, was to be executed on the spot. Martin Luther agreed. "On my deathbed I shall forbid my sons to read Erasmus' 'Colloquies.' " But Luther was then still professor of biblical exegesis at Wittenberg, an eminent member of the Catholic establishment. Within three years he would change his mind and, with it, the history of Western civilization. And Erasmus, though he denied it on his own deathbed, had sounded the claxon of religious revolution.

OF COURSE, "the great apostasy," as it came to be called in the Vatican, was no more the work of humanist scholars than it was an achievement of those godless descendants of Goths who had amused themselves by forging obscene propositions from the Blessed Virgin. The forces which fractured the unity of Christendom were enormously complex, and humanism, though a prime mover, was merely one current in the mighty wave which had just begun to form far out in the deep. One of its contributions was the revelation that art and learning had flourished before the birth of Jesus, when, it had been thought, such accomplishments were impossible. But men also wondered why God had allowed the triumph of the Muslims and the fall of Constantinople. And explorers returning from Asia and the Western Hemisphere reported thriving cultures which had either rejected Christ or never heard of him, thus discrediting those European Christian leaders who had held that belief in the savior was universal. It was an omen that Marguerite of Angoulême, the lovely Perle des Valois, sister of the king of France and herself queen of Navarre, became a skeptic. Once a woman of ardent faith, she now became a lapsed Catholic. In *Le miroir de l'âme pécheresse,* she acknowledged that she despised the religious orders, approved of attacks on the pope, thought God cruel, and doubted the Scriptures. Marguerite was accused of heresy before the Sorbonne, and a monk told his flock she should be sewn in a sack and flung into the Seine. As the sister of the French king she was never in peril, however; he adored her, and her championing of sexual freedom had enhanced her popularity in France.

The Vatican, with its population of bastards, was in no position to censure an advocate of infidelity. Marguerite's only real threat to Catholicism was her subsequent role as an accomplice of its enemies; she later provided sanctuary for fugitives from heresimach posses. One of them was John Calvin. It is instructive to note that Calvin was an ingrate. He rebuked his protectress for including, as guests of her court, Bonaventure Desperiers and Étienne Dolet, skeptics who mocked Catholics and Protestants alike. The dismal truth is that the new Christians would turn out to be at least as bigoted as the old.

However, their clergy were to prove neither corrupt nor depraved, and this, in that age, was refreshing. At a time when homicide, thievery, rape, and assassination reached shocking heights, loyal Catholics were most deeply distressed by the abuses of their own clergymen. Many of the clergy agreed. Abbot Johannes Trithemius of Sponheim condemned his own monks: "The whole day is spent in filthy talk; their whole time is given to play and gluttony. . . . They neither fear nor love God; they have no thought of the life to come, preferring their fleshly lusts to the needs of the soul. . . . They scorn the vow of poverty, know not that of chastity, revile that of obedience. . . . The smoke of their filth ascends all around." Another monk noted that "many convents . . . differ little from public brothels." According to Durant, Guy Jouenneaux, a papal emissary sent to inspect the Benedictine monasteries of France in 1503, described the monks as foul-mouthed gamblers and lechers who "live the life of Bacchanals" and "are more worldly than the mere worldling. . . . Were I minded to relate all those things that have come under my own eyes, I should make too long a tale of it."

In England Archbishop (later Cardinal) John Morton accused Abbot William of St. Albans of "simony, usury, embezzlement and living publicly and continuously with harlots and mistresses within the precincts of the monastery and without," and accused the country's monks of leading "a life of lasciviousness . . . nay, of defiling the holy places, even the very churches of God, by infamous intercourse with nuns," making a neighborhood priory "a public brothel." The bishop of Torcello wrote: "The morals of the clergy are corrupt; they have become an offense to the laity."

The public perception of the priesthood was in fact appalling. Eustace Chapuys, Charles V's ambassador in England, wrote the emperor: "Nearly all the people hate the priests." A Cambridge professor observed that "Englishmen, if called monk, priest, or clerk, felt bitterly insulted." Everywhere, wrote William Durand, bishop of Mende, the Church "is in ill repute, and all cry and publish it abroad that within her bosom all men, from the greatest even unto the least, have set their hearts upon covetousness. . . . That the whole Christian folk take from the clergy pernicious examples of gluttony is clear and notorious, since the clergy feast more luxuriously . . . than princes and kings." In Vienna the priesthood had once been the objective of ambitious youths. But now, on the eve of the religious revolt, it had attracted no recruits for twenty years.

In his fourteen-volume *History of the Popes,* Ludwig Pastor concludes that it was virtually impossible to exaggerate the "contempt and hatred of the laity for the degenerate clergy." Philip Hughes, historian of the Reformation in England, found that in 1514, when the chancellor of the bishop of London was accused of murdering a heretic, the bishop asked Cardinal Wolsey to prevent a trial by jury because Londoners were "so maliciously set in favor of heretical pravity that they will . . . condemn my clerk, though he were as innocent as Abel." Even Pope Leo, who, one would have thought, might have felt some responsibility for scandals committed in the name of the Church, observed in 1516, "The lack of rule in the monasteries of France and the immodest life of the monks have come to such a pitch that neither kings, princes, nor the faithful have any respect for them."

Priests by the thousands found it impossible to live in celibacy. Their solutions varied. In London it was not unknown for women entering the confessional box to be offered absolution in exchange for awkward, cramped intercourse on the spot. In Norfolk, Ripton, and Lambeth, 23 percent of the men indicted for sex crimes against women were clerics, though they constituted less than 2 percent of the population. The most common solution for men unable to bear the strain of continence was to take a mistress. Virtually all German priests kept women. The Roman clergy had a reputation for promiscuity, "but it is a mistake," writes Pastor, "to assume that the corruption of the clergy was worse in Rome than elsewhere; there is documentary evidence of the immorality of the priests in almost every town in the Italian peninsula. . . . No wonder, as contemporary writers sadly testify, the influence of the clergy had declined, and in many places hardly any respect was shown for the priesthood."

There was trouble in the convents, too. The problem seems to have been especially distressing in England. In 1520 eight nunneries there were closed, one because of "the dissolute disposition and incontinence of the religious women of the house, by reason of the vicinity of Cambridge University." After an examination of twenty-one convents in the diocese of Lincoln, fourteen were blacklisted for "lack of discipline or devotion." In several, nuns had been found who had been made pregnant by priests. Two reports told of prioresses living in adultery. A diocesan commission filed a separate account of one abbess who had presented a local blacksmith with three sons.

The failure of pontiffs to set a good example was heavily blamed. Egidio of Viterbo, general of the Augustinians, summed up Pope Alexander's Rome in nine words: "No law, no divinity; Gold, force and Venus rule." Guicciardini wrote: "Reverence for the Papacy has been utterly lost in the hearts of men." In 1513 Machiavelli charged that there could be no greater proof of papal "decadence than the fact that the nearer people are to the Roman Church, the head of their religion, the less religious they are. And whoever examines the principles on which that religion is founded, and sees how widely different from those principles its present practice and application are, will judge that her ruin or chastisement is near at hand."

IT WAS PRECISELY four years away, and the spark which ignited it was the sale of indulgences — specifically, the conduct of the *quaestiarii,* or pardoners, commissioned to distribute them, and the avarice of the papacy. Thomas Gascoigne, chancellor of Oxford, noted in 1450 that "sinners say nowadays: 'I care not how many evils I do in God's sight, for I can easily get plenary remission of all guilt and penalty by an absolution and indulgence granted me by the pope, whose written grant I have bought for four or six pence." The "indulgence-mongers," as Gascoigne scornfully called the *quaestiarii* in his account, "wander all over the country, and give a letter of pardon, sometimes for two pence, sometimes for a draught of wine or beer . . . or even for the hire of a harlot, or for carnal love."

John Colet, dean of St. Paul's Cathedral in the early sixteenth century, concluded that the commercialization of indulgences had transformed the Church into a "money machine." He quoted Isaiah: "The faithful city is become a harlot" — no one could doubt which city he meant — and then Jeremiah: "She hath committed fornication with many lovers. . . . She hath conceived many seeds of iniquity, and daily bringeth forth the foulest of offspring." He said, "Covetousness also . . . has so taken possession of the hearts of all priests . . . that nowadays we are blind to everything but that alone which seems able to bring us gain." In effect, the practice of indulgences was a form of religious taxation, and its weight bore heavily on those who could least afford it.

Informed Christians deeply resented the gulf between Europe's hungry masses and Rome's greed. In 1502 a procurer-general of the Parlement estimated that the Catholic hierarchy owned 75 percent of all the money in France; twenty years later, when the Diet of Nuremberg drew up its *Centum Gravamina* — Hundred Grievances — the Church was credited with owning 50 percent of the wealth in Germany.

Peter and Saul (later Paul) had lived in penury. The popes in the fifteenth and sixteenth centuries lived like Roman emperors. They were the wealthiest men in the world, and they and their cardinals further enriched themselves by selling holy offices. An ecclesiastical appointee had to send the Curia half his income during the first year of his appointment, and a tenth of it each year thereafter. Archbishops paid huge lump sums for their pallia, the white bands which served as the insignia of their rank. When Catholic officeholders died, all their personal possessions went to Rome. Judgments and dispensations rendered by the Curia became official when the applicant sent a gift in acknowledgment, with the Curia fixing the size of the gift. And every Christian was subject to papal taxes.

Even before he bought his pontificate, Cardinal Rodrigo Borgia's income had been 70,000 florins a year. But an occupant of Saint Peter's chair could do much better than that. Pope Julius

The traffic in indulgences

II formed a "college" of 101 secretaries who each paid him 7,400 florins for the honor. Leo X, more ambitious, created 141 squires and 60 chamberlains in his papal household, and, in return, received 202,000 florins.

Archbishops, bishops — even lower orders of the clergy — grew fat and frequently supported concubines on their fees and tithes. The laity had first protested their systematic impoverishment in the fourteenth century. Germans had seized tax collectors from Rome, jailed them, mutilated many, executed some. There, and elsewhere, brave prelates had supported the people. One, Álvaro Pelayo of Spain, declared: "Wolves are in control of the Church and feed on [Christian] blood!"; another, Bishop Durand of Mende, demanded that "the Church of Rome" remove "evil examples from herself . . . by which men are scandalized, and the whole people, as it were, infected."

The Vatican was unmoved. Over the years it had increased its levies, and that continued. In 1476 Pope Sixtus IV had proclaimed that indulgences applied to souls suffering in purgatory. This celestial confidence trick was an immediate success; David S. Schiff has described how peasants starved their families and themselves to buy relief for departed relatives. Discontent was growing when the wasteful Pope Leo found himself broke — undone by his war against the Duchy of Urbino. Going to the well once too often, on March 15, 1517, the Holy Father announced a "special" sale of indulgences. The purpose of this "jubilee" bargain (*feste dies*), as he called it, was to rebuild St. Peter's basilica. As an incentive donors would receive, not only "complete absolution and remission of all sins," but also "preferential treatment for their future sins."

There was, understandably, no mention of a secret agreement under which the Curia would split the jubilee's profits with young Albrecht of Brandenburg, archbishop of Mainz, who was deeply in debt to Germany's merchant family, the Fuggers. Albrecht had the pontiff's sympathy, and he was entitled to it. Albrecht had been obliged to borrow 20,000 florins because that was the price the pope had exacted for his confirmation as prelate.

The new archbishop chose as his jubilee's principal agent and hawker one Johann Tetzel, a Dominican friar in his fifties. There were *quaestiarii* whose traffic in indulgences was scrupulous, but Tetzel was not among them. He was a sort of medieval P. T. Barnum who traveled from village to village with a brass-bound chest, a bag of printed receipts, and an enormous cross draped with the papal banner. Accompanying him were a Fugger accountant and another friar, an assistant carrying a velvet cushion bearing Leo's bull of indulgence. Their entrance into a town square was heralded by the ringing of church bells. Jugglers performed and local throngs crowded around, waving candles, flags, and relics.

Setting up in the nave of the local church, Tetzel would begin his pitch by opening the bag and calling out, "I have here the passports . . . to lead the human soul to the celestial joys of Paradise." The fees were dirt-cheap, he pointed out, if they considered the alternatives. Christians who had committed a mortal sin owed God seven years' penance. "Who then," he asked, "would hesitate for a quarter-florin to secure one of these letters of remission?" Anything could be forgiven, he assured them, *anything*. He gave an example. Suppose a youth had slipped into his mother's bed

St. Peter's Square in Rome at the time of the coronation of Pope Sixtus V, in 1585.

and spent his seed inside her. If that boy put the right coins in the pontiff's bowl, "the Holy Father has the power in heaven and earth to forgive that sin, and if he forgives it, God must do so also." Warming up, Tetzel even appealed to the survivors of men who had gone to their graves unshriven: "As soon as the coin rings in the bowl, the soul for whom it is paid will fly out of purgatory and straight to heaven."

In Germany Tetzel exceeded his quota. He always did. This was his profession; he traveled from one diocese to another, raising funds as instructed by the Curia. Indulgences were popular among the peasantry, but less so among those who, in those days, formed the opinions of the laity. And this time he was in hostile territory. Northeastern Germany — Magdeburg, Halberstadt, and Mainz — had been chosen for this extortion because it was weak. France, Spain, and England were strong, and when they had asked that little be expected of them, pleading poverty, the pontiff had agreed. The decision was not without risk. Antipapal feeling was strong and vocal in Germany. The papal nuncio to the Holy Roman Empire was worried. That part of the Reich, he had written the pope, was in an ugly mood. He had therefore urged cancellation of the jubilee.

Leo had ignored him — unwisely, for presently ominous signs appeared. After watching Tetzel perform, a local Franciscan friar wrote: "It is incredible what this ignorant monk said and preached. He gave sealed letters stating that even the sins a man was intending to commit would be forgiven. The pope, he said, had more power than all the Apostles, all the angels and saints, more even than the Virgin Mary herself, for these were all subjects of Christ, but the pope was equal to Christ." Another eyewitness quoted the money-raiser as declaring that even if a man had violated the Mother of God the indulgence would wipe away his sin.

Nevertheless, Tetzel was probably acting within the letter of his archiepiscopal instructions, and he would have emerged triumphant once more had he not crossed, or at least approached, a political line. That was the boundary of Saxony, then ruled by Frederick III, also known variously as Frederick the Wise and, because he was among the privileged few entitled to choose a new Holy Roman emperor, as elector of Saxony. Frederick was no less

reverent than other rulers of his time, no less superstitious — he
had collected nineteen thousand saintly relics in Wittenberg's Castle Church — and, until now, no critic of *quaestiarii*. However,
accounts of Tetzel's extravagant claims had troubled him. He
wanted to keep Saxon coins in Saxon pockets. Therefore he had
declared the friar and his jubilee sale *non grata* in his territory. That
was where the peddler of paradise passports blundered. He knew
he wasn't wanted in Frederick's domain, but while working the
dioceses of Meissen, Magdeburg, and Halberstadt he came so close
to the border that some Saxons crossed over and bought his divine
wares.

Frederick was indignant. He considered this an affront. Of far
greater moment, several of these Saxon customers brought their
"papal letters" to a slender, tonsured monk of grave aspect and
hard eyes — Martin Luther — asking him, as a professor at Wittenberg, to judge their authenticity. After careful study Luther
pronounced them frauds. Word of this reached Tetzel. He made
inquiries. The professor, he was told — correctly — had no intention of offending the Church. Luther was an ardent Catholic,
though inclined, as an academic, to draw nice distinctions. Such
a man, Tetzel decided, would be easy to intimidate. Therefore, in
the most momentous decision of his life — and one of the most
momentous in the history of Christianity — he formally denounced him.

TETZEL BECAME the most famous man to misjudge Professor Martin Luther, but he was far from the first. Luther had always been
difficult. Few were close to him, and none — including, perhaps,
Luther himself — understood the tumultuous forces within him.
His genius is unquestioned. He had begun as an Augustinian friar.
In 1505, at the age of twenty-two, he was lecturing on the ethics
of Aristotle, using the original Greek text. Two years later he was
consecrated a priest, and the year after that, though he continued
to regard himself as a friar or monk, he was appointed by Frederick
to the chair of professor of philosophy at Wittenberg, on the Elbe,
about sixty miles southwest of Berlin. Later in his career he translated both the Old and New Testaments into New High German,
a language he virtually created, and composed forty-one hymns,

for which he wrote both the words and music. The most memorable of these, still sung around the world, is "A Mighty Fortress Is Our God."

In his early years Luther's loyalty to the Vatican was total; when he first glimpsed the Eternal City in 1511, he fell to his knees crying, "Hail to thee, O holy Rome!" He was already admired as a priest of narrow strength who had risen to early eminence as much by force of character as by intellect. Nevertheless, deep within him lurked a dark, irrational, half-mad streak of violence. This flaw, and it was a flaw, may be explained by his origins, which lay in the ignorant, superstition-ridden depths of medieval society. Luther was the product of a terrifying Teutonic childhood which would have broken most men.

He had been born in 1483, the son of a Mohra peasant who became a Mansfield miner, a husky, hardworking, frugal, humorless, choleric anticleric who loathed the Church yet believed in hell — which, in his imagination, existed as a frightening underworld toward which men were driven by cloven-footed demons, elves, goblins, satyrs, ogres, and witches, and from which they could be rescued only by benign spirits. It was Hans Luther's conviction that these good witches rarely interceded, though occasionally they could be propitiated by men living lives of relentless, joyless virtue.

Since children were born wicked, as Hans believed, it was virtuous to beat them senseless with righteous cudgels. However, Martin, the eldest of seven children, was never a submissive victim. He was not strong enough to overpower his father, but when the thrashings entered the realm of sadism, the two became, as he later recalled, open enemies. He received no sympathy from his mother. Though more timid, less irascible, and less worldly than her husband — she spent hours on her knees, praying to obscure saints — she shared Hans's convictions, including his belief in the salubrious effect of a vigorously applied lash. On one occasion, according to Luther, she caught him stealing a nut and whipped him to a bloody pulp.

The Church was the last career such parents would have chosen for their eldest son. He knew it, and that decided him. "The severe and harsh life I led with them," he wrote, "was the reason I afterward took refuge in the cloister and became a monk." Despite its inspirational beginning, his visit to the Vatican left a poor impression on him, but at the time he kept that to himself. His colleagues, dazzled by his treatises and his performances in his lecture hall, would have been astounded to learn that he had never shed the pagan superstitions infused in him even before he had reached the age of awareness — that a part of him was still haunted by pagan nightmares of werewolves and griffins crouched beneath writhing treetops under a full moon, of trolls and warlocks feasting on serpents' hearts, of men transforming themselves into slimy

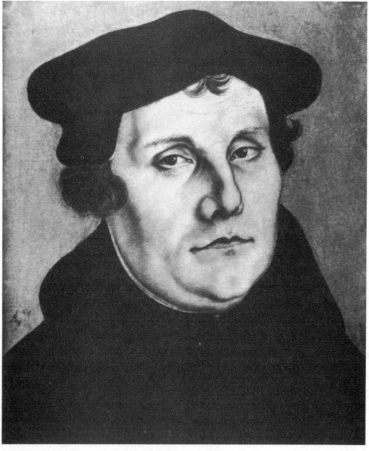

Martin Luther (1483–1546)

incubi and coupling with their own sisters while in a cave Brunhilde dreamed of the dank smell of bloodstained axes.

Luther was peculiar in other ways. His fellow monks spoke of
the devil, warned of the devil, feared the devil. Luther *saw* the
devil — ran into apparitions of him all the time. He was also the
most anal of theologians. In part, this derived from the national
character of the Reich. A later mot had it that the Englishman's
sense of humor is in the drawing room, the Frenchman's sense of
humor is in the bedroom, and the German's sense of humor is in
the bathroom. For Luther the bathroom was also a place of worship. His holiest moments often came when he was seated on the
privy (*Abort*) in a Wittenberg monastery tower. It was there, while
moving his bowels, that he conceived the revolutionary Protestant
doctrine of justification by faith. Afterward he wrote: "These
words 'just' and 'justice of God' were a thunderbolt to my conscience. . . . I soon had the thought [that] God's justice ought to
be the salvation of every believer. . . . Therefore it is God's justice
which justifies us and saves us. And these words became a sweeter
message for me. This knowledge the Holy Spirit gave me on the
privy in the tower."

Well, God is everywhere, as the Vatican conceded four centuries
later, backing away from a Jesuit scholar who had gleefully translated explicit excretory passages in Luther's *Sammtiche Schriften*.
The Jesuit had provoked angry protests from Lutherans who accused him of "vulgar Catholic polemics." Yet the real vulgarity
lies in Luther's own words, which his followers have shelved.
They enjoy telling the story of how the devil threw ink at Luther
and Luther threw it back. But in the original version it wasn't ink;
it was *Scheiss* (shit). That feces was the ammunition Satan and his
Wittenberg adversary employed against each other is clear from
the rest of Luther's story, as set down by his Wittenberg faculty
colleague Philipp Melanchthon: "Having been worsted . . . the
Demon departed indignant and murmuring to himself after having
emitted a crepitation of no small size, which left a foul stench in
the chamber for several days afterwards."

Again and again, in recalling Satan's attacks on him, Luther
uses the crude verb *bescheissen,* which describes what happens when
someone soils you with his *Scheiss*. In another demonic stratagem,

an apparition of the prince of darkness would humiliate the monk
by "showing his arse" (*Steiss*). Fighting back, Luther adopted
satanic tactics. He invited the devil to "kiss" or "lick" his *Steiss,*
threatened to "throw him into my anus, where he belongs," to
defecate "in his face" or, better yet, "in his pants" and then "hang
them around his neck."

A man who had battled the foulest of fiends in *der Abort* and
die Latrine was unlikely to be intimidated by the vaudevillian
Tetzel. Yet Luther's reply to the jubilee agent was not as dramatic
as legend has made it. He did not "nail" a denunciation of the
pope on the door of Frederick's Castle Church. In Wittenberg, as
in many university towns of the time, the church door was customarily used as a bulletin board; an academician with a new
religious theory would post it there, thus signifying his readiness
to defend it against all challengers.

Luther's timing was canny, however. He took advantage of
another tradition, the elector's annual display of his relics on All
Saints' Day, November 1. This always brought a crowd. Therefore at noon on October 31, 1517, he affixed his *Disputatio pro
declaratione virtutis indulgentiarum* (*Disputation for the Clarification of
the Power of Indulgences*) alongside the postulates of other theologians. He did something else. He prepared a German translation
to be circulated among the worshipers who would gather in the
morning. And he sent a copy to Archbishop Albrecht, sponsor
and secret beneficiary of Tetzel's carnival act.

Luther's theses — he had posted ninety-five of them — were
preceded by a conciliatory preamble: "Out of love for the faith
and the desire to bring it to light, the following propositions will
be discussed at Wittenberg under the chairmanship of the Reverend
Father Martin Luther, Master of Arts and Sacred Theology." It
did not occur to him that his position was heretical. Nor was it —
then. The pontiff, he agreed, retained the right to absolve penitents, "the power of the keys." He simply argued that peddling
pardons like Colosseum souvenirs trivialized sin by debasing the
contrition.

However, he then lodged an objection, one Rome could not
ignore. The papal keys, he pointed out, could not reach beyond
the grave, freeing an unremorseful soul from purgatory or even

decreasing its term of penance there. And while he absolved the
Holy See from huckstering indulgences, he added a sharp, significant observation, which, in retrospect, may be seen as the first
warning flash of the fury he had bottled up within since his hideous
childhood. It was, in fact, a direct criticism of the Apostolic See —
breathtaking because it could only be interpreted as the premed-
itated act of a heresiarch, and thus, a capital offense. He wrote:
"This unbridled preaching of pardons makes it no easy matter,
even for learned men, to rescue the reverence due the pope from
. . . the shrewd questionings of the laity, to wit: 'Why does not
the pope empty purgatory for the sake of holy love and of the
dire need of the souls that are there, if he redeems a . . . number
of souls for the sake of miserable money with which to build a
church?' "

THE SALE of indulgences plunged. Fewer and fewer quarter-florin
coins rang in the pontiff's bowl. The jubilee had virtually collapsed; Tetzel's spell had been broken. Luther was the new spell-
binder — divine or satanic, for opinion was deeply divided — and
accounts of his audacity spread across the continent with what
was, in the early 1500s, historic speed.

As long as a year would pass before the tidings of great events
reached the far corners of Europe. Except for the flatbed presses,
which moved at a lentitudinous pace, communications as we know
them did not exist. Information was usually carried by travelers,
and trips were measured by the calendar. The best surviving timetables start from Venice, then the center of commerce. A passenger
departing there could hope to enter Naples nine days later. Lyons
was two weeks away; Augsburg, Nuremberg, and Cologne, two
or three weeks; Lisbon seven weeks. With luck, a man could reach
London in a month, provided the weather over the Channel was
cooperative. If a storm broke in midpassage, however, you were
trapped. The king of England, leaving Bordeaux under fair skies,
did not appear in London until twelve days later.

Yet if news was electrifying, it could pass from village to village and even across the Channel, borne word-of-mouth. That is
what happened after Luther affixed his theses to the church
door. Before the first week in November had ended, spontaneous

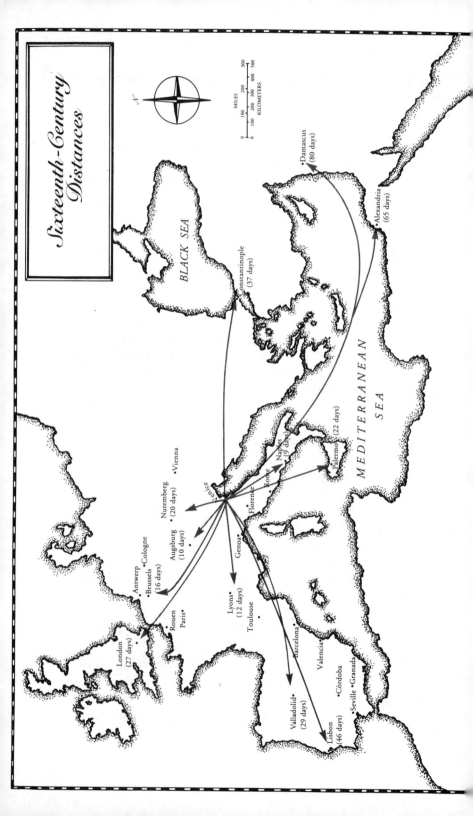

Sixteenth-Century Distances

MILES
KILOMETERS

BLACK SEA

MEDITERRANEAN SEA

Constantinople (37 days)

Damascus (80 days)

Alexandria (65 days)

Palermo (22 days)

Naples (19 days)

Rome

Florence

Venice

Vienna

Nuremberg (20 days)

Augsburg (10 days)

Antwerp
Brussels
Cologne (16 days)

Genoa

Lyons (12 days)

Toulouse

Rouen
Paris

London (27 days)

Barcelona

Valencia

Cordoba

Seville • Granada

Valladolid (29 days)

Lisbon (46 days)

demonstrations supporting or condemning him had erupted throughout Germany. Luther had done the unthinkable — he had flouted the ruler of the universe.

Penetrating the essence of the peasants' faith is difficult. Essentially it was belief in the supernatural. The lower orders of parochial clergy were regarded with contempt but also with affection. Bishops and archbishops, on the other hand, were less popular. In a study of Luther's homeland on the eve of his rise, Johannes Janssen, himself an eminent Catholic, found the prelates there obsessed with "worldly greed," while "preaching and the care of souls were altogether neglected." And, unlike priests faithful to their *Konkubinen,* they were notoriously promiscuous, sometimes traveling to federal or imperial diets with several mistresses in tow. The peasants' view of the pope is harder to define. They revered him, but not as the Vicar of Christ. He was more like a great magician. Now his powers had been impeached by a lowly Augustinian theologian. They expected a vengeful response. Its potency would sway their allegiance. If the pontiff's magic failed, they would begin to turn away from him.

In defying the organized Church, Luther had done something else. He had broken the dam of medieval discipline. By his reasoning, every man could be his own priest, a conclusion he himself would reach in 1520–1521. Moreover, as fragmentary accounts of the Gospels began to circulate, the peasantry learned that the sympathies of Christ and his apostles had lain with the oppressed, not with the princes who had presumed to speak in his name. Because church and state were so entwined in central Europe, Luther's challenge to ecclesiastical prestige encouraged a proletariat eager to demand a larger share in an increasingly prosperous Germany. Soon a pamphlet titled *Karsthans (Pitchfork John)* appeared in rural villages, pledging Luther the protection of the peasants. The assumption that he had become their champion was implicit.

The views of the upper classes were very different. Before the succession of disastrous popes their commitment to the Catholic hierarchy and the order of temporal life had been unwavering. Their lives were still guided by the dogmas of the Church, but the corruption in Rome and the flagrant misconduct of the clergy had angered them. It was also their "general opinion," in the words of Ludwig Pastor, "that in the matter of taxation the Roman Curia put on the pressure to an unbearable degree. . . . Even men devoted to the Church and the Holy See . . . often declared that the German grievances against Rome were, from a financial point of view, for the most part only too well founded." Now they listened attentively to the sermons of Luther's disciples touring Austria, Bohemia, Saxony, and the Swiss Confederation. The patricians, too, awaited a strong response from Rome.

ON APRIL 24, 1518, the German Augustinians, meeting in Heidelberg, relieved Luther of his duties as district vicar. It was a show of confidence, not a reprimand, and he used his new freedom well, delivering a closely reasoned denunciation of Scholastic doctrine as a pretentious "theory of glory." Printed copies were circulated across the Continent and discussed in widening circles, including the humanist community. Since the turn of the century humanist leaders had awaited a distinguished theologian with the courage to label Scholasticism as anti-intellectualism parading mindless shibboleths as philosophy. German scholars now published a sheaf of leaflets proclaiming themselves Lutherans.

In England John Colet, who had seen the revolt coming — yet whose loyalty to the papacy would remain unshaken throughout the coming tumult — saw the Curia engrossed not with good works and repentance, but with the size of the fees it could exact. Luther was discovering that he had become the voice of millions who suffered doubly from the Renaissance popes; impoverished by highwaymen like Tetzel, they also grieved for their beloved faith, desecrated by rogues in vestments. From this point forward, his wrath and theirs would join, gathering in volume and strength as together they confronted the most powerful symbol of authority Europe had ever known. Both sides would invoke the name of Christ, but in Germany, where first blood was being drawn, the spectacle invited parallels, not with the New Testament, but with *Das Lied vom huren Seyfrid,* the pagan fable first heard by Luther as a child, which reaches its climax when Siegfried buries his gory ax in the dragon Fafnir.

The gauntlet had been flung, but Pope Leo merely toyed with it. Archbishop Albrecht, alarmed, sent the theses from Mainz to

Rome accompanied by a forceful request that Luther be formally disciplined. Leo misinterpreted the challenge. Dismissing it as another dispute between Augustinians and Dominicans, he turned the matter over to Gabriel della Volta, the vicar general of Luther's order, instructing him to deal with it through channels, in this case Johann von Staupitz, the Augustinian responsible for Wittenberg. Della Volta's order may have wound up in some curial pigeonhole or file. Certainly it never reached Staupitz. In effect, the papacy had ignored the defiance in Wittenberg.

Elsewhere, however, the Catholic reaction was vehement. The universities of Louvain, Cologne, and Leipzig, strongholds of theological tradition, condemned the theses in their entirety. And Tetzel, feeling himself libeled, had decided to reply. Because he was an illiterate and ignorant of virtually every principle at stake, the Dominicans had appointed a theologian, Konrad Wimpina, as his collaborator, and in December 1517 *One Hundred and Six Anti-Theses* had appeared in Frankfurt under Tetzel's name. Unapologetic, unyielding, the friar defended his distributions of cut-rate salvation in an argument later described in the *Catholic Encyclopedia* as giving "an uncompromising, even dogmatic, sanction to mere theological opinions that were hardly consonant with the most accurate scholarship." The following March a hawker offered eight hundred copies of the leaflet in Wittenberg. University students mobbed him, bought the lot, and burned them in the market square.

Luther counterattacked in a tract, *Indulgence and Grace*. Now the rebelliousness in his tone was unmistakable: "If I am called a heretic by those whose purses will suffer from my truths, I care not much for their brawling; for only those say this whose dark understanding has never known the Bible." In the Curia wise men, realizing that Tetzel had become an embarrassment, told Leo that he had to go. The pope, agreeing, received Karl von Miltitz, a young Saxon priest of noble lineage now serving in Rome. Once the dust had settled, he told Von Miltitz, he wanted him to travel north and unfrock the discredited friar.

BUT ABANDONING TETZEL now — with orthodox German theologians fiercely defending him — was out of the question. Archbishop Albrecht had privately reprimanded the salesman for his excesses. In public, however, the leadership of the Catholic establishment there closed its ranks and its minds, refusing to discuss compromise. In Rome, a German archbishop called for heresy proceedings against Luther, and the Dominicans demanded his immediate impeachment. Dr. Johann Eck, vice chancellor of Ingolstadt University and perhaps the most eminent theologian in central Europe, attacked the theses in a leaflet, *Obelisks,* accusing their author of subverting the faith by spreading "poison." The Curia's censor of literature, concurring, issued a *Dialogue* reaffirming "the absolute supremacy of the pope," and Jakob van Hoogsträten of Cologne demanded Luther be burned at the stake.

Instead he kept scratching away with his pen. In April 1518, the month after Eck's blast, he published *Resolutiones,* a curious brochure whose ostensible purpose was to assure the Church of his orthodoxy and submission. In a copy sent to the pontiff he offered "myself prostrate at the feet of your Holiness, with all I am and have. Quicken, slay, call, recall, approve, reprove, as may seem to you good. I will acknowledge your voice as the voice of Christ, residing and speaking in you." Yet this inscription was wholly inconsistent with the text that followed. *Resolutiones* implicitly denied the pontiff's supremacy, suggesting he was answerable to an ecumenical council. The pamphlet went on to slight relics, pilgrimages, extravagant claims for the powers of saints, and the holy city ("Rome . . . now laughs at good men; in what part of the Christian world do men more freely make a mock of the best bishops than in Rome, the true Babylon?"). He declared the very foundation of the Curia's indulgences policy — stretching back over three centuries — null and void. The monk of Wittenberg was growing ever more confident, and as his confidence grew, so did his feelings of independence.

Leo was stunned. Abandon indulgences? Just as his pontificate was approaching bankruptcy? He was rebuilding a cathedral, waging wars, funding elaborate dinner parties while trying to keep Raphael, Lotto, Vecchio, Perugino, Titian, Parmigianino, and Michelangelo in wine. The Curia, juggling budgets, was swamped with bills. And now a German monk — a mere friar — had the audacity to condemn a prime source of Vatican revenue. The Holy Father summoned Martin Luther to Rome.

The invitation was declined. Acceptance might mean the stake — there were plenty of precedents for that. At the very least Luther might be assigned to an obscure Italian monastery, where, within a year, he and his cause would be forgotten. Instead he appealed to Frederick the Wise, submitting that German princes should shield their people from extradition. The elector agreed. He liked his controversial Augustinian. (One reason was that Luther's Wittenberg duties included keeping the university's books; unlike Leo, he had never resorted to red ink.) And

Pope Leo X (1475–1521)

Maximilian's advice, which Frederick sought, was decisive. The Habsburg emperor had only five months to live, but he had lost none of the political shrewdness which had forged an intricate dynastic structure, making his family dominant in central Europe. He was keeping a close watch on the interplay of German politics and religion. "Take good care of that monk," Maximilian wrote the elector. Handing Luther over to the pontiff, he explained, could be a political blunder. In his judgment, anticlerical sentiment was increasing throughout Germany.

Almost immediately an imperial diet, or Reichstag, confirmed him. The emperor, in summoning his German princes to Augsburg, was responding to a request from Rome. Leo had told him he was planning a new crusade against the Turks and wanted a surtax to support it. The diet rejected his appeal. The action was highly unusual, but not unprecedented; Frederick, after collecting a papal levy from his people, had decided to keep it and build the University of Wittenberg. His peers had been heartened. All the Vatican wanted from the princes, it seemed, was money, money, and more money. In their view the confirmation fees, annates, and costs of canonical litigation were already millstones around the empire's neck. Besides, they had sent the Curia revenues for other crusades, only to learn that the ventures had been canceled, while the funds, unreturned, had been spent on Italian projects. All previous crusades had failed anyway. And the princes weren't worried about Turks. The real enemy of Christendom, they decided, was what one of them called "the hell-hound in Rome." In a conciliatory letter to the Vatican, Maximilian assured the pope that he would move sternly against heresy. At the same time, he ventured to suggest that Luther be treated carefully.

AFTER MUCH THOUGHT, Leo agreed. Luther's summons to Rome was canceled. Instead, in the autumn of 1518 the pontiff ordered him to confer with a papal emissary — Tommaso de Vio, Cardinal Cajetan, general of the Dominicans — in Augsburg. On October 7 Luther arrived there with an imperial safe-conduct in his pocket. By now his life was in jeopardy, though Cajetan was no threat. The cardinal was a man of honor; he possessed a formidable intellectual reputation and had published a tremendous nine-volume commentary on Aquinas's *Summa theologica*. Their meeting, however, was barren of results, and since neither principal had been told its purpose, it ended in fiasco. Luther had come prepared to discuss an agenda of reforms, but the cardinal was an enforcer of ecclesiastical discipline. Considering his scholarly background, it seems odd that he ignored Luther's professorial appointment. Instead he acted in his role as a Dominican general, viewing the Wittenberg monk merely as a member of the lower clergy, who, having pledged obedience to prelates, could not criticize them publicly. The only issue, Cajetan said, was the sentence to be meted out.

He had, in fact, already reached his decision: the offender must immediately issue a public retraction and solemnly swear never again to question papal policy. Luther bluntly refused. His eminence, incensed, dismissed the impenitent priest and ordered him never to reappear in his presence unless he was on his knees, delivering an unconditional recantation. Then, alone, Cajetan scrawled a vehement denunciation of Luther and sent it at once, by special messenger, to Frederick the Wise.

Servants, watching this, reported it to Saxon councillors — in that age spies were ubiquitous; every European monarch maintained espionage rings in every other royal court, and the largest and most skillful were embedded deep in the Vatican. Rumors to the contrary, Cajetan did not actually try to arrest Luther, but concern for the monk's safety was genuine. After a reliable source reported plans to take him to Italy in chains, he was bundled out a side door, concealed in a farmer's cart, and hurried out of the city. It had been close; the trap had been about to spring. Cajetan wrote Frederick again, demanding that Luther be sent to Italy at once under armed guard. The elector refused. The monk was safe for the moment, but his situation was that of a fugitive living in a country which has decided, at least for the moment, not to extradite him.

Safely back in Wittenberg, he wrote a lively account of his confrontation with the cardinal and circulated it throughout Germany. To one friend he wrote: "I send you my trifling work that you may see whether or not I am right in supposing that, according to Paul, the real Antichrist holds sway over the Roman court."

Luther and his Lutherans were growing more intemperate in their language, and their private references to the pope were growing more irreverent. The pontiff again invited him to Rome for confession, offering to pay for the trip; Luther again decided that his security would be tighter in Wittenberg. The monk's peril had grown. The Holy Father and his prelates were omnipotent in the judgment of heresy. Every European sovereign was bound by law to deliver into their hands anyone branded an apostate by the ecclesiastic hierarchy. Lately the pope had become wary of exercising that right. As the prestige of the Holy Roman Empire weakened, it had become obvious that eventually a scofflaw ruler would defy him. But the line was only beginning to blur. No monarch had yet refused to hand over a heresiarch — and thousands of men had perished at the stake for offenses less flagrant than those already committed by Wittenberg's seditious professor. To challenge papal supremacy was, by definition, heretical and a capital offense. In the memory of living men four Germans had been martyred for apostasy, and the similarity of their offenses and Luther's was striking. Johan von Wesel of Erfurt, like Luther a professor, had rejected indulgences, telling his students: "I despise the pope, the Church, and the councils, and I worship only Christ." Despite a later recantation, he had been sent to his death. Condemnation had also awaited the brothers John and Lewin of Augsburg, for pronouncing indulgences a hoax, and Wessel Gansfort, who had rejected indulgences, absolution, and purgatory, calling the Bible the sole source of faith and salvation.

Luther later said of Gansfort, "If I had read his works before, my enemies might have thought that Luther had borrowed everything from [him], so great is the agreement between our spirits." That was also true of the others, and if they had been guilty of high crimes, so was he; he had defied the Vatican in print, on platforms, and from the pulpit. All that was lacking was a formal confession before an official ecclesiastical body, and on June 27, 1519, eight months after his flight from Augsburg, he unwittingly provided that in the great tapestried hall of Leipzig's Pleissenburg Castle.

Actually he could, with dignity, have absented himself from the Leipzig debate. The principal figure, in effect representing

Luther, was his senior colleague at Wittenberg, Andreas Boden-
stein, universally known, from his birthplace, as Professor Karlstadt. Karlstadt had run afoul of the Catholic hierarchy when
Obelisks, Johann Eck's polemical reply to Luther's theses, had appeared. At the time Luther himself had been packing for the Augustinian meeting in Heidelberg; his own comments had been
confined to a few scribbled notes at the bottoms of pages. But
Karlstadt, eager to join the struggle, had produced a manuscript
listing 379 new theses, to which he had added another 26 before
publication. And now, challenged by Eck, he found himself in
the middle of the battle.

EVERY SEAT was taken. Most of the audience comprised theologians
and nobles, but there was a large delegation of Wittenberg students
armed with clubs, prepared to fight for their professors. The
youths kept a wary eye on the presiding officer, Duke George of
Albertine Saxony. Duke George was a cousin of Frederick the
Wise, but, unlike the elector, he was also a fierce conservative and
therefore hostile to Luther. The only motive for Luther's presence
in the hall was personal loyalty. He was a fighter and an able
debater, and Karlstadt, though intellectually gifted, was neither.
The great Eck was expected to destroy him. Luther knew Eck
could do it, but meant to see to it that he left the hall bearing a
few bruises of his own.

As it turned out, Eck carried the day, scoring a greater victory
than anyone had anticipated. Afterward he boasted of a personal
triumph. He was right; it was. When Luther intervened, supporting his colleague, Eck skillfully maneuvered him far afield,
then to a quagmire, into which he sank. The catastrophe began
innocently, with a dispute over obscure issues raised a century
earlier at the ecumenical General Council of Constance, called to
reform the Church, bring an end to the Great Schism (there were
three rival popes at the time), and suppress heresy. Unaware of
where they were headed, Luther allowed Eck to lead him into a
candid discussion of a tragic victim of the council, the Bohemian
martyr Jan Hus.

Hus, the first great Czech patriot, had wanted to see the establishment of a Bohemian national church. After his ordination

he had dominated the ancient University of Prague as its rector and dean of the philosophy faculty. Delivering both lectures and sermons in Czech, he rode to a crest on the rising sense of Bohemian national identity. By attempting to end abuses of the clergy, he offended his ecclesiastical superiors. Excommunicated, he nevertheless continued preaching under the protection of Bohemia's weak King Wenceslas IV (Václav in Czech).

He then alienated powerful men in the Church and grievously offended the king. In 1411, the antipope John XXIII had demanded a large Czech sale of indulgences to finance new wars. Wars, Hus argued, were temporal; using ecclesiastical power to finance them was intolerable. Wenceslas, who had been promised a share in the proceeds of the sale, turned against him. Hus went into hiding and wrote tracts supporting his position, shielded by admiring peasants. Then, in 1414, when the Council of Constance was meeting, he was invited to address it. The reigning Holy Roman emperor, Sigismund, offered him a safe-conduct, and he accepted it, a suicidal error, for Sigismund betrayed him into the hands of the schismatic pope. Sentenced by a panel of judges, all his enemies, Hus went to the stake as a heretic.

Had Luther approved the condemnation of Hus, or even evaded the issue, his movement would have collapsed and he would have been scorned, even by his students, as craven and dishonorable. Being neither, he replied that even ecumenical councils could err. Hus had been right, he said; his doctrines had been sound; those who had broken faith with him, and then damned him, had behaved shamefully and disgraced the Church.

It was a brave reply. It was also calamitous. His differences with Rome had begun with a minor dispute over indulgences. Now he had challenged pontifical authority over Christendom, revealing himself before all Europe as an unshriven, unrepentant apostate. He knew it, and as he left Pleissenburg Castle, surrounded by his vigilant students, he was a badly shaken man.

ON THE DAY FOLLOWING Luther's humiliation, the seven electors of the Holy Roman Empire met in Frankfurt am Main to choose a new emperor, Maximilian having died six months earlier. The identity of the successor to *der gross Max* was far more engrossing to Pope Leo than the incipient split in the Catholic Church — a demonstration of how hopelessly the pontiff's priorities were askew. Historians agree that Luther could have been swiftly crushed had the pope moved decisively in his role as Vicar of Christ, the spiritual head of Christendom. Instead he dallied, vacillated, became engrossed in minor matters, and spent too many late evenings with his books. Leo X was no Borgia. In many ways he was more admirable than Martin Luther. Head of the Medici family, a poet and a man of honor, he was a leading patron of the Renaissance, a connoisseur of art, a scholar steeped in classical literature, and a pontiff tolerant enough to chuckle as he read the satires of Erasmus, appreciative that the humanist had observed the gentlemanly rule under which learned men of that time were free to write as they pleased, provided they confined themselves to Latin, leaving the unlettered masses undisturbed.

Those closest to the pope agreed that he was afflicted by three weaknesses: he was superficial, a spendthrift, and he lacked judgment. His poor judgment was to be his undoing, and it contributed heavily to the undoing of his Church. In the absence of decisive pontifical action, the Wittenberg abscess was spreading steadily. Oblivious to it, Leo waited nearly three years after the posting of Luther's Ninety-five Theses before issuing an ultimatum to their author. Meantime the situation within Germany had changed radically.

A pope who took his responsibilities more seriously would have stifled the revolt before the end of 1517 by ordering Frederick III to silence the mutinous Augustinian, imprison him, or cremate him. But Leo, for purely secular reasons, was courting Frederick. It had been clear for some time that the reign of the great Max was nearing its end. Any European prince was eligible to succeed him. The three obvious candidates, all mighty kings, were Henry VIII of England, Francis I of France, and young Carlos I of Spain.

Henry could be omitted. He lacked the wealth to compete in the election, and he wasn't much interested anyhow. Real power, not the illusion of it, attracted the vigorous British monarch, and he knew that despite its lustrous name the glitter of the imperial realm was fading. It was better known now as *die Romaisches Reich deutscher Nation,* a loose confederation whose leader, limited in his sovereignty, was voted into office by the archbishops of Mainz, Trier, and Cologne; the count palatine of the Rhine; the king of Bohemia; the margrave of Brandenburg — and the duke of Saxony, then Frederick III, Luther's patron.

Unlike Henry, the kings of France and Spain coveted the imperial title. Though reduced to a symbol, it was deeply invested with tradition and tied to the papacy in a hundred ways; as Maximilian had demonstrated, a shrewd diplomat could achieve much by manipulating its panoply. But Pope Leo wanted neither Charles nor Francis. The new emperor, if able, would control Germany, and any king who could unite Germany with either France or Spain would destroy the European balance of power that had preserved the shaky autonomy of the Italian states since 1494. Leo preferred a minor prince, and because Frederick of Saxony was the senior member of the electoral college, he settled on him. That explains his deference toward Frederick's lenient treatment of Luther. No other pontiff would have sent a cardinal to bargain with a monk — Cardinal Cajetan had misunderstood his mission to Augsburg, because it was, by all precedents, inexplicable — and none other would have tolerated the stream of abusive Lutheran pamphlets now issuing from Wittenberg. Committed to Frederick, Leo had even dispatched Von Miltitz to Wittenberg to offer him "the Golden Rose," an award popes conferred on princes as a sign of their highest favor. Leo hoped that would improve the Saxon elector's chances at Frankfurt am Main. Frederick, a man of honor, dismissed Miltitz and sent him back to Rome.

It had been a footling gesture. Carlos of Spain was not to be denied. He was prepared to become Emperor Charles V the way Borgia had become pope — by buying the imperial crown. He went deeply into debt to do it, but he had a lot of collateral. He ruled, not only Spain, but also Sicily, Sardinia, Naples, Spain's possessions abroad, the Habsburg holdings in Austria, the Netherlands, Flanders, and Franche-Comté. Still, the empire, though shopworn, did not come cheap; his *Trinkgeld* — bribes to electors who put their votes on the market — came to 850,000 ducats, of which he had borrowed 543,000 from the Fuggers.

German strength, which would prove indispensable to Luther, owed much to the new prosperity powered by the formidable Fuggers and their fellow merchants. Unintimidated by rank, they insisted that they be paid what was owed them, and on time; when the new emperor fell in arrears, Jakob Fugger II threatened to expose him: "It is well known that your Majesty without me might not have acquired the imperial honor, as I can attest with the written statements of all the delegates," he wrote, threatening to do exactly that unless Charles immediately issued an "order that the money which I have paid out, together with the interest on

Emperor Charles V (Carlos I of Spain) (1500–1558)

it, shall be repaid without further delay." Charles paid — mostly
by giving Fugger the right to collect various royal revenues in
Spain.

CHARLES HAD BEEN ELECTED, but his coronation was more than a
year away. That was long enough to form alliances, declare and
win wars, unseat dynasties — or nullify the choice of an emperor-
elect. Pope Leo, stubbornly refusing to concede defeat, continued
to neglect his office, by persevering in his courtship of Frederick
the Wise. He seemed prepared to endure the Wittenberg insubordination indefinitely, trusting that this lesser issue, which is how
he regarded it, would yield to a peaceful solution. Lutheran am-
bivalence encouraged him in this. Even before Leipzig, Luther had
been suffering through what might be called an identity crisis. He
had been trying to define the papacy and his relationship to it.
Meeting Von Miltitz in Altenburg in January 1518, he had appeared anxious to preserve the unity of Christendom, offering to
remain mute if his critics would also. He was prepared to issue
public statements acknowledging the wisdom of praying to saints
and the reality of purgatory. He was also willing to urge his
followers to make peace with the Church, and would even concede
the usefulness of indulgences in remitting canonical penances. To
Tetzel, lying on a monastic deathbed, he sent a gentle note, assuring him that the issue between them had been a minor incident
in a larger controversy, "that the affair had not been begun on
that account, but that the child had quite another father." In March
he even sent the pontiff a letter of submission.

    This was young Luther redux — a flashback to the moment
when, as a twenty-eight-year-old monk, he had first glimpsed the
capital of Catholicism and prostrated himself. Then a devout pilgrim, he had genuflected before saintly relics, worshiped at every
Roman altar, and scaled the Scala Santa on his knees. Now he
wrote the Holy See in the same exalted mood. The response from
the Vatican, prompt and friendly, invited him to Rome for confession. But by then Luther's inner struggle had resolved itself. Leo's
overture was declined once more. Wittenberg, after all, was still
safer for an avowed recreant, and as the dark doppelgänger within
him reformed, he made his final, irrevocable turn away from

Rome. The Luther who would make history was reemerging: willful, selfless, intolerant, pious, brilliant, contemptuous of learning and art, but powerful in conviction and driven by a vision of pure, unexploited Christianity.

In a brief, insightful passage he grasped this side of his temperament: "I have been born to war, and fight with factions and devils; therefore my books are stormy and warlike. I must root out the stumps and stocks, cut away the thorns and hedges, fill up the ditches, and am the rough forester to break a path and make things ready." Thus, within a month of repledging his allegiance to the Holy Father he wrote Georg Spalatin, chaplain to Frederick: "I am at a loss to know whether the Pope is Antichrist or his apostle." And in a more moderate but nevertheless revolutionary note, he suggested: "A common reformation should be undertaken of the spiritual and temporal estates."*

His followers, like him, were angry men; wrath was a red thread binding the Lutherans together. More and more — and especially after Leipzig — they resembled an insurgent army, with Wittenberg as its command post and new hymns which sounded like marches. Some members of his retinue left memorable contributions to polemical literature, but none could match the vehemence of their leader when fully aroused. After reading the Curia's continuing, uncompromising, absolute claims for the primacy and power of Catholic pontiffs, he published an *Epitome* which opened by describing Rome as "that empurpled Babylon" and the Curia as "the Synagogue of Satan." Three years earlier he would have been shocked to read such a diatribe, let alone write it himself. Now it was only an overture.

"The papacy," he wrote, "is the devil's church." And: "The devil founded the papacy." And: "The pope is *Satanissimus*." And: "The papacy is Satan's highest head and greatest power." And: "The pope is the devil incarnate." And: "The devil rules throughout the entire papacy." And: "The devil is the false God [*Abgott*] of the pope." And: "Because of God's wrath the devil has bedunged us with big and gross arses in Rome." Either Satan was

_____

*In a letter to Duke George of Saxony. Here, for the first time, he gave his movement the name by which history knows it.

the pope's excrement or the papacy was Satan's excrement, but it had to be one or the other. He wrote that unless "the Romanists" curbed their fury — as though his own tone were temperate — "there will be no remedy left except that" true Christians "girt about with force of arms . . . settle the matter no longer with words but by the sword. . . . If we strike thieves with the gallows, robbers with the sword, heretics with fire, why do we not much more attack in arms these masters of perdition, these cardinals, these popes, and all this sink of Roman Sodom which has without end corrupted the Church of God, and *wash our hands in their blood?*" (emphasis added).

Pope Leo's tolerance had seemed infinite, but this was too much. Protesting the abuse of indulgences had been heretical only in the eyes of precisians; Eck's coup, after all, had been based on an antecedent in which the Church could scarcely take pride. Incitement of homicide, however, was beyond tolerance. To propose slaughtering the pontiff and his cardinals would have been a high crime had the offender been an ignorant member of the laity. Here he was an accomplished theologian, and disciplining his apostasy was overdue. Furthermore, that same June the vigilant Eck, now in hot pursuit of heresiarchs, arrived in Rome with a copy of a new, splenetic Luther sermon openly questioning the power of excommunication. Accompanying it were detailed reports of Lutheran converts spreading dissent in central Europe and Switzerland. Reconciled at last to the coming coronation of Charles as the new Holy Roman emperor, the pontiff finally acted. On June 15, 1520, announcing that the papacy was in mortal danger from "a wild boar which has invaded the Lord's vineyard," he issued *Exsurge Domine,* a bull condemning forty-one of Luther's declarations, ordering the burning of his works, and appealing to him to recant and rejoin the faith. The German monk was given sixty days to appear in Rome and publicly renounce his heresies.

Sixty days passed, he remained in Wittenberg, and the Curia accordingly issued a bull of excommunication. It was not signed by the pope, and at his insistence it stopped short of the ultimate *Decet Romanum pontificem,* eternally damning the monk. Nevertheless Luther was named and condemned. All Christians were forbidden to listen to him, to speak to him, or even to look at him. In any community contaminated by his presence, religious services were to be suspended. He was declared a fugitive from the Church; kings, princes, and nobles were commanded to banish him from their lands or deliver him to Rome.

He responded with a series of caustic pamphlets. Then, told his books were being burned in Rome, he decided upon a dramatic act of defiance. At his suggestion, his faculty colleagues invited Wittenberg's "pious and studious" undergraduates to gather outside the city's Elster gate the next morning, December 10. A bonfire had been prepared. Cheering students emptied the university's library shelves and ignited the pile. Finally Luther, with his own hands, cast a copy of the papal bull into the flames, murmuring: "Because you have corrupted God's truth, may God destroy you in this fire." The blaze continued until nightfall. The following day Luther assembled them again. This time he announced that any man who refused to renounce the authority of the Holy See would be denied salvation. "The monk," Durant later wrote, "had excommunicated the pope."

BURNING A PAPAL BULL was, of course, a capital offense, but Luther had broken no law, because this bull was illegal. In the turmoil at the Vatican the Curia had been betrayed from within. The sixty-day countdown had begun June 15, the day of the *Exsurge Domine,* and damned Luther on August 14. But under their own laws, this period of grace did not start to run until he had been handed the bull. And there the saboteurs had been particularly effective.

He should have received it before the end of July. Summer had been dry; even a slow courier could have accomplished the journey from Rome to Wittenberg in less than seven weeks. Yet it did not reach him until October 10. In itself the injustice was slight; Luther was burning bridges as well as decrees. The significance of the delay lies in the identity of the obstructionists. German archbishops, serving in Rome, had held up the bull for nearly four months. In so intervening, they were representing the will of their countrymen. Luther was to be saved, not by the justice of his cause, but because in his fatherland, as all over Europe, the political vacuum being left by the ebbing Holy Roman Empire was being filled by a new phenomenon: the rising nation-states.

The tension between the peoples living on either side of the Alps was greater than the rivalry dividing Spain and Portugal. It was also much older. Piety and hostility toward the papacy had coexisted among central Europeans since the fifth century, when, they remembered with pride, Alaric had led their ancestors in sacking Rome. They also recalled — and this memory was bitter — how Pope Gregory VII had humiliated their leader six centuries later, forcing him to kneel in the snows of Canossa for three days before granting him absolution. Though Teutonic *Obrigkeit*, authority, remained in the hands of some three hundred independent princes, the *Volk* shared one language, one culture, and, increasingly, a sense of common identity. Their unanimity in the period may be overstated, but now that they were beginning to feel like Germans, Canossa and other old wounds were opened and nursed.

After the Church's jubilee of 1500, when Rodrigo Borgia, Alexander VI, was pope, German pilgrims recrossing the Brenner Pass had returned with wild stories of Vatican orgies, the poisoning of pontiffs, homicidal cardinals, pagan rites in the Curia, and nuns practicing prostitution in the streets of Rome. But the roots of Germany's burgeoning anticlericalism lay deeper than gossip. To a people united by a flickering new national spirit, the imperiousness of the Vatican had become intolerable. Rome had decreed that no sovereign was legitimate until he had been confirmed by the pope. In theory, a pontiff could dismiss any emperor, king, or prince if displeased with him. He wasn't even obliged to cite a reason. Clergymen, like later diplomats, were immune from civil law. No officer of the law could lay a hand on a priest guilty of rape or murder, and conflicts between civil and episcopal courts could be settled, by pontifical fiat, in favor of the clerics.

Maximilian had nearly broken with the Vatican. In 1508 he had been barred from attending his own coronation in Rome by hostile Venetians. The schismatic Council of Pisa offered him the papacy. He declined then, but a year later he briefly considered separating the German church from Rome. In the end he was persuaded that he couldn't rely on the support of German princes, but he went so far as to direct Jakob Wimpheling, the humanist, to draw up a list of Germany's grievances against the papacy.

Heading Wimpheling's complaints were protests against the Vatican's systematic looting of German taxpayers, industries, and the vaults of noblemen. Maximilian himself calculated that the papacy reaped a hundred times more in German revenues than he did himself — an exaggeration, of course; nevertheless, businessmen, the most vigorous men in the new German society, did find themselves competing with monastic industries whose profits, Rome had ruled, were exempt from taxation. Long before Luther arrived to lead his disgruntled countrymen, the chancellor to an archbishop of Mainz had angrily written an Italian cardinal that "taxes are collected harshly, and no delay is granted . . . and war tithes imposed without consulting the German prelates. Lawsuits that ought to have been dealt with at home have been hastily transferred to the apostolic tribunal. The Germans have been treated as if they were rich and stupid barbarians, and drained of their money by a thousand cunning devices. . . . For many years Germany has lain in the dust, bemoaning her poverty and her sad fate. *But now her nobles have awakened as from sleep; now they have resolved to shake off the yoke, and to win back their ancient freedom.*"

Among his countrymen, pastors and even prelates agreed. Archbishop Berthold von Henneberg wrote: "The Italians ought to reward the Germans for their services, and not drain the sacerdotal body with frequent extortions of gold." He was ignored. Relationships between pious churchgoers and the ecclesiastical hierarchy worsened. When Karl von Miltitz had journeyed to Altenburg to meet Luther, he had been astounded to find that half Germany seemed critical of the Vatican. So strong was antipapal feeling in Saxony that Miltitz evaded questions from natives, denied holding the pontiff's commission, and assumed a false identity.

A Catholic historian notes that "a revolutionary spirit of hatred for the Church and the clergy had taken hold of the masses in various parts of Germany. . . . The cry 'Death to the priests!' which had long been whispered in secret, was now the watchword of the day." Although the pope had remained ignorant of this festering discontent, the Curia knew of it. Rather than kindle an uprising there, the hierarchy had decided to exempt Germany from the Inquisition, and in 1516, the year before Luther posted his theses

on the Castle Church door, one of the ablest men around the
pontiff had warned him of imminent revolt in the heart of Europe.

🌢

HIS NAME WAS GIROLAMO ALEANDRO, Latinized to Hieronymus
Aleander. Then just forty, he was a handsome Venetian whose
arched brows, penetrating eyes, and thoughtful, pursed mouth
suggested a professorial life. In part this was justified. Aleandro
was an ecclesiastic of commanding intellect. A humanist and future
cardinal, he was a celebrated member of Europe's intelligentsia —
rector of the University of Paris, a colleague of Erasmus, fluent
in all classical tongues, and honored lecturer at Venice and Orleans.
He was also a man of action, however, and as such he would
become Luther's first formidable Catholic adversary. Aleandro had
anticipated the coming mutiny during an official visit to Austria.
There, he told Pope Leo, he had repeatedly overheard men muttering that they yearned for the emergence of a man brave enough
to lead them against Rome.

When the papacy issued a bull significant to one part of the
Church's vast realm, it was customary to dispatch eminent nuncios
from Rome with bales of copies, which they would post in major
population centers. Leo's *Exsurge Domine* was such a document,
and the dignitaries entrusted to inform all Germany of Luther's
shame were Aleandro and Johann Eck. To be chosen was regarded
as an honor, and Eck, remembering his triumph over Luther in
Leipzig the year before, set out with zest.

Aleandro, remembering his premonition, was less enthusiastic.
Earlier in the week word had reached the Vatican that their reception would be, at best, mixed; Luther had been degraded in
Rome, but he was no pariah to the north. Among his supporters
were Franz von Sickingen, imperial chamberlain and one of the
Holy Roman Empire's seven electors; Philipp Melanchthon, the
theologian; Lazaras Spengler, poet, and *Stadtrat* (councillor) of
Nuremberg; and Willibald Pirkheimer, the translator of Greek
classics into Latin. Albrecht Dürer was praying for Luther. Karlstadt, rallying to his cause, had published *De canonicis scripturis
libellus,* a slender volume commending the Bible and derogating
pontiffs, the Epistles, traditions, and ecumenical councils. In
Mainz even Archbishop Albrecht was flirting with the rebels.

These were prominent, conservative Germans. Ulrich von Hutten was prominent, but no conservative; he was writing with the slashing, polemical pen of the new Lutherans. Calling for Germans to free themselves from Rome, he published an ancient German manuscript and noted pointedly: "While our forefathers" — the Goths and Huns — "thought it unworthy of them to submit to the Romans when Rome was the most martial nation in the world, we not only submit to these effeminate slaves of lust and luxury, but suffer ourselves to be plundered to minister to their sensuality." Erasmus begged Hutten to mute his trumpet, but the poet laureate's notes grew harder and harsher; that spring of 1520, demanding independence from Rome in *Gespräche,* a verse dialogue, he called the Vatican a "gigantic, bloodsucking worm," adding: "The pope is a bandit chief, and his gang bears the name of the Church. . . . Rome is a sea of impurity, a mire of filth, a bottomless sink of iniquity. Should we not flock from all quarters to compass the destruction of this common curse of humanity?"

Eck and Aleandro began to move warily. At Döbeln, Turgau, and Leipzig the papal posters, with the distinctive red-letter imprint on each seal, were torn down. Eck was stunned. How could this happen in *Leipzig?* Debating Luther in this Catholic stronghold only a year earlier, he had scored a great triumph. By all the rules as he knew them, he should have been entitled to deference. But the Wittenberg heresy defied precedents. Humbling Luther in the great tapestried hall of Pleissenburg Castle had actually been a blunder. In Erfurt many professors, and even clergymen, scorned Eck and Aleandro and their pontifical proclamation; then a mob of students arrived and tossed all the remaining copies in the river. Eck panicked and fled.*

Aleandro was calmer — then. But less than six months later he too was appalled, writing the Curia from Hesse: "All Germany is up in arms against Rome. . . . Papal bulls of excommunication are laughed at. Numbers of people have ceased to receive the sacraments of penance. . . . Martin is pictured with a halo above his head. The people kiss these pictures. Such a quantity have been

---

*Most German universities remained loyal to the Church. Two exceptions were Erfurt, where Luther had been a student, and Wittenberg, where he taught.

sold that I am unable to obtain one. . . . I cannot go out in the streets but the Germans put their hands to their swords and gnash their teeth at me. I hope the Pope will give me a plenary indulgence and look after my brothers and sisters if anything happens to me."

In Wittenberg Luther was content. On June 11, 1520 — four days before the promulgation of *Exsurge Domine* in Rome — he had written Spalatin: "I have cast the die. I now despise the rage of the Romans as much as I do their favor. I will not reconcile myself to them for all eternity. . . . Let them condemn and burn all that belongs to me; in return I will do as much for them. . . . Now I no longer fear, and I am publishing a book in the German tongue about Christian reform, directed against the pope, in language as violent as if I were addressing Antichrist."

I AM PUBLISHING a book in the German tongue. . . . Although Martin Luther was a riddle of quirks and eccentricities, many wildly contradictory and some less than admirable, he was never a fool. At the outset he had been taken for one, but throughout 1520 events moved his way, partly because of the pope's dawdling but also because Luther possessed intuitive political skills. He not only grasped the powerful *Herrenvolk* spirit rising throughout the fatherland; he had conceived an ingenious way to exploit it.

As noted, the medieval elect, like imperial Rome, had kept the masses ignorant by a kind of linguistic elitism. Upper-class Romans had embraced Greek forms and grammatical laws, despite the fact that these clashed with the natural rhythms of the Latin language; as a consequence, serious texts had been unreadable to the vast majority of the empire's inhabitants. Their successors had followed the same pattern, adopting Latin as the tongue of men in power.

As new worlds of common speech struggled to be born, the humanists, with their veneration for antiquity, had actually played the role of obstructionists, fiercely criticizing Dante, Petrarch, and Boccaccio for writing in vernacular Tuscan, or Italian. The tide was beginning to run against them; sixteenth-century Italian intellectuals like Machiavelli, Ariosto, and Castiglione published in both Tuscan and Latin. In some parts of Europe — France, Castile,

Portugal, and to a lesser degree England — public documents were appearing in vernacular.

Elsewhere in Europe, however, those to whom Latin was gibberish — everyone, that is, except the higher clergy, the learned, and affluent noblemen — could not decipher a word of official pronouncements, laws, manifestos issued by their rulers; of the liturgies, hymns, and sacred rites of the Church; or, of course, of either Testament of the Bible. Contemporary books were equally unintelligible to them; so were political pamphlets. There were exceptions: the works of John Gower, Geoffrey Chaucer, and William Langland in England, and, across the Channel, those of François Villon. Villon, however, was virtually unique. Other Frenchmen, believing that serious "literature" could not be written in a common language, overloaded their work with Latinisms and were ridiculed as *grands rhétoriquers*.

In Luther's homeland Sebastian Brandt's *Das Narrenschiff* was a lonely masterpiece; even so, Brandt was no humanist and his work no triumph of the Renaissance; it was instead the last embodiment of medieval thought.· The Germans had developed a vernacular literature, but the books published by Gutenberg's successors were light entertainment — folktales, epics of ancient kings, the fantasies of Brunhilde — old wine, of poor vintage, rebottled for a people who could not even fathom the sermons read by their parish priests, let alone the tremendous issues raised in Wittenberg three years earlier and now keeping the new Holy Roman emperor awake nights.

Furthermore, and this was decisive for Luther, most Saxon, Austrian, Hessian, Pomeranian, Bavarian, Silesian, Brandenburg, and Westphalian nobles — the minor princes who would determine his fate during the coming winter — were equally handicapped. Only the wealthy could afford Latin teachers for their heirs. There were rich men in central Europe now, but they were in commerce; and trade, by tradition, was barred to the aristocracy. Von Hutten's vitriolic leaflets were as meaningless to them as to their peasants. But like the peasantry, they could be reached through the tongue they had learned as children. Latin was precise, balanced, logical; a feast for scholars. But Luther knew he could be more effective, more eloquent, more moving — and would possess a far larger megaphone — if he addressed his people in simple German, *einfach Deutsch.*

HIS FIRST APPEAL in German, *Sermon von den guten Werken,* was issued in June 1520, a few days after the pontiff's *Exsurge Domine* bull was proclaimed in Rome. It was followed by three defiant tracts, beginning with *An den christlichen Adel deutscher Nation* — in full, *An Open Letter to the Christian Nobility of the German Nation Concerning the Reform of the Christian Estate* — and ending with *Von der Freiheit eines Christenmanschen (Of the Freedom of a Christian Man).* In sum, they constituted an untempered (and often intemperate) assault on the Roman Catholic Church in all its guises, sacraments, theological interpretations, and conduct of Christian affairs on earth.

Each vehemently assaulted the papacy ("Hearest thou this, O pope, not most holy of men but most sinful? Oh, that God from heaven would soon destroy thy throne, and sink it in the abyss of hell!"), and all constituted naked appeals to German patriotism. Rome's greatest crime, if we are to judge it by these indictments, was neither scriptural nor theological; it was the exploitation of Germans, and particularly their economy, by Italian imperialists. Each year, Luther estimated, over 300,000 gulden found their way from Germany to Rome. He wrote: "*We here come to the heart of the matter.*"

Earlier, when he had posted his theses on the Castle Church bulletin board, readers left with the impression that indulgences had been the heart of the matter. Since then he had attacked four of the seven sacraments, defending baptism, communion, and, usually, contrition, but rejecting the others along with the doctrine of transubstantiation. Now his grievances were more comprehensible to Fuggers than theologians. "How comes it that we Germans must put up with such robbery and such extortion of our property at the hands of the pope? . . . If we justly hang thieves and behead robbers, why should we let Roman avarice go free? For he is the greatest thief and robber that has come or can come into the world, and all in the holy name of Christ and St. Peter! Who can longer endure it or keep silence?"

Not Martin Luther. He wanted papal legatees to be expelled from the land, German clergymen to renounce their loyalty to the Vatican, and a national church established, with the archbishop of Mainz as its leader. His thoughts were now ranging far beyond the pale, into territory never before explored by theologians, or at least theologians outside Rome. On October 6, 1520, while Aleandro and Eck were making their unpleasant tour of Germany, posting bulls damning him and watching them be torn down, he published a manifesto in Latin *and* German charging that the Church founded by Jesus Christ had suffered a thousand years of imprisonment under the papacy, shackled and corrupted in morals and faith. He denied that marriage was a sacrament and said any wife married to an impotent man should sleep around until she conceived a child, which she could pass off as her husband's. If he objected, she could divorce him, though Luther thought bigamy more sensible than divorce. At the end he repeated his defiance: "I hear a rumor of new bulls and papal maledictions sent out against me, in which I am urged to recant. . . . If that is true, I desire this book to be part of that recantation."

After reading this, Von Miltitz, astonishingly, still believed in the possibility of a reconciliation between the apostate monk in Wittenberg and the pontiff in Rome. On October 11, 1520, the young Saxon priest, now a spokesman for the pope, appeared in Wittenberg with a proposition: he would try to have the bull withdrawn if Luther would write the pope, denying malice in his assaults and presenting a reasonable case for reforms. Luther agreed, and in his letter he did, in fact, ask Leo to take none of his polemics personally ("Thy blameless life [is] too well known and too high to be assailed"). This, however, followed:

> But thy See, which is called the Roman Curia, and of which neither thou nor any man can deny that it is more corrupt than any Babylon or Sodom ever was, and which is, as far as I can see, characterized by a totally depraved, hopeless, and notorious wickedness — that See I have truly despised. . . . The Roman Church has become the most licentious den of thieves, the most shameless of all brothels, the kingdom of sin, death, and hell. . . . They err who ascribe to thee the right of interpreting Scripture, for under cover of thy name

they seek to set up their own wickedness in the Church, and, alas, through them Satan has already made much headway under thy predecessors. In short, believe none who exalt thee, believe those who humble thee.

Luther was now beyond redemption. This was the language of a fanatic, and deep in the bowels of the Curia papal clerks and chamberlains began, in their timeless way, to prepare his *Decet Romanum pontificem* — his absolute excommunication. Whether saboteurs were still entrenched there is unknown, but the bull was not ready for the pontiff's signature until late January 1521, and four months later, when Luther and the Holy Church finally parted, no copies of it had reached Germany.

In reality it would be only a technicality; the first bull had branded him an outlaw, banishing him from Christendom, and by both law and custom he should have been a runaway, the quarry of every European ruler. The fact that all were looking the other way — or that Rome wasn't prodding them — was no excuse in Aleandro's eyes. Seething over the injustice of it, he decided to corner the chief scofflaw, Frederick III the Wise, elector of Saxony. He found him in Cologne on October 23, 1520. The elector was in a foul mood. He had expected to be in Aachen, where Charles V, only twenty years old, was receiving the sacraments as Holy Roman emperor — the last of the line, as it would develop, with any genuine hope of achieving the medieval dream: a unified empire embracing all Christendom. Frederick shared the dream, had voted for Charles (without being bribed), and had been looking forward to the coronation all year. But he was nearly sixty, a great age then, and had always been an enthusiastic gourmand. Now he was paying the price. Immobilized by gout, he lay sprawled in an inn on the outskirts of the University of Cologne, attended by a professor of medicine, glaring at his swollen foot and groaning.

He received Aleandro ceremoniously; his respect for papal nuncios was great, and after ruling Saxony for thirty-four years he had learned to rally when called upon for decision. But he was not called the Wise for nothing. He knew how to distribute responsibility. After Aleandro had pleaded with him to arrest Luther, the elector said he wanted advice, which, fortunately, was available; Erasmus was lecturing nearby. Frederick sent for him, knowing the great humanist then shared his view of Luther and could express it more eloquently.

Erasmus did. An arrest of Luther was unjustified, he told Aleandro, because everyone knew that monstrous misconduct had shredded the Church's reputation, and attempts to mend the holy garment should be encouraged, not punished. The elector asked him what he considered Luther's major blunders. Wryly, Erasmus replied that he had made two: "He attacked the popes in their crowns and the monks in their bellies." As to *Exsurge Domine,* he doubted the bull was genuine. The pope was a gentle man; it did not sound at all like him. According to Pastor, the Catholic historian, Erasmus said he suspected a conspiracy in the Curia. Frederick then gave Aleandro his decision. Luther, he said, had appealed the bull; meantime he should remain free.

He added — and this exasperated the nuncio — that if it came to a trial, the court would sit in Germany, not Rome. Hurrying to Aachen, Aleandro appealed this matter to the new emperor, Charles, who, to his consternation, confirmed Frederick. Charles didn't like it. The powers of his new office were overshadowed by his role as king of Spain, where the situation was unlike that in Germany, and the Church's challengers were few and weak. Spanish prelates would never put up with a sovereign tolerant of heresiarchs. Furthermore, war between Spain and France was imminent, and he was trying to negotiate an alliance with the Vatican, an arrangement which would include papal funds for his armies. Finally, as a condition of his election in Frankfurt am Main, he had agreed that no German could be convicted without a fair hearing in his own country. The emperor therefore had no choice. Luther, he said, would have to be tried before an imperial diet, which would convene in Worms on January 27, 1521.

SITTING ON THE LEFT BANK of the Rhine, some ten miles northwest of Mannheim, the ancient city of Worms (pronounced *Vurmz*) was rich in Roman, ecclesiastical, and folk history; its destruction by the Huns had been immortalized in *The Nibelungenlied,* and only twenty-six years earlier Maximilian had presided over the most recent diet to be held there, proclaiming, as its ultimate achievement, "perpetual public peace" (*ewiger Landfriede*).

Now the irony of those words lay heavy over the eminent assemblage gathering in response to the imperial decree — the empire's archbishops, bishops, princes, counts, dukes, margraves, and representatives of free cities, one of which Worms itself had been for nearly four centuries. Their mood now was anything but peaceful. To the dismay of the twenty-year-old emperor, they were obsessed with one topic: the fate of Martin Luther. Charles intended to try the heretical professor here (and meant to see him convicted), but that had not been his purpose in convening the Reichstag. He wanted to mobilize the people for the coming conflict with France and to strengthen the empire's administration, moral discipline, and ties with the Vatican, whose support he needed to shield Hungary from the infidel Turks.

The prospects for papal appropriations were dimmed even before the first session opened. To the emperor's horror — and the rage of Aleandro — "the great body of the German nobles," writes a Catholic historian, "applauded and seconded Luther's attempts." Aleandro himself reported that the air was thick with leaflets denouncing Rome. One, written in Von Sickingen's castle at Ebernburg, a few miles from Worms, was from the irascible Ulrich von Hutten. Hutten demanded that the nuncio and his Roman entourage leave German soil: "Begone, ye unclean swine! Depart from the sanctuary, ye infamous traffickers! Touch not the altars with your desecrated hands! . . . How dare you spend the money intended for pious uses in luxury, dissipation, and pomp, while honest men are suffering hunger? The cup is full. See ye not that the breath of liberty is stirring?"

Alarmed, the new emperor's confessor — Jean Glapion, a Franciscan — met privately with Frederick's chaplain, Spalatin. Glapion believed a confrontation with Luther under these circumstances would be disastrous for the Church. The only solution lay in compromise. In his opinion, he confided, many Lutheran calls for ecclesiastical reform were justified; indeed, he had warned Charles V that he would face divine punishment if Catholicism was not purged from such "overweening abuses." In five years, he promised, imperial power would be used to sweep them away. But Luther had not been blameless — his *Babylonian Captivity* had made Glapion feel "scourged and pummeled from head to foot." Some sort of recantation would be necessary. Spalatin sent the Franciscan's proposition to Wittenberg by horseman; in three weeks the rider returned with a blunt rejection.

In any event, neither the Franciscan nor his august penitent could speak for the pontiff, and Aleandro, who could, was in no mood to bargain. On March 3, appearing before the diet, the nuncio demanded the immediate condemnation of Luther. He was turned down, however, on the ground that "the Wittenberg monk," as the accused was now known throughout Germany, was entitled to a hearing. Accordingly, another swift horseman was dispatched to Saxony, this one bearing an imperial invitation to testify. Charles added: "You need fear no violence nor molestation, for you have our safe-conduct."

This assurance was received skeptically in Wittenberg. Just such a pledge, it was remembered, had been Hus's undoing. And in fact the emperor's old tutor Adrian of Utrecht, now a cardinal, was urging an encore — he wanted Charles to break his word, arrest Luther as he approached the diet, and send him to Rome. The emperor refused, but Spalatin, informed of the ruse by spies, rushed a warning to Saxony. Luther ignored it: "Though there were as many devils in Worms as there are tiles on the roofs, I will go there." On April 2 he left home — a crowd including forty professors cheered him off — and two weeks later a band of German knights clattering alongside in full armor, brandishing sharpened swords, escorted him to the diet. People lining the streets cheered the spectacle. Aleandro was deeply offended. Yet in light of Adrian's abortive plot, the precaution does not seem to have been excessive.

The diet setting was spectacular: the monk, appearing in his simple plain robe, faced his inquisitor, Johann von der Ecken, a functionary of the archbishop of Trier, and behind him, the court. This body comprised, first, a panoply of prelates in embroidered, flowered vestments and, second, secular rulers and their ambassadors in the most elaborate finery of the time — short furred jackets bulging at the sleeves, silk shirts with padded shoulders,

velvet doublets, brightly colored breeches, and beribboned, be-
jeweled *braquettes,* or codpieces. (They were of course padded. It
would have been ignoble for a nobleman not to appear to be what
the Germans called *grosstiftung:* grossly well endowed.) Titled lay-
men wore coronets, tiaras, diadems; young Charles, presiding on
a throne as supreme civil judge, wore his imperial crown; prelates
wore miters, and burghers furred and feathered hats.

Luther's head was uncovered and tonsured. Nevertheless he
was the commanding figure there, and everyone seemed to realize
it. But when Ecken gestured sweepingly toward a table piled with
the monk's published works and ordered him to retract the heresies
in them, Luther, for the first time in his public life, hesitated.
Nodding slowly, he acknowledged the tracts. As to the retraction . . . he faltered and asked for time. The emperor granted him
a day. That night several members of the diet surreptitiously visited his simple lodging, and Hutten sent a note from Von Sickingen's nearby castle. All begged him to hold his ground.

And in the morning he did. When Ecken again demanded re-
pudiation, Luther replied that those passages describing clerical
abuses were just. At that point the multilingual Charles cried:
"*Immo!*" — "No!" Luther personally reproached him: "Should I
recant at this point, I would open the door to more tyranny and
impiety, and it would be all the worse if it appeared that I had
done so at the insistence of the Holy Roman Empire." Pausing
and setting himself, he agreed to withdraw anything contrary to
Scripture.

Ecken, ready for this, replied: "Martin, your plea to be heard
from Scripture is the one always made by heretics." In reality, he
added, the right to scriptural interpretations was reserved to ecumenical councils and the Holy See: "You have no right to call
into question the most holy orthodox faith" which had been "defined by the Church . . . and which we are forbidden by the Pope
and the Emperor to discuss, lest there be no end to debate." Once
more he asked: "Do you or do you not repudiate your books and
the errors which they contain?"

Until now all exchanges had been in Latin. This time, however,
Luther replied in German. He rejected the authority of popes and
councils, which had contradicted one another so often. He recanted

nothing. To do so would violate his conscience; it would not, he added cryptically, even be safe. He ended: *"Hier stehe Ich, Ich kann nicht anders."* ("Here I stand. I can do no other.") Then, turning, he departed alone.

It was, Thomas Carlyle would write, "the greatest moment in the modern history of man." Certainly it was the most astonishing moment in young Charles's life. To rebuke a Holy Roman emperor! To defy the glittering array of ecclesiastical authority! The next day he summoned his most powerful princes and read aloud a statement he had written in French, expressing regret that he had not acted against the heretical monk's "false teaching" with greater alacrity. He told them that although Luther could return home under his *sauf-conduit,* he would be forbidden to preach or make any disturbance along the way. "I will proceed against him as a notorious heretic," he said and added, gratuitously, he thought, "I assume you will do the same."

To his further amazement, only four of his electors agreed; among those declining were Frederick the Wise and Ludwig of the Palatinate. That night placards bearing the image of a peasant's shoe — the German symbol of revolution — appeared all over Worms, including the door of the Rathaus (town hall). Bishops, frightened for their safety, implored Luther to make peace with the diet, but he refused, and, after a week left on his trip home. Pope Leo had sent his personal guarantee of the imperial safe-conduct, but it would expire on the tenth day of Luther's journey, and Frederick, taking no chances, disguised a troop of his soldiers as highwaymen and staged a false ambush on May 6. Luther was spirited away to Wartburg Castle, near Eisenach, in the Thuringian Forest, and hidden from the world under the alias Junker Georg.

In Worms his princely allies had already begun to slip away. On the day of his disappearance only a rump diet remained in session. Nevertheless Charles convened it to deliver a vitriolic denunciation of the rebel monk, drafted by the frustrated Aleandro. The diatribe charged, among other things, that Luther had "sullied marriage, disparaged confession, and denied the body and blood of Our Lord." It continued: "He is a pagan in his denial of free will. The devil in the habit of a monk has brought together ancient errors into one stinking puddle and invented new ones. . . . His teaching makes for rebellion, division, war, murder, robbery, arson, and the collapse of Christendom. He lives the life of a beast."

On the emperor's instructions, pursuit of the monk and his accomplices was to begin immediately. His writings were to be "eradicated from the memory of man." Aleandro ordered Luther's books burned. Those members of the diet still in the city ratified the imperial decision, and three weeks later it was formally promulgated. Meantime Pope Leo, who had been closely following the preparations for war in France and Spain, switched his allegiance from Francis to Charles, encouraging a preemptive strike by Spain. That was all the emperor salvaged from the Diet of Worms.

Had Charles remained in Germany to enforce his edict, he would have been unchallenged. His spies could have quickly found their man in Wartburg. After all, several bands of Lutheran admirers did. But lawmen would have been unnecessary anyway. Luther's temperament wouldn't permit him to hole up indefinitely, bored in the woods. Within a few months he left his lair to deliver a series of eight sermons in Wittenberg. Yet the emperor was already gone. Preoccupied by his conflict with the French, he absented himself from central Europe for ten years. By the time he returned, it was too late. Europe had changed. Somewhere in the continent a kind of universal joint — one of those suspicious devices whose design could be found among Leonardo's papers — had shifted. German princes, the king of France — even the pope — were loath to give Charles the powers he needed to suppress Luther. Moreover, the monk and the movement he had launched had grown too powerful to be suppressed. The emperor tried mightily, but it would be his dying effort, and medieval Christendom would die with him.

COAXED BACK into hiding by his frantic protector, Junker Georg reluctantly grew a beard and wore knightly attire as a disguise. He slept poorly, ate too much, grew fat, and suffered familiar hallucinations — he told his bodyguards that an apparition of the devil had appeared, stinking up the place, but he had replied in kind, routing the demon *"mit einem Furz"* ("with a fart"). To Spalatin he sent a treatise on monastic vows, repudiating celibacy as a trap of Lucifer's and declaring sexual desire to be irrepressible. (Spalatin, embarrassed, hid the tract.) Finally Luther settled down on a stump, surrounded himself with foolscap, and began compounding his crimes by translating the New Testament into German. But he remained restless. "I had rather burn on live coals," he wrote, "than rot here. . . . I want to be in the fray."

Actually no one was thicker in it. Luther's movement was sweeping northern Europe: first the free cities, led by Nuremberg; then Saxony, Brandenburg, Prussia, Württemberg, Hesse, Brunswick, and Anhalt; then half Switzerland; then Scandinavia. Italy and Spain never threatened to defect. Nor, after England turned, did Ireland; whatever the English were for, the Irish were against. But for a time Catholicism seemed a lost cause in Bohemia, Transylvania, Austria, and even Poland. Converts could be found in the unlikeliest places. Maximilian's granddaughter Isabella — sister of Charles V, the Holy Roman emperor — was converted to Lutheranism. And the king of France tolerated Lutheran propaganda, decided purgatory did not exist, and turned against the pope, though he never became a closet Protestant.*

Early Protestant strength sprang from tradesmen; from anticlericals; from the educated middle classes, whose humanistic studies had convinced them that Catholicism was rooted in superstition; and, in Germany, from the nobility, whose first acts, upon renouncing allegiance to Rome, were to appropriate all Church wealth within their domains, including land and monasteries. This was a powerful incentive to break with Rome; overnight a prince's tax revenues increased enormously, and as he appointed magistrates to fill the void left by ousted papal and

---

*Appearing this early, the word "Protestant" is slightly anachronistic. It would not enter the language for another eight years. In 1529 at a Speyer Reichstag, a Catholic bloc voted to rescind toleration of Lutheranism, which had been granted three years earlier. The protesting minority were called Protestants. The term is introduced here because even at the outset of the Reformation not all Protestants were Lutherans.

episcopal appointees, his prestige among his people rose. They, however, had nothing to say about all this. The decision was completely his. His subjects adopted whatever faith he chose; the various diets and councils which met throughout the century to discuss tolerance — and eventually granted it, accepting the historic schism — were discussing the rights of rulers, not the ruled. Religious freedom for the individual lay centuries away. It did not even exist as an abstraction.

Had men been offered choices, the result would have been chaotic. Protestantism was already confusing enough as it was. All converts agreed on certain principles: renunciation of papal rule; replacing Latin with common tongues; the abandonment of celibacy, pilgrimages, adoration of the Virgin and the saints; and, of course, condemnation of the old clergy. However, because the religious revolution also aroused advocates of panaceas, divisions appeared quickly, and ran deep. Presently Protestants were at each other's throats.

Perhaps the most popular Protestant dogma — and a striking illustration of how far removed that century was from this — was predestination: the tenet that God, being omniscient and omnipotent, is responsible for every action, virtuous and vile, and man is without choice. Luther, the ultimate determinist, could not grasp the concept of moral freedom. In *De servo arbitrio* (1525) he wrote: "The human will is like a beast of burden. . . . God foresees, foreordains, and accomplishes all things by an unchanging, eternal, and efficacious will. By this thunderbolt free will sinks shattered in the dust."

But, dissenters replied, if no man's actions can alter his fate — if his salvation or damnation are foreordained — why resist wicked temptations, or toil to improve the human condition, or even go to church? They argued furiously and endlessly, but never reasonably. Thus Protestantism was divided at its birth. There was the Lutheran Church, and there was the Reformed. As other major figures emerged — Huldrych Zwingli of Switzerland, for example; John Calvin, a native of France; and the Scotsman John Knox — new sects formed, each with its own views of worship, each as intolerant of the others as it was of Rome, each as repressive

as Catholicism. Anabaptists appeared, and Mennonites, Bohe-
mians, and the forerunners of Baptists, Congregationalists, Pres-
byterians, and Unitarians.

In the spirit of the time, they celebrated their spiritual rebirths
violently. Tirades led to recriminations, then to public executions.
Autos-da-fé were more popular than ever. Peasants would walk
thirty miles to hoot and jeer as a fellow Christian, enveloped in
flames, writhed and screamed his life away. Afterward the most
ardent spectators could be identified by their own singed hair and
features; in their eagerness to enjoy the gamy scent of burning
flesh, they had crowded too close. Ultimately this fascination with

The Reformation Monument, Geneva

death, as ordinary then as it seems extraordinary now, led to
massive butchery — to spreading bloodstains of religious wars
which crossed national frontiers and carried over into a new age.

No ONE HAS calculated how many sixteenth-century Christians
slaughtered other Christians in the name of Christ, but the gore
began to thicken early. Within a year of Worms, Von Sickingen
was in the field, fighting an army led by the archbishop of Trier —
the prelate turned out to be the better general; the knight fell
mortally wounded — and within four years the number of Germans killed or executed approached a quarter-million. Their faith
cannot be indicted for their deaths. The homicidal lust had long
been latent. Before the revolution, Christendom's common people, as brutal as their leaders, had enjoyed the sport known to the
Germans as *Bärenhetze* — setting famished dogs loose on a bear
chained in a pit and watching them eat him alive. A part of them
had wanted to be down in the pit, too. They had been awaiting
an excuse for a rampage, and Worms would have provided it,
whatever the outcome: the knights of Luther's volunteer escort
had sworn to kill him unless he refused to recant.

Even as word of his successful defiance spread across Germany,
the mayhem had begun. Erfurt heard the news in the last days of
April; a mob demolished forty houses belonging to the Church,
burned rent rolls, razed a library, and, invading the university,
killed a humanist scholar. In Wittenberg another mob, brandishing
daggers and rocks, invaded a parish service; women kneeling before an image of the Madonna were stoned, and the priest driven
out. The following day a band of students destroyed the altars of
the city's Franciscan monastery. Shortly thereafter, a leader of the
local Augustinian congregation mounted a stump and called upon
all who could hear him to follow their example — to roam the
countryside, applying the ax to Catholic images, altars, and sacred
paintings, and then feeding them to flames. Luther's colleague,
Professor Karlstadt, led students in assaults on local churches,
tearing crucifixes and pictures from the walls and stoning priests
who tried to intervene. Wearing civilian clothes, Karlstadt said the
Mass in German and invited his congregation to celebrate holy
communion by drinking from the chalice and taking the bread in

their own hands — sacrilege in the eyes of Rome. He persuaded Wittenberg's Ratsversammlung, the town's council, to ban music at all religious services. Both monks and priests, he argued, should be *required* to wed, and he observed his fortieth birthday by setting an example, marrying a fifteen-year-old girl.

It was these disorders which had flushed Luther out of his sanctuary in the Thuringian Forest. His attitude toward violence had always been ambivalent. No Protestant, not even Hutten, had published prose as incendiary as *Adel deutscher Nation,* but now, confronted with the consequences, he drew back. It proved to be only the temporary lapse of a revolutionary. Nevertheless it was impressive. He preached: "Do not suppose that abuses are eliminated by destroying the object which is abused. Men can go wrong with wine and women; shall we then prohibit wine and ban women? The sun, the moon, the stars, have been worshipped; shall we then pluck them out of the sky?"

Under his direction, both old and new communion rites were made available to Wittenbergers, and worshipers who cherished crucifixes, religious images, and holy music were left alone; as a composer of hymns, he himself approved of such solace. The Ratsversammlung, reversing itself, drove Karlstadt out of town. Unchastised, he took a pulpit in nearby Orlamünde to condemn Luther as a "gluttonous ecclesiastic . . . the new Wittenberg pope." His congregation was swayed. Frederick the Wise, fearing an uprising — and it was coming — asked Luther to make the burghers of Orlamünde see reason. He tried, but nothing was sacred anymore, not even the man who, more than any other, had inspired them; the Orlamünders, refusing to listen to him, stoned him and pasted him with mud until he withdrew.

Hearing of the incident, Thomas Müntzer, another former Lutheran turned radical Anabaptist, published a pamphlet calling his former idol "Dr. Liar [*Dr. Lügner*]," a "shameless monk" who spent his time "whoring and drinking." Müntzer was openly calling on the serfs to revolt; in a leaflet, *Ermahnung zum Frieden (Admonition to Peace),* Luther begged them to be patient. They rose anyway, and when their rebellion collapsed — nearly 100,000 peasant deaths later — Karlstadt was threatened with prosecution as an instigator. Ironically, he turned to Luther for refuge. It was

quickly granted, and Karlstadt, weary of struggle, hoarse from
his polemics, and exhausted by the demands of his teenaged bride,
returned to teaching. He died, an obscure professor in Basel, fifteen
years later. Müntzer was less fortunate. He led rebellious peasants
against seasoned troops in Saxony. The defeat of the rebels was
followed by an orgy of medieval brutality; five thousand men
were put to the sword. Some three hundred were spared when
their women agreed to beat out the brains of two priests suspected
of encouraging the uprising. Then Müntzer himself was tortured
to the point of death and beheaded.

LUTHER had been among the captivated readers of Erasmus's *Encomium moriae.* The eminent humanist was now busy at the University of Louvain's Collegium Trilingue, with professorships in
Greek, Latin, and Hebrew, and on March 18, 1519, Luther had
written him there, humbly soliciting his support. It was a curious
appeal, revealing a total misunderstanding of everything Erasmus
represented. Replying on May 30, the scholar suggested that it
"might be wiser of you to denounce those who misuse the Pope's
authority than to censure the Pope himself. . . . Old institutions
cannot be uprooted in an instant. Quiet argument may do more
than wholesale condemnation. Avoid all appearance of sedition.
Keep cool. Do not get angry. Do not hate anybody."

Erasmus continued to defend Luther. In the *Axiomata Erasmi,*
a statement addressed to Frederick of Saxony, he declared that
men who loved the gospel were those least resentful of the Wittenberg monk; Christians were demanding evangelical truth, he
added, and could not be suppressed. To Lorenzo Cardinal Campeggio he sent a long letter which began with the observation that
during his travels "I perceived that the better a man was, the less
he was Luther's enemy. . . . If we want truth, every man ought
to be free to say what he thinks without fear. If the advocates of
one side are to be rewarded with miters, and the advocates of the
other side with rope or stake, truth will not be heard." He now
knew that the *Exsurge Domine* had been genuine, but believed that
"nothing could have been more invidious or unwise than the
Pope's bull. It was unlike Leo X, and those who were sent to
publish it" — Eck and Aleandro — "only made things worse."

He concluded: "You may assure yourself that Erasmus has been, and always will be, a faithful subject of the Roman See. But I think, and many will think with me, that there would be a better chance of settlement if there were less ferocity."

But thus far the greater ferocity had come from Rome's critics. If Luther had badly misjudged Erasmus, Erasmus's misjudgment of Luther was complete. There is no other way to interpret his May 30, 1519, letter to him. It was an offer of reasonable advice to an unreasonable fundamentalist. As such, it was not only wasted but probably incomprehensible to the monk, whose sensible preaching to the Wittenbergers had been out of character; who, most of the time, spoke the language of invective. The monk in Wittenberg was by nature everything the scholar in Louvain asked him not to be: inflammatory, passionate, seditious, hot, furious, and a born hater. That was his magic, and it was also part of his genius. Erasmus had deplored injustice without result; Luther hated it with great results. One man was thoughtful, the other intuitive.

However, intuition, though it fuels action, is volatile and therefore dangerous. And Luther's sense of justice was selective. Though he was outraged by the peasant revolt, he remained silent on the one early excess of Protestantism which offended learned Europeans most. The Erfurt mob's murder of a humanist, an innocent bystander, was an omen to his fellow humanists. Intellectuals everywhere were caught *entre deux feux* — in peril, as, in times of bloodlust, they have always been. By exposing Roman corruption and eroding blind acceptance of medieval superstition, thoughtful men had opened the way for reform, but the reformers, being emotional men, did not acknowledge the debt. On the contrary; the "Martinians," as Luther's followers called themselves, accepted what was coming to be known as the Zwickau Dogma, named after the town in which it originated. The dogmatists held that God spoke directly to simple men in simple language, that they instinctively understood him, and that the true Christian spurned literature, even reading and writing. Karlstadt, though learned, had first destroyed his own books and then declared that true believers should confine themselves to tilling the ground or working with their hands. George Mohr, a colleague and protégé, resigned from the faculty to preach the joys of illiteracy, and a number of Wittenberg undergraduates, seeing no point in further study, left their lecture halls to become craftsmen.

Intolerance, contempt for learning, the burning of religious art, the rejection of classical culture as pagan, and the adoption of primitive papal tactics — book burning, excommunication, even death at the stake — alienated humanists who had at first defended Luther: Johannes Cochlaeus, dean at Frankfurt am Main; Johannes Reuchlin, who had stopped the burning of Luther's books and as a result faced trial as a heretic; Willibald Pirkheimer, the Nuremberg merchant, scholar, and friend of Dürer, whom Erasmus had called "the chief glory of Germany" and who had been excommunicated for his open defense of Luther; Conradus Mutianus Rufus of Gotha; and Erasmus himself.

The Vatican had shielded scholars and sponsored their successful searches for the lost treasures of classical learning, provided, of course, they confined themselves to Latin and Greek. The humanists had approved of reforming the Church, but had not bargained for Protestant ravings about predestination and hell and demons and all the baggage of supernaturalism which, to them, signified a reactionary return to medievalism. Mutianus had called Luther "the morning star of Wittenberg." Now, according to Durant, he decided that he behaved with "the fury of a maniac." Cochlaeus, another early admirer of Luther, wrote him: "Christ does not teach such methods as you are carrying out so offensively with 'Antichrist,' 'brothels,' 'Devil's nests,' 'cesspools,' and other unheard-of terms of abuse, not to speak of your threatenings of sword, bloodshed, and murder," adding: "O Luther, you were never taught this method of working by Christ!" Pirkheimer wrote: "Things have come to a pass that the popish scoundrels are made to appear virtuous by the Evangelical ones. . . . Luther, with his shameless, ungovernable tongue, must have lapsed into insanity, or been inspired by the Evil Spirit."

When Erasmus agreed, Luther denounced him as a quixotic dreamer who "thinks that all can be accomplished with civility and benevolence." Erasmus was offended. He was, and knew himself to be, the most eminent scholar of his time. But other Martinians were harder on him than their leader. Some scorned him as a renegade; others, in the words of a later critic, as "a begging parasite, who had [sense] enough to discover the truth, and not enough to profess it." Still others denounced him as a Vatican stooge, on the pope's payroll. That was terribly unjust. It was true that in Louvain Erasmus was as dependent upon Catholic wealth as Michelangelo in Rome; true also that he owed his bread, his books, and his very clothing to pensions from an archbishop, a baron, and the Holy Roman emperor, all loyal to the Holy See. However, he had accepted them only on the condition that he would retain his intellectual independence. And he continued to exercise it. In Cologne, in Frederick III's inn rooms — where he had saved Luther, who never thanked him, and enraged Aleandro, who never forgave him — he had shown that he was no papal pawn. That was merely an omen; as the interfaith conflict grew, so did his courage.

ERASMUS was not without weakness. He was guilty of all the familar academic sins. He overestimated the power of logic, assumed that intelligent men are rational, and believed that through his friendships with the European elite — the emperor, the pope, King Francis I, King Henry VIII, Italian princes, German barons, the lord chancellor of England, and virtually every learned man on the Continent — he could alter events. Although he privately regarded conventional religion as a stew of superstitions, he could envisage no institution which would replace the Roman faith as an enforcer of social discipline and private morality. In Christendom's widening civil war, he foresaw only madness, and he believed the Catholic infrastructure could be set aright if he brought his wisdom to bear on its flaws. Hans Holbein's portrait in oils, now in the Louvre, captures the inner Erasmus: thin-lipped, long-nosed, the eyes hooded, the expression forbidding. It may be seen as a study in intellectual arrogance. "I do not admit," he wrote, "that my doctrine can be judged by anyone, even by the angels."

But he *was* wise. No other figure on the European stage saw the religious crisis so clearly; if he was vain to suppose that he could impose his solution on it, the fact remains that no other solution made sense. And despite the judgment of his contemporaries, Protestant and Catholic alike, he was no weakling. In rejecting Luther's overture he had assured his own isolation, for obscurantist Catholic theologians deeply distrusted him. They not only blamed Erasmus for Luther's defection; they suspected him of being his amanuensis. "These men," he had written to Luther, "cannot by any means be disabused of the suspicion that your works are written by my aid, and that I am, as they call it, the standard-bearer [*vexillarius*] of your party. . . . I have testified to them that you are entirely unknown to me, that I have not read your books, and neither approve nor disapprove of your writings, but that *they* should read them before they speak so loudly. . . . It was no use; they are as mad as ever. . . . I am myself the chief object of animosity."

That animosity grew, for although he would not abandon Rome — "I endure the Church till the day I shall see another [better] one," he wrote — he refused to mute either his suggestions for Catholic reforms or his criticism of those who had dishonored their vows. The Vatican should encourage tolerance, he wrote; its hostility toward all change was senseless. He offered suggestions. The Church was too rich; vast tracts of its arable land should be turned over to those who farmed them. The clergy ought to be allowed to marry. Worshipers might be offered alternate forms of communion. Predestination appalled him, but he thought it should be studied, discussed, and debated by priests with open minds. And something *must* be done about promiscuous nuns and lecherous, thieving, forging, drunken monks; "in many monasteries the last virtue to be found is chastity," and "many convents" had become "public brothels."

HE CONTINUED to correspond with Pope Leo X and, later, his successors, Adrian VI and Clement VII. All instructed the Curia to extend him every courtesy, but they were ignored. The fog of religious strife was, if anything, thicker than those of secular wars; obscurant theologians in Rome and hard-liners in the dioceses abroad saw the widening apostasy as an opportunity to stifle dissent. In Catholic Louvain they were particularly active, even among Erasmus's colleagues, and their suspicion of him rose on October 8, 1520, when Aleandro arrived there to promulgate Luther's excommunication. He spread word that the great scholar was the secret mastermind behind Protestant revolts. The faculty, reasoning that the nuncio ought to know, was preparing to expel its most learned colleague when, anticipating his critics, he abruptly left.

Erasmus moved to Cologne, then still loyal to the pontiff. Rumors that he was a closet Lutheran followed him, however; strangers accosted him with the charge that he had laid the egg Luther hatched. "Yes," he would wryly reply, "but the egg I laid was a hen, whereas Luther has hatched a gamecock." By late 1521 he was fed up with them; in mid-November he renounced his pensions, moved up the Rhine to Basel, Switzerland, and settled among a nucleus of humanists. Here he enjoyed a respite; elsewhere priests were using his name as a synonym for treachery, but the Swiss, committed to Protestantism in various forms, left him alone.

They did not, however, leave Catholicism alone. Inflamed by evangelist preachers, a Basel mob rioted, broke into every Catholic church in the vicinity, and destroyed all religious images. As it happened, Erasmus himself had recently impeached the veneration of images, writing that "people should be taught that these are no more than signs; it would be better if there were none at all, and prayer were addressed only to Christ." He had, however, added: "But in all things let there be moderation." The immoderate, rioting vandals had ruptured the thin membrane of civility which he cherished. Disgusted, he showed Switzerland his heels, moving this time to Freiburg im Breisgau, in Catholic Austria. By now Christendom was so confused that no one thought his source of support odd. Actually his bills were being paid by the Fuggers, staunch Catholics who were, at the same time, quietly supporting Protestants in Catholic Venice.

Nevertheless he found no peace there, either. Austrian opinion about him was divided. Freiburg's Stadtrat (town council), welcoming Europe's most illustrious intellectual, moved him into Maximilian's imperial palace, but the local Augustinians were aware of, and resented, his presence among them. During his Swiss idyll, hereticators had been smearing him all over the Continent. Using techniques which would reemerge in later ages, they identified him as the leader of apostate conspiracies, muttering, in Europe's many tongues, one of mankind's oldest and most insidious apothegms: *Es gibt keinen Rauch ohne Feuer* — Where there's smoke, there must be fire.

Erasmus was now approaching seventy. Racked with pain from several afflictions — gallstones, ulcers, gout, dysentery, respiratory disease, arthritis, and pancreatitis — he also felt suffocated by suspicion. In his final flight he returned to Basel. There, after years of wandering, pursued by lies, he passed away in the home of Jerome Froben, son of the scholar-publisher Johann, who had first published his Latin translation of the Greek New Testament.

Erasmus died a martyr to everything he had despised in life: fear, malice, excess, ignorance, barbarism. And his martyrdom did not end at the grave. He had known that his life was ebbing, yet asked for neither priest nor confessor. Word that he had refused last rites found its way to Spain, where the rekindled Inquisition, having completed a systematic study of his books, began formal proceedings against the doyen of humanism, thereby setting in motion wheels which, eight years later, would grind out a formal denunciation of Erasmus. He was excommunicated and branded a heretic. Under the violent reactionary Pope Paul IV, who as a cardinal had reorganized the Inquisition, everything Erasmus had ever published was consigned to the *Index Expurgatorius,* which meant that any Catholic who read the prose which had once delighted a pontiff would be placing his soul in jeopardy.*

ERASMUS WAS the most eminent intellectual victimized by the revolution, but he was far from alone. Indeed, once the lines of battle had been drawn, humanists everywhere were hostages to one side or the other, and sometimes to both. Reason itself had become suspect: tolerance was seen as treachery. Luther, once he had survived Worms, was shielded by Frederick the Wise and the gathering armies of Protestantism. Catholics could find refuge in monasteries, with sympathetic sovereigns or princes, in the papal states, or among the thousandfold sanctuaries of the Holy Roman emperor. The intellectuals were usually without champions, unarmed in a Europe bristling with weapons, and at times it seemed

---

*In the 1560s the Council of Trent, after rescinding many of the bans, allowed dissemination of most of his works in expurgated editions.

that every man's hand was against them. Very few were to be untouched during the disorders. Some, like Erasmus, fled from one asylum to another; some were executed; others survived torture but were horribly maimed, their noses torn away, foreheads branded, hands cut off at the wrist, or nipples plucked out by pincers.

At the outbreak of the revolution most of the humanists had been ordained priests, and several, because of their eminence, were picked by their superiors to serve as blacklisters, leading the Church's counterrevolution. Suspecting Protestant sympathies among his clergy, the bishop of Meaux appointed Jacques Lefèvre d'Étaples his vicar general with instructions to weed them out. Lefèvre, then approaching seventy, was professor of philosophy at the University of Paris, the author of works on physics, mathematics, and Aristotelian ethics, and a Latin translation of Saint Paul's Epistles. His former pupils — the bishop was one of them — revered him without exception.

But although he wore vestments and celebrated Mass, Lefèvre was above all a humanist. To expose medieval myths, he proposed a clearer version of the original New Testament. He was working on a French translation of the Bible, and — like Luther — he believed that the Gospels, not papal decrees, should be the ultimate court of theological appeal. Lefèvre was incautious enough to observe also that he thought it "shameful" that bishops should devote their days to hunting and their nights to drinking, gambling, and mounting *putains* — a criticism which was ill received in Meaux. Suddenly the hunter of heretics was himself condemned as one, and by the Sorbonne at that. Fleeing Paris, he found sanctuary in Strasbourg, in Blois, and, finally, in Nérac, with Marguerite of Angoulême, queen of Navarre and protectress of the revolution's humanist refugees. There he resumed his scholarship and died quietly, of natural causes, five years later.

Lefèvre was one of Marguerite's successes. She also had her failures, notably Bonaventure Desperiers and Étienne Dolet. Both were given her best efforts; nevertheless both died violently in Lyons. Desperiers had been guilty only of bad timing; had he published his *Cymbalum mundi* before Luther challenged Rome, the Curia would have ignored it. Written in Latin and addressed

to fellow humanists, it noted the flagrant contradictions in the
Bible, deplored the persecution of heretics, and mocked miracles.
There was nothing new here. The satires of Erasmus and the
German heretics, making the same points, had been more caustic.
But in the new age of intolerance, *Cymbalum* was denounced by
both sides — the Catholic witchhunters in the Sorbonne and the
Protestant Calvin. Then it was publicly burned by the official
hangman of Paris. Desperiers became too hot even for Marguerite;
she was forced to banish him from Nérac. She sent him money,
but the pressure was too much for him. On the run, threatened
and hounded, he died, reportedly by his own hand. Dolet, on the
other hand, courted death. A printer as well as a Ciceronian
scholar, he clandestinely published books on the *Index Expurgatorius* until he was summoned before the Inquisition, found guilty,
and, despite Marguerite's attempts to intervene, burned alive.

Some humanists were victims; some became leaders of the revolt. All, when captured, met hideous deaths. Those who had led
became martyrs, but the deaths of leaders and led seem equally
senseless. In his *Christianismi restitutio* (*The Restitution of Christianity*) the Spanish-born theologian and physician Michael Servetus dismissed predestination as blasphemy; God, he wrote,
condemns only those who condemn themselves. Servetus was
naive enough to send a copy to a preacher who believed in predestination as the revealed word and who, knowing which church
Servetus would attend and when, had him ambushed at prayer.
A Protestant council sentenced him to death by slow fire. Now
terrified, aware of his blunder, the condemned author begged for
mercy — not for his life; he knew better than that; he merely
wanted to be beheaded. He was denied it. Instead he was burned
alive. It took him half an hour to die.

The Catholics who quartered the body of the Swiss Huldrych
Zwingli and burned it on a pyre of dried exrement were equally
merciless; so was Martin Luther, who had regarded Zwingli as a
rival and called his ghastly death "a triumph for us." In the darkness enveloping Christendom no one recalled that as a young priest
the slain Swiss had taught himself Greek to read the New Testament in the original and possessed a profound knowledge of

Tacitus, Pliny, Homer, Plutarch, Livy, Cicero, and Caesar. All they remembered was that he had said he would prefer "the eternal lot of a Socrates or a Seneca than of a pope."

Perhaps the most poignant figure in the strife — and certainly one of the most tragic — was Ulrich von Hutten. Once he had distinguished himself as a humanist, a Franconian knight, a brilliant satirist, and one of the first scholars in central Europe to cherish the vision of a unified Germany. Like Luther, he had abandoned Latin to help shape the German language as it is spoken today; his *Gesprächbüchlein,* published the year after Worms, was a greater contribution to linguistics than to theology. But Hutten was one of the committed humanists, and like most Reformation zealots he displayed more enthusiasm than judgment. Unwisely, he had cast his lot with Von Sickingen, whose defeat transformed him into a penniless fugitive robbing farms for food as he fled toward Switzerland. Reaching it, he headed straight for Basel, and Erasmus. He expected his fellow humanist to support him, but that was asking too much. Not only had his vehement rhetoric offended the man who preached moderation and tolerance; Hutten had denounced Erasmus as craven for not supporting Luther. Now, in Basel, the victim of his abuse refused to receive him, wryly explaining that his stove provided too little heat to warm the German's bones.

Angry, desperate, and ill — his affliction was venereal — Hutten abandoned both dignity and decency by turning to extortion. He wrote a scurrilous pamphlet about Erasmus (*Expostulation*) and offered to suppress it in exchange for money. Erasmus indignantly refused. Then Hutten began circulating it privately. The local clergy asked Basel's city fathers to expel the polemicist, and it was done. Hutten moved to Mulhouse and sent his manuscript to the press. A mob drove him out. In the summer of 1523 he stumbled into Zurich, only to find that there, too, the city council was preparing a motion of expulsion. Homeless, broke, banished from society, he retreated to an island in the Lake of Zurich, and there, aged thirty-five, he succumbed to syphilis. His sole possession was his pen. Valuable only a year earlier, it was now worthless.

ALL PROTESTANT regimes were stiffly doctrinal to a degree unknown — until now — in Rome. John Calvin's Geneva, however, represented the ultimate in repression. The city-state of
Genève, which became known as the Protestant Rome, was also,
in effect, a police state, ruled by a Consistory of five pastors and
twelve lay elders, with the bloodless figure of the dictator looming
over all. In physique, temperament, and conviction, Calvin (1509–
1564) was the inverted image of the freewheeling, permissive,
high-living popes whose excesses had led to Lutheran apostasy.
Frail, thin, short, and lightly bearded, with ruthless, penetrating
eyes, he was humorless and short-tempered. The slightest criticism
enraged him. Those who questioned his theology he called "pigs,"
"asses," "riffraff," "dogs," "idiots," and "stinking beasts." One
morning he found a poster on his pulpit accusing him of "Gross
Hypocrisy." A suspect was arrested. No evidence was produced,
but he was tortured day and night for a month till he confessed.
Screaming with pain, he was lashed to a wooden stake. Penulti-
mately, his feet were nailed to the wood; ultimately he was decapitated.

Calvin's justification for this excessive rebuke reveals the mind-
set of all Reformation inquisitors, Protestant and Catholic alike:
"When the papists are so harsh and violent in defense of their
superstitions," he asked, "are not Christ's magistrates shamed to
show themselves less ardent in defense of the sure truth?" Clearly,
he would have condemned the Jesus of Matthew (5:39, 44) as a
heretic.* In Calvin's Orwellian theocracy, established in 1542, acts
of God — earthquakes, lightning, flooding — were acts of Satan.
(Luther, of course, agreed.) Copernicus was branded a fraud, attendance at church and sermons was compulsory, and Calvin himself preached at great length three or four times a week. Refusal
to take the Eucharist was a crime. The Consistory, which made
no distinction between religion and morality, could summon anyone for questioning, investigate any charge of backsliding, and
entered homes periodically to be sure no one was cheating Calvin's

---

*"Resist not evil; but whosoever shall smite thee on thy right cheek, turn to him
the other also," and "Love your enemies, bless them that curse you, do good
to them that hate you, and pray for them which despitefully use you, and
persecute you."

God. Legislation specified the number of dishes to be served at each meal and the color of garments worn. What one was permitted to wear depended upon who one was, for never was a society more class-ridden. Believing that every child of God had been foreordained, Calvin was determined that each know his place; statutes specified the quality of dress and the activities allowed in each class.

But even the elite — the clergy, of course — were allowed few diversions. Calvinists worked hard because there wasn't much else they were permitted to do. "Feasting" was proscribed; so were dancing, singing, pictures, statues, relics, church bells, organs, altar candles; "indecent or irreligious" songs, staging or attending theatrical plays; wearing rouge, jewelry, lace, or "immodest" dress; speaking disrespectfully of your betters; extravagant entertainment; swearing, gambling, playing cards, hunting, drunkenness; naming children after anyone but figures in the Old Testament; reading "immoral or irreligious" books; and sexual intercourse, except between partners of different genders who were married to one another.

To show that Calvinists were merciful, first offenders were let off with reprimands and two-time losers with fines. After that, those who flouted the law were in real trouble. The Consistory made no allowances for probation, suspended sentences, or rehabilitation programs, and Calvin assumed that everyone enjoyed community service without being sentenced to it. Excommunication and banishment from the community were considered dire, though those living in a more permissive age might find them less appalling. In any event, there were plenty of other penalties, some of them as odd as the offenses they punished. A father who stubbornly insisted upon calling his newborn son Claude spent four days in the canton jail; so did a woman convicted of wearing her hair at an "immoral" height. A child who struck his parents was summarily beheaded. Abortion was not a political issue because any single woman discovered with child was drowned. (So, if he could be identified, was her impregnator.) Violating the seventh commandment was also a capital offense. Calvin's stepson was found in bed with another woman; his daughter-in-law, behind a haystack with another man. All four miscreants were executed.

Of course, it proved impossible to legislate virtue. Some of Calvin's devoted followers insisted that it was possible, that the Consistory's moral straitjacket worked; Bernardino Ochino, an ex-Catholic who had found asylum in the city-state, wrote that "Unchastity, adultery, and impure living, such as prevail in many places where I have lived, are here unknown." In fact they were widely known there; the proof lies in the council's records. A remarkable number of unmarried young women who worshiped with Ochino managed to carry their pregnancies to term unde-

John Calvin (1509–1564)

tected. Some abandoned their issue on church steps or alongside forest trails; some named their male co-conspirator, who then married them at sword's point; some lived as single parents, for not even Calvinists could orphan an innocent infant.

On other issues they were adamant, however. The ultimate crime, of course, was heresy. It was even blacker than witchcraft, though sorcerers could not be expected to appreciate the distinction; after a devastating outbreak of plague, fourteen Geneva women, found guilty of persuading Satan to afflict the community, were burned alive. But because the soul was more precious than the flesh, the life expectancy of the apostate was even shorter. Anyone whose church attendance became infrequent was destined for the stake. Holding religious beliefs at odds with those of the majority was no excuse in Geneva or, for that matter, in other Protestant theocracies. It was a consummate irony of the Reformation that the movement against Rome, which had begun with an affirmation of individual judgment, now repudiated it entirely. Apostasy was regarded as an offense to God and treason to the state. As such it was punished with swift, agonizing death. One historian wrote, "Catholicism, which had preached this view of heresy, became heresy in its turn."

THE POPE, AFTER ALL, was a Catholic, if not a very good one, and because his Church hadn't changed its view of heresy, one might have expected him to have met the Protestant revolt with a terrible swift response. The dimensions of the threat were staggering. But Leo failed to perceive this; he had learned nothing since Worms. To him the great split in his realm was still "a squabble among monks," and he assumed that all pious men were governed by Augustine Triumphus's *Summa de ecclesiastica potestate* (1326), promulgated two centuries earlier by Pope John XXII, which had decreed that as God's vice-regent on earth, a pontiff must be obeyed, even when he is a great sinner.

Leo wasn't a great sinner, but religion ranked rather low in his priorities, below learning, living well, serving as head of the Medici family, and making war. He was one of history's great squanderers; according to Francesco Cardinal Armellini Medici, treasurer of the Holy See, he spent 5 million ducats during his seven years in the Vatican and left debts exceeding 800,000. How much of this went into supporting Charles V's imperial armies is unknown, but Leo was committed to France's defeat, not because of Francis I's secret sympathies for Protestantism — he had no inkling of that — and not even because, like Pope Julius, he was pursuing realistic political goals. Despite Charles's military successes, which would culminate in his great victory over the French at Bicocca, Leo's only spoils were two provinces in northern Italy, hardly worth the loss of Germany, Switzerland, and Scandinavia to Protestantism.

Nevertheless an excuse for a celebration was a temptation Leo could not resist. On the last evening in November 1521 he held an all-night banquet at the Vatican, complete with fine wines, champagne, gambling, music, theatricals, acrobats, fireworks, and his many *nipoti*, including three nephews and two cousins, all wearing the cardinals' hats he had bestowed upon them. As always, he had a marvelous time, though the price turned out to be extravagant, even by his standards. At dawn, as his guests departed, he withdrew, explaining that he felt ill. He had caught a chill. By noon he was running a fever, which, by nightfall, had killed him.

He was forty-six years old. He was also bankrupt. Armellini found there wasn't enough money in the pontiff's vaults to provide candles for Leo's coffin; he had to use melted-down stubs from the last cardinalate funeral. Had the dead pope been spared, Roman wags said, he would have sold Rome, then Christ, then himself. He had sponsored magnificent painting and sculpture, which should have counted for something, but there were few kind words for him that bleak December. Because he had mishandled the Protestant apostasy, wrote Francesco Vettori, a contemporary historian, Leo had left the papacy in the "lowest possible repute." In the streets of Rome men hissed the sacred college on its way to choose his successor.

Their contempt was unjustified. For the first time in nearly a century their eminences chose well. They hadn't meant to; the outcome was unexpected, the consequence of a three-way deadlock. In a move to break it, someone nominated Adrian Cardinal Boeyens of Utrecht, the emperor's childhood mentor, who wasn't even present. Rival blocs, trying to outmaneuver one another, wound up outfoxing their own interests; to their horror, they found they had actually elected the unknown prelate, who thereby became Adrian VI, the only Dutch pope in history — "the Barbarian," as Romans immediately began calling him.* That is precisely what he was not. A former professor of the University of Louvain, Adrian was exactly what Catholicism desperately needed: a reformer.

In his first speech to the cardinals he bluntly told them that corruption in the Church was so rife that "those steeped in sin" could "no longer perceive the stench of their own iniquities." Under his predecessor, he said, "sacred things have been misused, the commandments have been transgressed and in everything there has been a turn for the worse." They eyed him stonily. He moved decisively to end the sale of indulgences, outlaw simony, cut the papal budget, and assure that only qualified candidates for the priesthood were ordained, but his orders always miscarried. Unable to bridge the cultural barrier with the Italians around him — only two of his aides were Dutch — he was thwarted at every turn by the entrenched Curia, and after a year in office he died, unmourned, having been, wrote Vettori, "a little and despised pope."

THE ITALIAN CARDINALS, grateful for the chance to rectify their mistake so soon, now turned to one of their own: Giulio de' Medici, a cousin of Leo X, who became Pope Clement VII (r. 1523–1534). Weak and vacillating, Clement tried to play Charles V and Francis I off against one another. He entered into secret treaties with each, and was exposed, thereby earning the distrust of both. Italy became a bleak battleground. Two Englishmen crossing Lombardy wrote home of starving children in Pavia, adding that "the most goodly countree for corne and vynes that may be seen is so desolate that in all that ways we sawe [not] oon man or woman in the fylde, nor yet creatour stirring, but in great villages five or six myserable persons."

It never seems to have occurred to this pope that Rome itself

---

*He was also the last non-Italian elected pope until John Paul II (Karol Wojtyla of Poland) in 1978.

was vulnerable to mayhem — that his fellow Christians might repeat the Visigothic sack of the Eternal City. Yet his alliances with France offended Romans loyal to the Holy Roman emperor, and as a Medici he had inherited enemies, among them Cardinal Pompeo Colonna, a feuder, a hater, and an ambitious prelate who had his eye on the papal tiara. Colonna plotted Clement's assassination. Rallying imperialists, he led a raid on the Vatican in 1526. Several members of the papal household were killed, but the pope

Pope Clement VII (1478–1534)

himself escaped through a secret passageway built for this express purpose by the Borgia pope, who had been better at this sort of thing than he was.

The pontiff and the ferocious cardinal reached terms and the raiders withdrew, whereupon Clement, after granting himself absolution, hired a band of mercenaries and leveled Colonna's properties. He felt victorious, and congratulated himself. Yet the sacrilegious behavior of the raiders should have warned him of worse to come. Donning the Holy Father's robes while he escaped through the hidden passage, they had pranced about the piazza of St. Peter's, mocking the Vicar of Christ. A papal secretary of state wrote the papal nuncio in England — where the devout King Henry VIII worried about the safety of His Holiness — "We are on the brink of ruin."

The seeds of ruin lay in the ill-disciplined, famished, unpaid troops of Charles V, who had outfought King Francis's army, crossed the Alps, and were at large in northern Italy. Led by the Constable de Bourbon, a French renegade, their spearhead was formed of *Landsknechte* (mercenaries) from central Europe, and the defenders heard a cry which one day would intimidate all Europe, the roaring *"Hoch! Hoch!"* of charging German infantry. As Protestants, these Teutons affected to despise the pope as a heretical ally of their enemy, but their chief inspiration was less lofty. It was greed: the prospect of plunder and ransoms in Florence and Rome, promised them by their commanders. Charles himself seems to have been unaware of this. His own reverence for the See of St. Peter led him to grant his foes an eight-month armistice in exchange for 60,000 ducats, to be distributed among his troops. It wasn't enough. Enraged, believing themselves betrayed, men of the imperial army mutinied and marched on the capital of Christendom, given free passage and even food by Italian princes who had been victims of Medici popes. On May 6, 1527, they burst into Rome. One of the first victims of the assault was the Constable de Bourbon, killed by a sniper on the Roman walls. Any hope of disciplining the mutineers died with him. They pillaged house to house, murdering anyone who protested. Buildings were put to the torch. Then the dying began.

Clement, most of the sacred college, and many Curia officials found sanctuary in the fortress of Sant' Angelo, though they barely made it — one cardinal was hauled to safety in a basket after the portcullis had been dropped. But the rest of the population was helpless. Women of all ages were raped in the streets, nuns rounded up and herded into bordellos, priests sodomized, civilians massacred. After the first, week-long orgy of destruction, more than 2,000 bodies were floating in the Tiber, some 9,800 others awaited burial, and countless thousands of corpses lay sprawled in the city's ruins, their bloated, stinking remains eviscerated by rats and hungry dogs.

The soldiers had come for money, and they got it — between 3 million and 4 million ducats in ransoms alone. The rich were scourged, and the lucky, who could pay, freed. Those who produced no ransom were tortured to death. But the plunder did not stop there. No source of loot was overlooked. Tombs were broken open for treasure, relics stripped of their jeweled covers, monasteries, palaces, and churches rifled for their gems and plate.

The fortress Castel Sant' Angelo, Rome

There was also sacking for the sheer wicked joy of desecration. Archives and libraries went up in flames, with manuscript pages saved only to be used as bedding for horses. The Vatican was turned into a stable. Drunken *Landsknechte* strutted around in the red hats and vestments of cardinals, parodying holy rites, with one, wearing the pontiff's vestments, riding an ass. All this continued, off and on, for eight months, until the food ran out and plague appeared. Only then did the mutineers withdraw, having transformed the glory that was Rome into a reeking slaughterhouse.

As news of the sack spread across Europe, Protestants interpreted it as an act of divine retribution. And some Catholics agreed. A senior officer in Charles's army, while deploring "these outrages on the Catholic religion and the Apostolic See," commented, "In truth everyone is convinced that all this has happened as a judgment of God on the great tyranny and disorders of the papal court." Cardinal Cajetan, who had met Luther in Augsburg nine years earlier, agreed. "We who should have been the salt of the earth," he wrote with heavy heart, "have decayed until we are good for nothing beyond outward ceremonials."

BUT MOST MEMBERS of the Catholic hierarchy saw it differently. Now, they believed, they had seen the faces of the Protestant heresy — the fact that half the looting troops had been Spanish Catholics was ignored — and now they would move with just as much vigor, intolerance, and brutality as those rebelling against their God. Sir Isaac Newton would not discover his Third Law until a generation later, but it was already in effect: henceforth every action by the insurgent Christians would provoke an equal and opposite reaction in Rome. And the Church's reflexive responses to dissent matched those of the schismatics. The same doom, in the same guise, awaited those who had betrayed Rome: torture, drawing and quartering, the noose, the ax, and, most often, the stake. In that age the world was still lit only by fire. At times it seemed that the true saints of Christianity, Protestant and Catholic alike, had become blackened martyrs enveloped in flames.

In vain enlightened Catholics urged internal disciplinary reforms, curing the blight which had driven good Christians from their ancestors' faith — the corruption of the clergy, the luxurious lives led by prelates, the absence of bishops from their dioceses, and nepotism in the Holy See. At the very least, they argued, pontiffs should rededicate themselves to devotional lives, good works, and the reaffirmation of beliefs under attack by Protestants: for example, the real presence of Christ in the Eucharist, the divinity of the Madonna, the sanctity of Peter.

Instead the Vatican committed its prestige to reaction, repression, and military and political action against rulers who had left the Church. As always, when scapegoating has become public policy, the Jews were blamed. In Rome they were confined to a ghetto and forced to wear the Star of David. Meantime, Catholic princes were persuaded to make war in the name of the savior, or

Lutheran satire on papal reform

even to send hired assassins into the courts and castles of the Protestant nobility. Every aspect of Protestantism — justification by faith alone, exaltation of the Lord's Supper, the propriety of clerical marriage — was condemned in a stream of bulls. Nevertheless the rebel faiths continued to prosper. In 1530 Charles V, at the insistence of the Curia, signed a decree directing the Imperial Chamber of Justice (Reichskammergericht) to take legal action against princes who had appropriated ecclesiastical property. They were given six months' grace to comply. None did.

The Spanish Inquisition is notorious, but the Roman Inquisition, reinstituted in 1542 as a pontifical response to the Reformation, became an even crueler reign of terror. All deviation from the Catholic faith was rigorously suppressed by its governing commission of six cardinals, with intellectuals marked for close scrutiny. As a consequence, the advocates of reform, who had proposed the only measures which might have healed the split in Christendom, fell under the dark shadow of the hereticators' suspicion. No Catholic was too powerful to elude their judgment. The progressive minister of Naples, disgusted with the venal Neapolitan church court, began trying indicted ecclesiastics in the city's civil court. For thus violating the *privilegium fori,* he was summarily excommunicated. The liberal Giovanni Cardinal Morone was imprisoned on trumped-up charges of unorthodoxy. Another cardinal, who had actually reconverted lapsed Catholics, ran afoul of the Vatican by attempting to prevent war between the Habsburgs and France. He was recalled to Rome, accused of heresy, and ruined. The archbishop of Toledo, because he had openly expressed admiration of Erasmus, was sentenced to seventeen years in a dungeon, and after the death of Clement VII another Erasmian — Pietro Carnesecchi, who had been the pope's secretary — was cremated in a Roman auto-da-fé.

In the opinion of the Apostolic See, most Catholic rulers, including the Holy Roman emperor, were far too tolerant of heresy. Francis I was particularly disappointing, and the Vatican was delighted when, after his death at Fontainebleau in 1547, he was succeeded by the devout and murderous Henry II, at whose side lay the even more homicidal Diane de Poitiers, royal mistress and enthusiastic *Inquisiteuse.* Together they planned a grand strategy to crush all French apostates. The printing, sale, or even the

possession of Protestant literature was a felony; advocacy of heretical ideas was a capital offense; and informers were encouraged
by assigning them, after convictions, one-third of the condemneds'
goods. Trials were conducted by a special commission, whose
court came to be known as *le chambre ardente,* the burning room.
In less than three years the commission sentenced sixty Frenchmen
to the stake. Anne du Bourg, a university rector and a member
of the Paris Parlement, suggested that executions be postponed
until the Council of Trent defined Catholic orthodoxy. Henry had
him arrested. He meant to see him burn, too, but destiny — the
Protestants naturally said it was God — intervened. The king was
killed in a tournament in 1559. His queen, his mistress, and the
Vicar of Christ mourned him. Du Bourg, of course, did not,
though he went to his death anyway as a *martyr luthérien.*

HENRY II OF France had been admired, applauded, and blessed in
St. Peter's, but in the twelve years following the rise of Luther
the sovereign most cherished in Rome was Henry VIII of England.
Henry seemed, indeed, the answer to a Holy Father's prayers. The
fact that his handsome features, golden beard, and athletic build
also made him the answer to maidenly and unmaidenly prayers
appeared to be irrelevant; the Apostolic See was in no position to
condemn royal lechery. More important, before the death of his
elder brother made him heir to his father's throne, he had been
trained to be a priest.

By the time he mounted the throne, in 1509, he could and did
quote Scripture to any purpose, and after the monk of Wittenberg
had posted his Ninety-five Theses on the Castle Church door,
Henry had denounced him in his *Assertio septem sacramentorum contra
M. Lutherum,* a vigorous defense of the Catholic sacraments, probably ghostwritten by Richard Pace, Bishop John Fisher of Rochester, or, possibly, Erasmus. In it he asked, "What serpent so
venomous as he who calls the pope's authority tyrannous?" and
declared that no punishment could be too vile for anyone who
"will not obey the Chief Priest and Supreme Judge on
earth . . . Christ's only vicar, the pope of Rome."

Luther, replying with his typical grace, referred to his critic as
that "lubberly ass," that "frantic madman . . . that King of Lies,

King Heinz, by God's disgrace King of England," and continued: "Since with malice aforethought that damnable and rotten worm has lied against my King in heaven, it is right for me to bespatter this English monarch with his own filth." He then sponsored a Protestant conspiracy in the heart of London, the Association of Christian Brothers. The association circulated anti-Catholic tracts and reached its climax the year before Rome's sack with the publication of William Tyndale's famous — infamous in the Vatican — English translation of the New Testament, which made the thirty-four-year-old British clergyman an archenemy, not only of the Apostolic See, but also of his then-Catholic sovereign.

Tyndale was a humanist, and his tale is an example of the deepening hostility between men of God and men of learning. English humanists had rejoiced at Henry's coronation. Lord Mountjoy had written Erasmus of the "affection [the king] bears to the learned." Sir Thomas More said of the new monarch that he had "more learning than any English monarch ever possessed before him," and asked, "What may we not expect from a king who has been nourished by philosophy and the nine muses?" Henry's invitation to Erasmus, urging him to leave Rome and settle in England, appeared to confirm the enthusiasm of English scholars. It seemed inconceivable that the popular monarch, faced with a choice between faith and reason, should choose faith.

But Erasmus, after accepting the invitation, found that the king had no time for him. And as the religious revolution grew in ferocity, Henry's commitment to Catholicism deepened. Lord Chancellor More, with royal encouragement, imprisoned the Christian Brothers and other heretics. And the Tyndale affair, which appalled English intellectuals, seemed to align him with the most reactionary heresimachs.

William Tyndale had conceived his translation while reading ancient languages at Oxford and Cambridge, and he had begun work upon it shortly after his ordination as a priest in 1521, the year of Luther's condemnation at Worms. A Catholic friend reproached him: "It would be better to be without God's law than the pope's." Tyndale replied: "If God spare me, ere many years I will cause the boy that driveth the plough to know more of the Scripture than you do."

Had he valued his own years on earth, he would have heeded
his friend. It was one thing for Erasmus to publish parallel texts
of the Gospels in Latin and Greek; few, after all, could read them.
This was another matter altogether. It was actually dangerous; the
Church didn't want — didn't permit — wide readership of the
New Testament. Studying it was a privilege they had reserved for
the hierarchy, which could then interpret passages to support the
sophistry, and often the secular politics, of the Holy See.

Tyndale had been warned that finding a printer for his completed manuscript would be difficult. Luckless in England, he
crossed the Channel and found a publisher in Catholic Cologne.
The text had been set and was on the stone when a local dean
heard of it, grasped the implications, and persuaded authorities in
Cologne to pi the type. Fleeing with his manuscript, Tyndale
found that he was now a police figure; had post offices existed,
his picture would have been posted in them. The Frankfurt dean
sent word of his criminal attempt to Cardinal Wolsey and King
Henry, who declared Tyndale a felon. Sentries were posted at all
English ports, under orders to seize him upon his return home.

But the fugitive was less interested in his personal freedom than
in seeing his work in print. He therefore journeyed to Protestant
Worms, where, in 1525, Peter Schöffer published an octavo edition
of his work. Six thousand copies had been shipped to England
when Tyndale was again spotted. He was on the run for the next
four years. Then, believing himself safe, he settled in Antwerp.
However, he had underestimated the gravity of his offense and
the persistence of his sovereign. British agents had never ceased
stalking him. Now they arrested him. At Henry's insistence he
was imprisoned for sixteen months in the castle of Vilvorde, near
Brussels, tried for heresy, and, after his conviction, publicly gar-
rotted. His corpse was burned at the stake, an admonition for any
who might have been tempted by his folly.

The royal warning was unheeded. You can't kill a good book,
including the Good Book, and Tyndale's translation was excellent;
later it became the basis for the King James version. Despite a
lengthy *Dialogue* by More, denouncing the translation as flawed,
copies of the Worms edition had been smuggled into the country
and were being passed from hand to hand. To the bishop of Lon-

don this was an intolerable, metastasizing heresy. He bought up all that were for sale and publicly burned them at St. Paul's Cross. But the archbishop of Canterbury was dissatisfied; his spies told him that many remained in private hands. Protestant peers with country houses were loaning them out, like public libraries. Assembling his bishops, the archbishop declared that tracking them down was essential — each was placing souls in jeopardy — and so, on his instructions, dioceses organized posses, searching the homes of known literates, and offered rewards to informers — sending out the alarm to keep Christ's revealed word from those who worshiped him.

Henry's blows against Lutheranism and English heresy were appreciated in Rome. The king had expected them to be, and had

King Henry VIII of England (1491–1547)

let Rome know that he would welcome a quid pro quo. Earlier pontiffs had designated the rulers of Spain as "Catholic Sovereigns" and French monarchs as "Most Christian." Henry wanted something along that line, and Pope Leo gave it to him, bestowing upon him and his successors the title *Defensor Fidei,* Defender of the Faith. Henry ordered this struck on all English coins, and because kings rarely return anything once it is in their grasp, the rulers of England have kept the honorific ever since,* though within a dozen years of its conferral the Holy See very much wanted it back.

IN THE POPULAR imagination, Henry VIII and Martin Luther have been yoked as leaders of the Reformation, though each would have deeply resented the coupling, and in fact they do not belong together. Luther was a theological rebel. Henry remained a faithful Catholic in every particular except one. He rejected the supremacy of Rome because the pontiff — for political, not religious reasons — resisted what the king regarded a royal prerogative. There is much to be said in Henry's behalf and very little in the pope's, but the motives of both have been muddied, as often happens when romance rears its violin-shaped head.

The immediate issue was Henry's decision in 1527 to dissolve his eighteen-year-old marriage to Queen Catherine, Catherine of Aragon, the daughter of Ferdinand and Isabella of Spain. His motive would not be acceptable to later ages, but it was then. Medieval sovereigns were expected to function as national stallions, providing heirs for their thrones. This was particularly important in Henry's case. The dreary, thirty-one-year War of the Roses between the Yorkists and the Lancastrians had ended only six years before his birth, and his family's claim to the monarchy was shaky; if he died without male issue, England would almost certainly be ravaged by civil war again.

Unfortunately Catherine, now forty-two, had proved an incompetent conceiver of healthy boys. Her only child to survive

---

*"Elizabeth II, by the Grace of God, of the United Kingdom of Great Britain and Northern Ireland and of Her Other Realms and Territories Queen, Head of the Commonwealth, Defender of the Faith."

infancy was a girl. Henry knew the problem did not lie with him.
In 1519 he had sired a bastard boy by his first royal mistress,
Elizabeth Blount, the sister of William Blount — Lord Mountjoy,
Erasmus's patron. Though adulterous, this and Henry's other affairs were sanctioned by custom; unwritten law held that when
royal marriages had been contracted for reasons of state, either
party might seek diversion elsewhere. But there was another consideration. Assuming that his queen would bear children of both
sexes, the king had betrothed their small daughter, Mary, to the
dauphin of France. Should Henry die without leaving a son, Mary
would inherit the English throne, and when her husband was
crowned king of France, the British island would, in effect, become
a province of France.

The annulment he sought required Rome's consent, but that
should have presented no problem. Papal dispensations were not
uncommon; the usual procedure was to find some flaw in a marriage which would permit an annulment or a divorce. In Henry's
case the flaw was genuine. Catherine was the widow of his older
brother Arthur, and English canon law prohibited such a marriage,
taking its precedent from the book of Leviticus (20:21): "If a man
shall take his brother's wife it is an unclean thing . . . they shall
be childless." The Vatican had provided a dispensation permitting
Henry to wed her, but it was doubtful that the pontiff had possessed the power to overrule the scriptural ban, particularly since
the queen's fruitlessness seemed to have fulfilled its prophecy. The
king said that the dispensation, and therefore his union with Catherine, had been illegal. Theologians on both sides of the Channel
agreed with him.

In Rome, however, the prospect of an English royal divorce
bore distasteful political implications. Pope Clement was struggling to recover from the sack of the holy city, where, largely as
a result of his own blundering, his situation had become highly
complicated. If the pontiff agreed, he could anticipate a highly
unpleasant confrontation with a ruler even more powerful than
Henry: the Holy Roman emperor, whose domains sprawled across
the Continent, and whose armies had now twice defeated the
French in disputes over Milan, Burgundy, Naples, and Navarre.
The undisputed master of Italy, Charles V literally surrounded the

Vatican and therefore was, in proximity alone, bound to intimidate any pontiff, particularly at a time when the papacy was deeply involved in regal intrigues. Clement was a captive pope, and the emperor's views would be given great weight, especially if they were strongly held.

In this case they were. Charles's childhood tutor, the future Pope Adrian, had instilled in him a solemn reverence for the Vicar of Christ. Catherine was his aunt, and he was incensed by the argument — unwisely presented to the Vatican by Henry's legate — that because she had been Arthur's widow, her marriage was not only invalid but actually incestuous. Should the Vatican accept this reasoning, she would be reduced to the level of a discarded concubine, and her daughter, Mary, England's heir apparent, Charles's cousin, would become illegitimate. If Clement denied papal permission, Henry would be blocked — unless, of course, he quit the Church, a possibility which seems to have occurred to no one except him until he had publicly committed himself. It came as a shock to prominent English Catholics, confronting them with an agonizing choice between their faith and their monarch. No one who knew Henry expected royal sympathy for their dilemma, and there was none; when the humanist Juan Luis Vives spoke up for Catherine, he was dismissed as Mary Tudor's teacher and banished from the court.

None of Henry's predecessors would have dreamed of breaking with Rome, but he was a man of immense determination, and his resolve was strengthened by his choice of, and infatuation with, Catherine's successor: Anne Boleyn, a nobly born nineteen-year-old girl remarkable for her flashing eyes, long, flowing hair, and vivacity. Here his judgment was gravely flawed. Superficially, Anne seemed qualified for the throne. The daughter of a viscount and granddaughter of a duke, she had been educated at a Paris finishing school and had served as lady-in-waiting, first to Marguerite of Navarre and then, back in England, to Catherine. She was witty and gay. But she was also flighty, self-centered, and, by all accounts, lascivious.

It was her sexuality which had attracted Henry to her. The Boleyn women were noted for their libidos; both Anne's mother and her older sister had slipped naked into the king's bed, to his subsequent delight, but her lovemaking skills eclipsed theirs. To him this wanton girl seemed built to breed. He was convinced that once the Holy See had sanctioned a royal annulment, freeing him to wed her, crown her, and impregnate her with a scion, England would be guaranteed a future sovereign to rule an England at peace. What he did not know — then — was that despite her youth she was as experienced as he was. Before she seduced him, her many lovers had included the poet Thomas Wyatt and Henry Percy, the future Earl of Northumberland. Even in what one historian of Hampton Court describes as "exceedingly corrupt court revels," she was notoriously available to both single and married courtiers. Indeed, there is evidence that when the king designated her his queen-elect, she and Percy were already secretly married.

Because of this — and much more of the same, which was to follow — the king's decision to abandon Catherine led to the messiest divorce in history. Yet had Anne Boleyn never existed, Henry would still have found a new queen. He had begun to consider changing wives as early as 1514, when Anne was a child of seven; when he quit Catherine's bed in 1524, it was to sleep with Mary Boleyn, not her younger sister. Three more years passed before he took Anne as his mistress and made the first, tentative inquiries about a dispensation from Rome.

His hopes were vested in his lord chancellor, Cardinal Wolsey. Wolsey sympathized with the king's yearning for a son and had his own candidate for the succession, the French princess Renée, daughter of King Louis XII. Privately the cardinal was appalled by Anne. He was familiar with her reputation, and by now the king must have heard at least a whisper of it. But to a monarch with Henry's pride it would have been inconceivable that any queen of his would be tempted — let alone dare — to contemplate infidelities. Furthermore, by now he was in love with her.

Wolsey badly needed a success. Once considered invincible, the lord high chancellor was now seen as a leader of lost causes. His wars had alienated the Commons and the merchants, his dictatorial manner had offended the clergy, and his foreign policy — rejecting Charles V for a French alliance — had proved disastrous. Had he been wise, he would have been unobtrusive. Yet he could not

hide his lack of enthusiasm for what the royal court was calling
"the king's great matter." Henry, impatient, bypassed the cardinal
and sent his own secretary, William Knight, to Rome. Knight,
speaking for his sovereign, submitted his case to Pope Clement.
The pontiff, he argued, should declare Henry's present marriage
invalid. In any event, he proposed, the matter should be decided
in England. His Holiness agreed. Knight then suggested that an
eminent prelate serve as judge and make the final ruling. He had
Wolsey in mind. The pontiff knew it. He also knew that for seven
months of the previous year he and his retinue had been holed up
in Sant' Angelo while Rome was sacked. The troops still surrounded the city, and their commander was the English queen's

Anne Boleyn (1507–1536)

nephew. If Clement yielded to Knight's other point, he would be inviting the wrath of Charles V. Yet he could not leave the English cardinal out. Therefore, Clement ruled that *two* members of the sacred college should preside. Wolsey would be joined by an Italian cardinal, Lorenzo Campeggio. This was a stunning loss of face for Wolsey, and when Anne turned against him he was a ruined man. Henry seized his palace at Whitehall and stripped him of his secular offices. He was allowed to retain the archbishopric of York. After a year the king ordered his arrest. Ill, Wolsey died on the way to London.

In the meantime, Cardinal Campeggio had found the English sovereign immovable. "This passion," he wrote the pope, "is the most extraordinary thing. He sees nothing, he thinks of nothing but his Anne; he cannot be without her for an hour." Nevertheless Henry, willful but astute, had been proceeding shrewdly. He had appointed a commission to gather legal opinions from Catholic scholars all over Europe, and confronted the pontiff's representative with the fact that they backed him, without exception. Campeggio agreed that England deserved a fertile queen. He urged Catherine to retire to a nunnery. She agreed — provided Henry enter a monastery. The cardinal was offended. He knew she could not be serious; the thought of Henry VIII resigning himself to obedience, chastity, and poverty was absurd. What the cardinal did not realize was that Catherine's intractability, supported by her imperial nephew and his captive pope, meant that from this point forward the likelihood of England's defection from Catholicism would increase month by month.

HENRY IS OFTEN depicted as short-tempered, a man who was determined to have his way whatever the consequences. The determination was there, but in pursuing his desires he also showed remarkable patience. His reply to Luther — the work of a staunch Catholic sovereign — was written in 1521. In 1522 Anne Boleyn, aged fifteen, became a lady-in-waiting to Queen Catherine, and it was there that she caught the king's eye. He had already despaired of Catherine's infertility, but five years passed before he secretly began to seek to annul their marriage. For six years the pope, under pressure from her nephew Charles, ignored Henry's appeals.

It was in 1533 that he married Anne, now twenty-six, and was excommunicated by the pope. Parliament passed the Act of Succession in 1534; it declared the king's marriage to Catherine invalid, recognized Anne as the new queen, made questioning her marriage to Henry a capital crime, and required all Henry's subjects to take an oath of loyalty to him. Nor was the tale told. The king's disillusionment with Anne, among other consequences, lay ahead.

In the beginning the king had assumed that the pope would swiftly grant his request, dissolving his barren marriage. All precedents were on his side. Even Campeggio, who first came to London in 1528, agreed with him. But the pope, to Henry's growing frustration, seemed incapable of making up his mind. Campeggio knew how little weight an Italian cardinal carried in London. If he ruled in Catherine's favor, he would simply be banished. Therefore he appealed for instructions from the Vatican. Clement's frantic reply reflects his helplessness. He told his cardinal "not to pronounce sentence without express commission hence. . . . If so great an injury be done to the Emperor, all hope is lost of universal peace, and the Church cannot escape utter ruin, as it is entirely in the power of the Emperor's servants. . . . Delay as much as possible." By this and other byzantine maneuvers the pope bought time — five more years of it.

Eventually there was no time left to buy. Anticipating a dispensation, the king had fitted up splendid apartments for Anne adjacent to his own at Greenwich; courtiers reported to her, as though she had already been crowned; crowds gathered outside her windows, ignoring Catherine. Often Henry would not leave Greenwich until noon. But papal politics made this bedfellowship perilous. The issue became critical when Anne discovered that she was with child. Thomas Cranmer, a Cambridge theologian, had drawn up a new array of arguments; a team of negotiators, now hastily dispatched by the king, presented them in Rome. Still the pontiff hesitated. Anne was beginning to show, and no infant could succeed to the monarchy unless born to a queen.

Henry could wait no longer. He appointed Cranmer archbishop of Canterbury, invested him with extraordinary powers, and urged him to place the broadest possible interpretation on his new office. The new prelate moved swiftly, ruling that the pope was incompetent to grant a dispensation. He declared Catherine a divorcée, secretly married Henry to his mistress, and in May 1533, on Whitsunday of her twenty-seventh year, when she was in the seventh month of her pregnancy, crowned her with great ceremony in Westminster Hall.

Nothing could stop the split in the Church now. The king's blood was up. He had already summoned a special session of Parliament. Working on the anticlerical feelings of the MPs — and despite the opposition of Sir Thomas More, his new high chancellor — he had rammed through a brutal legislative program limiting the powers of tᴉᴇ clergy, increasing taxes on the Church, and cutting the annates paid to Rome to 5 percent. This last act was the sort of insubordination which deeply wounded the Holy See. Clement had dawdled for years over the divorce petition from London, but he had also drafted a bull excommunicating the king. Now the Vatican executed it.

The king's response was just as vehement. Following his lead, Parliament passed thirty-two religious bills, which, among other things, cut off *all* revenues to Rome, and confiscated all Church lands — by a conservative Catholic estimate, 20 percent of the land in England. Other measures suppressed monasteries, decreed that spiritual appeals by English Christians must be made to Canterbury or the king, required new clergymen to swear loyalty to the crown before they could be consecrated, and stipulated that only royal nominees could become bishops and archbishops. Then Henry took the ultimate step. In the Act of Supremacy (November 1534) he abandoned Rome completely, founding a new national church, Ecclesia Anglicana, and appointing himself and his successors its supreme head.

Sir Thomas More, Wolsey's successor as high chancellor, had followed Henry for a time, but he had been in agony, trapped between conflicting loyalties. More was the king's humble servant. However, he was also a devout Catholic. The less his sovereign saw of him, he reasoned, the better. Therefore he resigned the chancellorship in 1532. It was in vain. He could not hide; he was too eminent; the king was watching him closely. His personal crisis reached a climax in the spring of 1534. When the king demanded that his subjects take an oath to obey the Act of Succession,

he was asking more than More could give. It meant swearing fealty
to Henry and repudiating the papacy. Most of the English clergy
meekly obeyed. More didn't protest; he simply remained mute.
He condemned neither the oath nor those who had taken it, but
though remaining loyal to the crown in word and deed, he refused
to renounce Rome — a devastating silence, because Henry was
taking an enormous risk. Although he was a powerful monarch,
his reign was confined to the living. England's rising national spirit
supported him, as Germany's had supported Luther, but if the
pope excommunicated his entire kingdom, condemning every Englishman to eternal flames, the possibility of an uprising would
be far from remote. In this exigency the king could not hesitate.

More had already opposed Henry's marriage to Anne and refused to attend her coronation, a mortal insult. Any tolerance of
further lèse majesté by Henry would be interpreted as weakness,
especially since the former chancellor, garlanded with royal honors, was the most influential man in English public life. The king
could be merciless or he could forfeit his crown, and for this king
that was no choice. More was charged with treason and imprisoned
in the Tower of London.

At his trial More finally spoke out. Splitting the Church was
a tragic crime, he said; he could not, in all conscience, be an
accomplice to it. Nor, he added, could he bring himself to believe
that "any temporal man could be the head of the spirituality." He
was one of the most eloquent men of his generation, but he spoke
in a hubbub and could scarcely be heard. The hearing was a for-
mality. The verdict had already been decided. His judges included
Anne's father, her uncle, and her brother, Lord Rochford. They
condemned him to be "hanged, drawn, and quartered" — the
extreme penalty for betrayal of the sovereign. It meant that the
chancellor's shrunken cadaver, cut into four parts, would be left
to rot on the London docks.

That was too much for the king. As Anne sulked — Sir Thomas
had succeeded Wolsey as the object of her malice — Henry
changed the sentence to simple beheading. The scholar who had
served him so faithfully went to the ax with his head high. As he
mounted the scaffold it trembled and seemed about to collapse.
Turning to a king's officer he said calmly, "I pray you, Mr. Lieu-

tenant, see me safe up, and for my coming down let me shift for myself." Then, altering the ghastly ritual by blindfolding himself, he asked the hushed crowd to witness his death "in the faith and for the faith of the Catholic Church, being the King's good servant, but God's first." He died. Afterward his head was affixed to London Bridge.

England was shocked. No one in the kingdom believed the former lord chancellor even capable of betraying crown and country. Erasmus mourned his friend, "whose soul was more pure than any snow, whose genius was such that England never had and never again will have its like." The Vatican proclaimed him a Christian martyr. In time the papacy beatified and then canonized him.

LESS THAN A YEAR later Anne Boleyn followed him to the block. Her thousand-day reign had been a disaster, so calamitous that the prestige of the papacy was enhanced; only divine intervention, men reasoned, could have visited such punishment upon the rebel monarch in London. His conviction that she would present him with an heir had been wrong. Her first baby, like Catherine's, was female. No one could blame her for that, but the failure of her womb was the least of it. Once on the throne she seemed to change personality. Her gaiety vanished and was replaced by temper tantrums, sharp-tongued imperiousness, and innumerable petty demands which left the king exasperated. Catherine at least had been gentle, and he began to miss that; when she died, he wept, and ordered the court to go into mourning. Anne refused. After she presented him with a second, dead child — a boy, born prematurely and badly deformed — he no longer desired her. He told friends Anne had bewitched him, and cited the baby's deformities as evidence of her sorcery. To her fury, he began sliding his hand under the skirts of one of her maids, the nobly born Jane Seymour.*

If the evidence later arrayed against her is to be believed, Anne

---

*Who became Henry's third wife and deserves to be remembered as one of the few genuine ladies of the age. The sister of the duke of Somerset, Jane spurned the king's advances as long as his queen lived. She asked him never to speak to her when they were alone and returned his letters and gifts unopened. Her first act as queen was to reconcile Henry and Catherine's daughter.

was the last wife in England entitled to protest her husband's dalliance. According to sworn testimony, she had scarcely recovered from her daughter's birth when she began taking lovers, and her intrigues continued through her three-year marriage. If a youth aroused her desire, witnesses declared, she would invite him to her bedchamber by dropping a handkerchief at his feet; if he picked it up and wiped his face, her proposition had been accepted, and her personal maid would be alerted to his arrival that evening at midnight.

These charges may have been trumped up — later it was said that several of the men accused of sleeping with the queen were homosexuals — but this was not apparent at the time. Henry, according to the record, learned that he was being cuckolded. Told of the handkerchief signal, he watched it happen, moved in that night with armed yeomen, and struck hard. The new lord chancellor took Anne to the Tower and read out the charges against her. She fell to her knees, sobbing and protesting her innocence.

In the preliminary hearing three knighted gentlemen of the privy chamber and a court musician confessed to "criminal intercourse with the queen." Then the earl of Northumberland, as he now was, testified that he, too, had been intimate with her. The greatest sensation came at the end, when Lord Rochford, Anne's brother — who had found Sir Thomas More guilty — was led into the dock and accused of coupling with his own sister, a charge supported, by what is said to have been convincing evidence, by Rochford's wife. Tried by a jury which included Anne's father, the musician pleaded guilty and, as a commoner, was merely hanged. The knights then were beheaded.

Three days later, twenty-six peers, chaired by Anne's uncle, the duke of Norfolk, sat in judgment of her and her brother. Both were found guilty of adultery and incest and condemned to death by their uncle. Violent death being commonplace and a life hereafter assumed, the condemned in that age often accepted their fate with an insouciance which would be astonishing today. After praying that she be forgiven her crimes, Anne, still only twenty-nine, asked that her head be struck off as soon as possible. She remarked wryly that she drew comfort from the thought that "the executioner I have heard to be very good, and I have a little neck," then laughed. On the scaffold she asked the crowd to pray for the king: "A gentler and more merciful prince there never was, and to me he was ever a good, a gentle, and sovereign lord." She and Rochford were decapitated within a few minutes of each other, the queen, by precedence of rank, meeting the blade first.

This extraordinary cataract of events, precipitated by a king's yearning for a male heir, led, ironically, to two royal heiresses, each of whom reigned memorably. Catherine's daughter, Mary, survived her mother's humiliation and briefly visited a terrible retribution upon those she held responsible for it. The fears of Charles V were at first realized; after the divorce Mary was declared illegitimate. Later, however, after the birth of a male heir to Henry — the future Edward VI, his son by Jane Seymour — Parliament relented, passing a complex act which, among other things, restored Catherine's daughter to the royal line of succession and permitted her to occupy the throne for five years, beginning in 1553, as Queen Mary I.

Mary was not a beloved sovereign, nor did she mean to be. Popularity was not among her priorities. Juan Luis Vives had done his work well; she had never renounced her Roman Catholicism, nor — understandably — had she forgiven the zealous new Protestants who had refused to let her visit her mother, even when Catherine had lain on her deathbed. As sovereign she swore to turn back the clock, wiping out the Reformation. It was impossible, but she tried very hard. As her chief adviser she appointed Reginald Cardinal Pole, an English cardinal who had remained loyal to Rome, and whom the pope designated as Mary's papal legate. Pole shared her bitterness. He had quarreled with Henry over the divorce and predicted, in the king's presence, that he would be consigned to hell.

That had been lèse majesté with a vengeance, and it had been swiftly punished. The angry sovereign had set a price on Pole's head; the cardinal had fled for his life, eluding capture but suffering nevertheless, for during his fugitive years both his mother and brother were beheaded. Now, at his urging, Mary made her attempt to restore papal supremacy over England. The penal laws against heresy were revived. On her orders, Archbishop Cranmer was burned at the stake — other famous martyrs were Bishops

Ridley and Latimer — and Pole was then consecrated in Canterbury as Cranmer's successor. Over three hundred Englishmen, whose only crime had been following Mary's father out of the Roman Church, were also executed. Perhaps her most significant achievement, which she shared with Henry, was her demonstration that England could be just as barbaric as the rest of sixteenth-century Europe. Even today she is remembered as Bloody Mary.

THE IMMORTAL Maid of Orleans still dominated memories of the prior century. But now the sixteenth was more than half gone and it had produced no woman to match her; indeed, no heroines at all. Then, late in its sixth decade, irony intervened to produce a woman who would rank with the greatest sovereigns in English history, giving her name to a new age which would redeem the squalor of the old. She was the daughter of the disgraced Anne Boleyn, who had lain in Anne's womb, awaiting birth, during the coronation Sir Thomas More had ignored. On the day of her birth, she had been declared illegitimate by the Vatican. In the wake of her mother's execution the archbishop of Canterbury — after ruling that Anne had, in fact, been married to Percy at the time of her royal wedding and had thus been bigamous as well as adulterous and incestuous — had concurred with Rome, pronouncing the child a bastard.

Anne having been formally declared a common slut — thus placing her far beneath Catherine, whose status as a divorcée was relatively respectable — the royal solicitors concluded that Henry's second marriage had had no legal status whatever. Since it had never occurred, the three-year-old waif who had been its only issue had no legal existence. Like her half-sister, however, and indeed because of her, Anne's daughter was to be rescued from oblivion. The restoration of Mary's legitimacy created a precedent. After Jane Seymour's death in childbirth, Parliament, bowing to Henry's will, recognized all three of his children, conceived in various wombs, thus establishing the final order of Tudor succession: first Edward, son of Jane; then Mary, daughter of Catherine; and finally, Elizabeth, daughter of Anne.

Crowned in 1558 at the age of twenty-five, Elizabeth I restored Protestantism, revived her father's Act of Supremacy, and reigned over England for forty-five glorious years. In light of the tragic consequences of her parents' sexual excesses, which had typified European nobility in their time — the promiscuity, the proliferation of bastards, the hasty coupling in palace antechambers — she was perhaps wise to live out her long life unaccompanied by a connubial consort, and to be remembered in history as the Virgin Queen.

ONE MAN ALONE

IN THE TEEMING Spanish seaport of Sanlúcar de Barrameda it is Monday, September 19, 1519.

Capitán-General Ferdinand Magellan, newly created a Knight Commander of the Order of Santiago, is supervising the final victualing of the five little vessels he means to lead around the globe: *San Antonio, Trinidad, Concepción, Victoria,* and *Santiago.* Here and in Seville, whence they sailed down the river Guadalquivir, Andalusians refer to them as *el flota,* or *el escuadra:* the fleet. However, their commander is a military man; to him they are an armada — officially, the Armada de Molucca. They are a battered, shabby lot, far less imposing than the flota Christopher Columbus led from this port twenty-one years ago, leaving Spain for his third crossing of the Atlantic.

Nevertheless the capitán-general's armada is more seaworthy than it appears — he has seen to that. Now approaching his forties, the man who will become the greatest of the sixteenth-century explorers is a precise, even fastidious mariner. Every plank and rope has been personally tested by him; he has directed the replacement of all rotten timbers and overseen the installation of new shrouds and new sails of strong new linen, each stamped with the cross of St. James, patron saint of Spain. Each of the five requires a lot of looking after. The small ships — *San Antonio,* the largest, displaces only 120 tons — are actually *naos,* three-masted, square-rigged hybrid merchantmen derivative of fourteenth-century cogs and Arabian dhows. Unless carefully attended, all are potential shipwrecks. Therefore they have been repeatedly scoured and caulked from stem to stern. Now their grizzled commander is patiently checking the stores for a two-year expedition — never dreaming that the great voyage will take three years, and that he will not survive it.

Physically Magellan is unimpressive. He was born to one of
the lower orders of Portuguese nobility, but his physique is that
of a peasant — short, swart, with a low center of gravity. His skin
is leathery, his black beard bushy, and his eyes large, sad, and
brooding. Long ago his nose was broken in some forgotten brawl.
He bears scars of battle and walks with a pronounced limp, the
souvenir of a lance wound in Morocco. He had acted recklessly
then (and will again, in the last hours of his life), but he is rarely
impulsive. On the contrary; his reserve approaches the stoical. He
is a man who lives within, saving the best of himself for himself,
enjoying solitude. As a commander he can be ruthless — "tough,
tough, tough," in the words of a fellow captain. Subordinate
officers dislike this *dureza*, though they concede his supreme com-
petence and the quickness with which he rewards those who perform well — rare traits among commanders of the time. Because
of this, he is popular among his crews.

Proud of his lineage, meticulous, fiercely ambitious, stubborn,
driven, secretive, and iron-willed, the capitán-general, or admiral,
is possessed by an inner vision which he shares with no one. There
is a hidden side to this seasoned skipper which would astonish his
men. He is imaginative, a dreamer; in a time of blackguards and
brutes he believes in heroism. Romance of that stripe is unfashionable in the sixteenth century, though it is not altogether dead.
Young Magellan certainly knew of El Cid, the eleventh-century
hero Don Rodrigo, whose story was told in many medieval bal-
lads, and he may have been captivated by tales of King Arthur.
Even if he had missed versions of Malory's *Morte d'Arthur,* he
would have been aware of Camelot; the myths of medieval chivalry had persisted for centuries, passed along from generation to
generation. Arthur himself was a genuine, if shadowy historical
figure, a mighty English *Dux Bellorum* who won twelve terrible
battles against Saxon invaders from Germany and was slain at
Camlann in A.D. 539. Less real, but enchanting to children like
the youthful Magellan, was the paladin Lancelot du Lac, introduced in 1170 by the French poet-troubadour Chrétien de Troyes.
De Troyes was also celebrated for his *Perceval, ou Le Conte du
Graal,* the first known version of the Holy Grail legend, which
was retold in 1203 by the German poet Wolfram von Eschenbach

as the story of *Parzival*. Both De Troyes and Von Eschenbach were translated into other European languages, including Portuguese. And there were others. At his death in 1210 Gottfried von Strassburg left his epic *Tristan und Isolde*. In 1225 France's Guillaume de Lorris wrote the first part of the allegorical metrical romance *Roman de la Rose,* distantly based on Ovid's *Ars Amatoria.* Chaucer translated it in the next century. And in 1370 or thereabouts *Sir Gawain and the Green Knight,* a poetic parable of Arthur's elegant nephew, appeared in England.

Magellan, a man of boundless curiosity, has found reality equally enthralling, devouring the works of Giovanni da Pian del Carpini, who in 1245 had traveled east to Karakorum in central Asia, and Marco Polo's account of his adventures in the Orient,

Ferdinand Magellan (c. 1480–1521)

dictated to a fellow prisoner in 1296. More important, the commander of the five little ships has been inspired by the feats of Columbus and the discoverers since. Other Europeans have dreamed of following their lead. What sets Magellan apart is his unswerving determination to match them and thus become a hero himself. Erasmus and his colleagues are admirable, but they are writers and talkers; Magellan believes that deeds are supreme. He would agree with George Meredith — "It is a terrific decree in life that they must act who would prevail" — and in his struggle for dominance his most valuable possession will be his extraordinary will. He can endure disappointment and frustration, but can never accept defeat. He simply does not know how.

Yet thus far his career has been one of unfulfilled promise. Although he craves recognition, his very directness — his complete lack of guile, or even tact — has repeatedly cost him the support of those in a position to honor him. In Lisbon, for example, he disdained the silken subtleties at the royal court, and, as a result, encountered disaster. To the urbane courtiers surrounding the fatuous king, he seemed an awkward boor. Having suffered from a false accusation of larceny, and having then cleared his name, he sought an audience with Dom Manuel I, the Portuguese sovereign. He wanted royal support for his great voyage. Both Portugal and Spain coveted the Spice Islands; Magellan urged the king to help him stake Portugal's claim there. But he had handled the interview badly. Manuel, a fop, expected his subjects to fawn over him. Ignoring court protocol, Magellan went straight to the point. His sovereign responded by dismissing him in the rudest possible manner, turning his royal back while the courtiers tittered. His Majesty had even told the supplicant that the Portuguese crown had no further need for his services — that he could take his proposal elsewhere. Magellan, single-mindedly pursuing his vision, then put himself at the disposal of Spain's eighteen-year-old King Carlos I, soon to become Holy Roman Emperor Charles V. On March 22, 1518, acting in his own name and that of his insane mother Johanna, Carlos signed a formal *Yo el Rey* agreement, or *capitulación,* underwriting the capitán-general's voyage and appointing him governor-to-be of all new lands to be discovered by the expedition.

Now Magellan moves from vessel to vessel, counting first the stores needed to feed the 265 members of his crews — quantities of rice, beans, flour, garlic, onions, raisins, pipes and butts of wine (nearly 700 of them), anchovies (200 barrels), honey (5,402 pounds), and pickled pork (nearly three tons); then the thousands of nets, harpoons, and fishhooks which will be needed to supplement diets; next, astrolabes, hourglasses, and compasses for navigation; iron and stone shot for his cannon, and thousands of lances, spikes, shields, helmets, and breastplates, should they land on hostile shores, as is likely; forty loads of lumber, pitch, tar, beeswax, and oakum, hawsers, and anchors are insurance against shipwrecks; mirrors, bells, scissors, bracelets, gaily colored kerchiefs, and brightly tinted glassware are intended to befriend natives in the East. . . . The inventory goes on and on. It seems endless, but the admiral's interest never flags.

IN ROME MICHELANGELO, having completed *Moses* and the Sistine Chapel, is dedicating a sonnet to his lifelong idol, Dante. The paint is still drying on Sebastiano del Piombo's *Christopher Columbus.* Titian has just finished *The Assumption,* Raphael a portrait of Leo X with his sacred College of Cardinals, and Dürer a miniature of Jakob Fugger, the German merchant prince, intimate of popes and sovereigns. Earth is fresh on the graves of Leonardo da Vinci, dead at sixty-seven in a French castle near Amboise; the emperor Maximilian I, who died in his sixtieth year at Wiener Neustadt; Johann Tetzel, the indulgence hawker, gone at fifty-four in Leipzig; and the once lovely Lucrezia Borgia, who succumbed in northern Italy at the age of thirty-nine. Lucrezia's last years were devoted to piety and the education of her son Giovanni, whose father, Pope Alexander VI, was also his grandfather.

Jakob Fugger is not dead, but he is approaching the end, making more money every day. His colossal fortune is estimated at 2,032,652 guilders. In England Lord Chancellor Wolsey has just moved into Hampton Court palace. Among the works now popular with literate Europeans are More's *Utopia,* Alexander Barclay's *The Shyp of Folys of the Worlde,* and Machiavelli's *Il principe.* Erasmus is enjoying his third popular success, *Colloquia familiaria.* Inspired by his renown, satire and morality plays are fashionable in the theater. Among the stage triumphs are Peter Dorland van Diest's *Everyman,* John Skelton's *Magnificence,* and Gil Vicente's *Auto da Glória.*

Among the least-read works of the time are Copernicus's *Little Commentary* and the Borgia pope's bulls apportioning the New World between Spain and Portugal. Spain and France are arming heavily, preparing for a new war over Italian spoils. All crowned heads are ignoring the growing signs of a far greater conflict, the religious revolution, although nearly two years have passed since Luther posted his theses on the door of the Wittenberg church. Now he is drafting *An den christlichen Adel deutscher Nation,* calling on the German nobility to rise against Rome.

How MUCH Magellan is aware of all this is unknown. Probably very little. He has never been much interested in public affairs, and even if he were, following them closely would be impossible for him. For example, he will be at sea, beyond anyone's reach, when Luther takes his stand at Worms. Thus he will die ignorant of Christendom's coming schism, a tragedy for devout Catholics like him; he would have readily sacrificed his life defending the Church. Most of the rest of the contemporaneous tumult in Europe would seem irrelevant to him, although he would be wrong. All these events form a mosaic, and his expedition will become part of it. History is not a random sequence of unrelated events. Everything affects, and is affected by, everything else. This is never clear in the present. Only time can sort out events. It is then, in perspective, that patterns emerge.

The patterns of Magellan's age are now clear. Its clarifying event was the shattering of the medieval world — *medium aevum,* as Renaissance humanists called it. That historic collapse was the legacy of countless events and influences, which combined to create the greatest European upheaval since the barbarians' conquest of Rome. The religious revolution — which destroyed the Renaissance — was merely the most conspicuous thread in a very long rope. Others were the fall of Constantinople to Muhammad II in 1453, the humanists' discovery of wisdom in the values of classical civilization, thereby dooming Scholasticism, a medieval attempt to fuse pagan learning and Christianity. As the Church relinquished its monopoly of education, renascent Europe became aware of a widening, unbridgeable gulf between reason and faith. The masses remained pious; the learned found serenity in rational thought.

Meantime the growth of commerce, particularly the prosperity of England and Germany, expanded the middle and merchant classes. These, growing in power and influence, became exasperated with the arrogant prelates even as the supernational authority of Roman pontiffs was being challenged by rising nation-states and strengthened monarchies. Secularism spread, fueled by the invention of printing, the growth of literacy, and the wider knowledge of the Scriptures in vernacular versions. All these forces raised doubts, discredited custom, bred skepticism, loosened standards, undermined the comfort and support of tradition, and, as Christendom decayed as a distinctive civilization, led to the emergence of modern Europe.

All this meant change, and was therefore resented by the medieval mind. It is perhaps significant that the science which showed the least progress in these years was geology. Because of its divine authorship, the biblical account of creation was above criticism. "If a wrong opinion should obtain regarding the creation as described in Genesis," declared Pietro Martire Vermigli, the Italian reformer, "all the promises of Christ fall into nothing, and all the life of our religion would be lost."

The menace of Copernicus was even greater. The Scriptures assumed that everything had been created for the use of man. If the earth were shrunken to a mere speck in the universe, mankind would also be diminished. Heaven was lost when "up" and "down" lost all meaning — when each became the other every twenty-four hours. "No attack on Christianity is more dangerous," Jerome Wolf wrote Tycho Brahe in 1575, "than the infinite size and depth of the universe."

Finally, the exploration of lands beyond Europe — of which Magellan's voyage was to be the culmination — opened the entire world, thus introducing the modern age. The discoveries also undermined pontifical dogma on the character of the globe, introducing yet another threat to papal prestige. One of Rome's oldest arguments was that the Church's teachings must be true because everyone believed in the divinity of Christ. That had been plausible in the Middle Ages, but now, as reports poured in from navigators, travelers, conquistadores, and even missionaries, Europeans realized that other religions flourished in newly discovered lands, and those who worshiped alien gods there appeared to be none the worse for it.

DURING THE DARK AGES literal interpretation of the Bible had led the Church to endorse the absurd geographical dicta of *Topographia Christiana,* a treatise by the sixth-century monk Cosmas. Cosmas, who had traveled to India and should have known better, held that the world was a flat, rectangular plane, surmounted by the sky, above which was heaven. Jerusalem was at the center of the rectangle, and nearby lay the Garden of Eden, irrigated by the four Rivers of Paradise. The sun, much smaller than the earth, revolved around a conical mountain to the north. The monk's arguments were fragile, and not everyone accepted them — the Venerable Bede, among others, insisted that earth was round — but Cosmas scorned them. Rome, agreeing with him, rejected their protests as an affront to common sense.

This patristic dismissal of so elementary a fact was a sign of how deep the wisdom of the ancient world had been buried. More than three hundred years before the birth of Christ, Aristotle had determined that the planet must be a sphere; after an eclipse he had pointed out that only an orb could throw a circular shadow on the moon. The existence of India and Spain was known in Athens. However, few other geographical or scientific facts were available to Aristotle, and this led him into error. Holding that land was heavier than water, and that the masses of each must balance, he had inferred that the distance between the Iberian Peninsula and the Indian subcontinent could not be great, and that, consequently, there was no land between them — that is, no North or South America. Therein lay the origin of Columbus's error, which others would challenge and which Magellan, ultimately, would discredit.

Aristotle's spherical theory of the globe had been the cornerstone of classical geography. The Greeks arbitrarily divided the planet into five zones, two of them polar, too cold to be inhabitable; two others temperate; and one an equatorial region. Albertus Magnus and Roger Bacon, their medieval successors, later concluded that the equator, because of its great heat, must be incapable of sustaining life. Their conviction that man could not survive in the tropics, widely accepted, persisted until the fifteenth century.

With the exceptions of Pliny, Macrobius, and Agrippa, whose contributions were slight, the Romans added nothing to geographical knowledge. However, in Alexandria, on the outskirts of the empire, a school of Egyptian astronomers led by Ptolemy and Hipparchus flourished four centuries after Aristotle. Their calculation of the earth's circumference (twenty-five thousand geographical miles) was surprisingly accurate. They also partitioned the globe into 360 degrees, lined its surface with parallels of latitude and meridians of longitude, and, with their invention of the astrolabe, which measured latitude by "shooting the sun," provided an instrument which was to be used by mariners, including Magellan, until the Elizabethan Age.

But the Alexandrians, like the Greeks, erred. They concluded that the earth was both immovable and the center of the universe. Furthermore, Ptolemy's *Geógraphiké hyphégésis* (*Guide to Geography*), which greatly influenced medieval geographers, inferred that Asia extended much farther east than it actually does. Here again, those who were misled included Columbus, whose belief that Asia could be reached by sailing westward was thereby strengthened. Any doubts in his mind were resolved by *Imago mundi*, a comprehensive world geography by Pierre d'Ailly, a fourteenth-century cardinal and master of the College of Navarre. D'Ailly took the Aristotelian view that Europeans could reach India by sailing westward. *Imago mundi* became Columbus's favorite bedside book. His copy, with heavy marginal scribblings, is preserved in Seville's Biblioteca Colombina.

During the long medieval night, Hellenic and Egyptian learning was preserved by Muslim scholars in the Middle East, where it was discovered by early Renaissance humanists. After poring over it, Pope Pius II, Cardinal Borgia's early critic, wrote his influential *Historia rerum ubique gestarum*. Though largely a rehash of Ptolemy, Pius's *Historia* was by no means uncritical; earlier works notwithstanding, he reached the startling conclusion that Africa could be circumnavigated. His premise that an equator existed, even though it was invisible, went unchallenged; by then the spherical shape of the planet, and the Greek partition of it into climatic zones, was accepted except by those who insisted upon literal interpretation of the Scriptures.

THAT IS, it was accepted by scholars. Average people still assumed that the earth was flat, and their knowledge of the world beyond the horizon was largely derived from mythical lore. The sources of these fables were protean. Some could be traced to Homer. Others derived from romantic yarns told by wanderers; or the legends of Alexander the Great and Saint Thomas the Apostle; or the imaginative figments of Ctesias, a Greek who lived in the Persian court four centuries before Christ; or the Roman concoctions of Pliny and Gaius Julius Solinus; or in the extraordinarily popular fourteenth-century hoax *Voyage and Travels of Sir John Mandeville, Knight*. Written in the Anglo-French of the time, the *Travels* is purportedly a collection of true narratives, retold by Mandeville. Actually all are fictive, but the narratives are so persuasive that "Sir John Mandeville" (or, in some versions, "Johan Maundville, chevaler") was often believed where the Marco Polo genuine article was not.

Most medieval myths were set in Asia, which fascinated men then. Until the Tatar Peace of the mid-thirteenth century, no European had traveled east of Baghdad. The crusades and pilgrimages had provided some grasp of Palestine and Syria, but the Orient — "Cathay" — was considered magical, fantastic, and endowed with incredible wealth. Paradise was thought to be there somewhere, and it says much for medieval knowledge of the mysterious East that long after the first reports of Genghis Khan's terrible campaigns reached the Continent in 1221, he was believed to be a great Christian monarch who was devoting his life to the conversion of infidels.

Thus credulous men swallowed whole the stories of the giants Gog and Magog, of a jungle race with long teeth and hairy bodies, of griffins, of storks who fought with pygmies, of people who created their own shade by lying down and blotting out the sun with an enormous single foot, of men with dogs' heads who barked and snarled, and of the opulent *patria* of Ophir, in whose storehouse lay King Solomon's jewels and gold. Ophir was only one of many fabulous lands which existed only in fantasy. Others were the lost continent of Atlantis, a legend dating back to Plato; El Dorado; Rio Doro, the River of Gold; the Empire of Monomotapa; the Island of the Seven Cities of Cibola, said to have been discovered in the Atlantic by seven bishops, fugitives from Moorish Spain; and St. Brendan's Isle, based on the implausible tale of Saint Brendan, who was said to have found an enchanted land in the waters northwest of Ireland. In Magellan's time many of these places could be found in atlases. Portugal's Prince Henry the Navigator encountered a sea captain who said he had landed on the Island of the Seven Cities. As late as 1755 St. Brendan's Isle was believed to be situated five degrees west of the Canary Islands, and Brazil Rock, also imaginative, was not stricken from Britain's admiralty charts until 1873.

These were typical of the phantoms which confused and misled explorers sailing into unknown waters. Given the state of maps then, it is hardly surprising that so many ships failed to return; the wonder is that any of them found anything. Africa was shown as adjacent to India. The Indian Ocean and the Red Sea were small bodies of water. Egypt was placed in Asia; so was Ethiopia. Navigators poring over charts found such bewildering legends as "India Ethiope" and "India Egyptii," and the fourteenth-century Catalan Atlas, which may be seen today in Paris's Bibliothèque Nationale, is a farrago of distortions and inventions, including islands of griffins, the realm of Gog and Magog, a land of pygmies placed between India and China, an island called "Iana" where Malaya should be, and another island, "Trapobana," where there is nothing but open sea.

ALTHOUGH the rest of Europe was unaware of them, a few adventurous souls living on the western and northern edges of the continent had been venturing into the unknown since the Dark Ages. Beginning in the sixth century, Irishmen had first visited, and then settled, the Orkney, Shetland, and Faeroe islands. Undoubtedly the Irish reached farther than that, for Vikings occupying

Iceland in the ninth century found them already there. Then the
Norsemen took over. After a thousand-mile voyage through
some of the most dangerous seas in the world, Norway's Erik the
Red landed on Greenland at the end of the tenth century. Circa
A.D. 1000, Erik's son Leif reached North America. These feats
were a prelude to the expansion of Europe, but they cannot be
regarded as the first stages of that expansion. Ireland itself was
virtually undiscovered, and to people south of Scandinavia the
Vikings were pagan plunderers, almost as remote as Orientals and
certainly not part of the civilized world. Moreover, Norse and
Celtic medieval discoveries were never followed up. Since they
were scarcely known outside the ranks of the explorers, they had
no impact on the rest of the continent.

The Middle East was another matter. While the vast majority
of Europeans knew almost nothing of the real Asia, some of them
had been toiling busily on its fringes for three centuries. They
were traders, which is significant; profit, not curiosity, was to be
the prime motive behind the age of exploration. Because they
were Genoese, Venetian, and, to a lesser degree, Pisan, and because
they were highly successful, these merchants became major stokers
of Italy's prosperity. Their subsequent decline — after audacious
Spaniards and Portuguese had discovered new ways to reach the
Orient — dealt a mortal blow to that boom. The slump that followed was as responsible for the end of the Italian Renaissance as
the religious rebellion against Rome.

Beginning with the crusades — from A.D. 1100 to nearly
1300 — Oriental goods had reached the West through three main
arteries. One was overland, on caravan roads across northern
China and central Asia to the shores of the Black Sea. The other
two reached the Middle East via the Indian Ocean. Cargoes were
either sailed around the southern tip of the Arabian Peninsula, past
Yemen, up the Red Sea, and from there by land to Alexandria
and Gaza; or — this way was favored by dealers in the highly
profitable spice trade — up the Persian Gulf and thence by caravan
to the Levantine coast. The entrepreneurs who awaited them at
the end of each route transshipped the goods to Italy, southern
France, and the Iberian Peninsula. There wagons took over, haul-
ing the payloads to northern Europe.

Competition between the Italians for this lucrative traffic was fierce. Even if only one out of five dhows survived a three-year voyage, the trader owning the fleet was enriched; a sack of pepper, cinnamon, ginger, or nutmeg was worth more than a seaman's life, and a shipment from Araby would include fragrant ambergris, musk, attar of roses, silks, damasks, gold, Indian diamonds, Ceylonese pearls, and, very likely, hallucinogenic opiates. Shrewd merchants greased palms at every stage of a journey. In Middle Eastern wars they chose sides, knowing they would be rewarded by the winners. The Venetians were granted trading privileges during the fifty-seven-year Latin occupation of Constantinople, but they lost these after 1261, when the city fell to Greek troops led by Michael Palaeologus — henceforth the Byzantine emperor Michael VIII. Enterprising Genoese then replaced the Venetians by strengthening their ties with the Palaeologi. Using Constantinople as a base, they penetrated northern Persia, the Crimea, and distant reaches of the Black and Caspian seas; so ingenious were they, and so vigorous, that their central Asian contacts survived the breakup of the Mongol Empire. In Africa they sailed up the Nile as far as Dongola, in the Sudan; thrusting out from Tunis, they explored the Sahara and the Niger basin. Meantime the Venetians had established a monopoly in the Egyptian trade. Their cargoes came from South Asia — from the Moluccas, Malaya, and India's Malabar Coast. Then, in the fifteenth century, such Venetians as Niccolò de' Conti and John Cabot (he was born Giovanni Caboto) began penetrating the Orient directly from the west.

Yet even then the Atlantic beckoned. The traditional arteries of trade were cumbersome. Indian spices had to pass through at least twelve hands before they reached the consumer. The farther merchants were from the Middle Eastern scene, the greater their handicap. Spain and Portugal were particularly ill situated, but the Italians also suffered. Men groped toward a more direct route. In 1291 Genoese vessels had become the first to sail through the Straits of Gibraltar, bypassing Iberian ports and proceeding through the English Channel to Dutch anchorages. If the Portuguese and Spaniards were to harvest profits from seaborne commerce, they would have to find a new route to Asia. It was a challenge, and not for the fainthearted. In the same year that Gibraltar lost its virginity, two Genoese brothers, Ugolino and Guido Vivaldo, vowed to reach India by finding and doubling Africa's southern tip. Bravely sailing out through the straits, they headed south — and were never heard from again. Another century would pass before the riddle of the Cape of Good Hope was solved, and by then Italy would have lost the baton of leadership.

AT THIS POINT in the history of exploration an eminent fourteenth-century Englishman appears in an unexpected role. He is Geoffrey Chaucer (1342–1400). Like most writers in all ages, Chaucer remained solvent by finding other employment from time to time. In 1368 he became an esquire of the royal household; later he was appointed clerk of the King's Works. One of his royal admirers was Philippa, daughter of John of Gaunt and granddaughter of King Edward III. Chaucer's avocation was the study of navigation. He modestly described himself as an "unlearned compiler of the labors of old astrologiens," and in fact much of his *Treatise on the Astrolabe* was adapted from a Latin translation of the *Composito et operato astrolabii* of Messahala, an eighth-century Arabian astronomer. Nevertheless Chaucer was an enthusiast, and his enthusiasm was infectious. Young Philippa caught it. She became intrigued by his lessons in navigation. Later, as queen of Portugal, she taught them to one of her sons, Henry, who, sharing her enthusiasm, grew up to act upon it. He is remembered in history as Prince Henry the Navigator (1394–1460). Although the prince himself did little navigating, he sponsored voyages of discovery, encouraged seaborne commerce, developed the sailing vessel known as the Portuguese caravel, and designed a grand strategy to outflank Islamic power by establishing contact, first with Africa south of the Sahara, and then with the Orient. Islam survived his challenge, but in the process seamen inspired by Henry established the Portuguese overseas empire, which subsequently became the most extensive in the world, dominating European trade with India and the East Indies for 150 years.

In retrospect, their accomplishments seem almost miraculous, for despite the efforts of men like Chaucer and Prince Henry, navigation remained a highly inexact science. The prince is said to have improved the instruments used by navigators. One can only wonder what they were like before him. To be sure, latitude could be measured with any one of several versions of the astrolabe, chiefly the English cross-staff, a forestaff, or, in Magellan's case, a calibrated backstaff. All, like their Egyptian forerunner, were primitive quadrants that measured the angle between the sun and the horizon. First-rate astronomers could also make an educated guess at longitude — if they were on land. But there was no way a man at sea could determine the longitude of his ship. To do that, he needed to read the position of the stars, which required knowledge of the precise time — an impossibility, since accurate clocks, with balance wheels and hairsprings, would not be invented until the middle of the next century. Of course, every captain had a compass, and all could compute dead reckoning. None, however, knew the difference between magnetic north and true north, or realized that dead reckoning suffered from disastrous errors arising from the drift of the water.

In the days of al-Idrisi, the twelfth-century geographer, Arabs had taught Sicilians how to sail boats, and Sicilians had passed the knowledge along to the Genoese, who had taught the Spaniards and Portuguese. But although the shores washed by the Mediterranean had been mapped, few captains had ventured beyond it. Even where coastlines could be found on charts, water depths were rarely shown. This massive lack of information, together with the abundance of misinformation, put a premium on the experience of seamen who, venturing into unknown waters, hoped to make it home.

Pilots on exploratory voyages carefully documented the progress of each expedition. When the leaders' hopes were justified — when they reached strange lands and returned — these records, or rutters, became invaluable. Each was a detailed, step-by-step chronicle of the journey out and the journey back. Specific information included tides, reefs, channels, magnetic compass bearings between ports and headlands, the strength and direction of winds, the number of days a master kept his vessel on each tack, when he heeled it over for repairs, where he found fresh water, soundings measured in fathoms and speed in knots, measured by comparing the time required for a sandglass to empty with the progress of

knots which were tied, at intervals, on a rope attached to a small
log that was thrown overboard and paid out. Everything went in,
everything — even the changing color of the sea — which might
conceivably be useful to another pilot trying to reach the same
destination.

Rutters were copied by hand and translated under supervision,
but those opening new trade routes never reached the hands of
printers. They were too precious. Some were sold. Others were
declared to be state secrets; divulging their contents was punishable
by death, for a rival captain with a rutter in his cabin could exploit
another's dearly bought knowledge. Once a way had been found,
dangers were minimal, but the perils of the original explorers can
scarcely be exaggerated.

It is a remarkable fact that virtually all of them came from one
corner of Europe. Portugal and Spain had contributed little to
Western civilization before then. In the five centuries since then
they have produced several brilliant artists; apart from that, their
achievements have been less than awesome. But this, incontest-
ably, was Iberia's hour. Within thirty years — a single generation — a few hundred small ships weighing anchor in Lisbon,
Palos, and Sanlúcar discovered more of the world than had all
mankind in all the millennia since the beginning of time.

THE FIRST probing voyages were cautious, even hesitant, and in
perspective their accomplishments seem slight. In 1460, when
Prince Henry died, Portuguese mariners had made only six unimpressive discoveries: three small archipelagoes off their own
coast — the Azores, Madeiras, and Canaries — and, in northern
Africa, Cape Verde's fertile promontory, the Senegal River, and
the port of Ceuta. The prince had been in his grave eleven years
when João de Santarém became the first European to cross the
equator and return unscathed. Another eleven years passed before
Diogo Cão found the mouth of the Congo River. Finally, in 1486,
a half-century after the prince's first expedition, Bartolomeu Dias
made a major discovery. Struggling through a mighty storm, he
rounded the southern tip of Africa. He was anxious to sail on,
convinced that India lay ahead, but his exhausted men forced him
to return home. There King John II, after congratulating him,

named the tip the Cape of Good Hope. To Dias's dismay, however, his countrymen were indifferent to the implications of his rutter — an all-water route to India, outflanking the Middle Eastern merchants dealing in spices, perfumes, silks, drugs, gold, and gems.

Six years later the initiative passed to Spain, whose Castilian adventurers, having completed their conquest of the Moors' last stronghold, were ready for new challenges. Because Arab traders had passed along fragments of Asian geography, Europeans had a general idea of the continent's chief coastal features: India, China, Japan, the East Indies. Paolo Toscanelli, a Florentine scholar, had concluded that the Orient lay only 3,000 nautical miles west of Lisbon. Toscanelli strengthened the confidence of Genoa's Christopher Columbus. Columbus had raised 500,000 maravedis for an expedition. He won over Louis de Santangel, Spain's royal treasurer, and Santangel persuaded the crown to invest another 1 million maravedis — roughly $14,000 — in a Columbian attempt to reach the East by crossing the Atlantic.

Off the Genoese seaman went, navigating by dead reckoning and, legend has it, crying to his men, *"Adelante! Adelante!"* ("Forward! Forward!"). Returning early in 1493, he electrified Christendom by reporting complete success. In Barcelona Isabella and Ferdinand held a grand reception for him. Honoring him with the titles Viceroy of the Indies and Admiral of the Ocean Sea (*Almirante del Mar Océano*), they told him to organize more expeditions to the Orient. Actually he couldn't. He had found, not Asia, but the Bahama island of San Salvador. He refused to abandon his claim to the discovery of Cathay, however, and although he returned to the New World three times, he never changed his mind. He called the natives he encountered Indians, which is why the Caribbean Islands have been known as the West Indies ever since. In 1496, he was unable to sail around Cuba. His officers explained that they were thwarted by bad weather, but Columbus rejected the explanation. The real reason, he said, was that they were lying off an Oriental peninsula. He thought it was probably Malaya.

His claims continued to be accepted. In Lisbon King Manuel, ascending the throne in 1495, assumed that the Spaniards had stolen a march on him. Jealous, and aware of the pleas of Bartolomeu

Dias, he gave Vasco da Gama four vessels and instructions to reach
India via the Cape of Good Hope. Da Gama is not among the
attractive figures of the age, although in many ways he was typical
of it. Brawny, brutal, cruel, and vindictive, he sought to dominate
strange lands by terrifying the inhabitants. Once he deliberately
set fire to an Arab ship, burning alive some three hundred pas-
sengers, including women and children. Nevertheless he earned
the rank of *almirante,* bestowed upon him by his grateful sovereign, for Portugal's rise as a world power owed much to him.
On November 22, 1497, he rounded the cape Dias had found.
Equipped with an Arab map and accompanied by an Arab navigator, he pushed on, first reaching Mozambique and Kenya on
Africa's east coast, and then, after a twenty-three-day run across
the Indian Ocean, Calicut on the southwest shore of India.

THE PORTUGUESE had finally found a new passage to India, one
free of the costly transshipment and tolls exacted by the old routes
from Egypt, Arabia, and Persia via Italy. For more than a century
the economic consequences of this commercial revolution — for
that is what it amounted to — were more spectacular than the
discoveries of Columbus and his successors in what was coming
to be known as the New World. While Spanish navigators were
floundering about in the Caribbean "Indies," the vaults of Lisbon's
banks were filling up with profits from the new trade. Indeed,
until the turn of the sixteenth century the Portuguese scarcely
thought of the possibilities lying on the far side of the Atlantic
and even then Manuel's ministers were preoccupied with the mar-
kets created by vessels doubling the Cape of Good Hope.

Afonso de Albuquerque took office as governor of Portuguese
India in 1509. His duties were more military than civil; fighting
Hindus and Muslims, he captured and fortified both Goa and, on
the Arabian coast, Aden; then he landed on Ceylon and moved
on to seize Malacca on the Malayan Peninsula, the center of the
East Indian spice trade. From Malacca alone he sent home $25
million in loot. His Excelência roamed all over the underbelly of
Asia. He dispatched twenty ships to the Red Sea, and, in 1512,
planted Manuel's colors in Celebes and the Moluccas. The Portuguese expansion continued to pick up momentum; in 1516

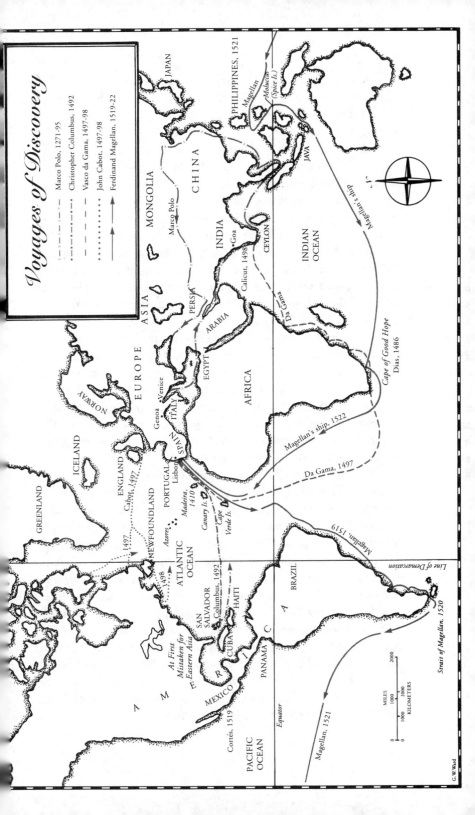

Voyages of Discovery

- —·—·—·— Marco Polo, 1271-95
- —·—··—··— Christopher Columbus, 1492
- —·—·—·—· Vasco da Gama, 1497-98
- — — — — John Cabot, 1497-98
- ·········→ Ferdinand Magellan, 1519-22

GREENLAND

ICELAND

NORWAY

EUROPE

ENGLAND

Cabot, 1497

NEWFOUNDLAND

ATLANTIC OCEAN

Azores

PORTUGAL
Lisbon

SPAIN

Genoa
Venice
ITALY

EGYPT

ARABIA

PERSIA

ASIA

MONGOLIA

Marco Polo

CHINA

INDIA

Goa

Calicut, 1498

CEYLON

JAPAN

PHILIPPINES, 1521

Magellan

Moluccas
(Spice Is.)

JAVA

INDIAN OCEAN

Da Gama

Magellan's ship

Cape of Good Hope
Dias, 1486

AFRICA

Da Gama, 1497

Magellan's ship, 1522

Madeira,
1410

Canary Is.

Cape
Verde Is.

1497

1498

At First
Mistaken for
E Eastern Asia

SAN
SALVADOR

Columbus, 1492

CUBA

HAITI

PANAMA

MEXICO

Cortés, 1519

A
M
E
R
I
C
A

BRAZIL

Line of Demarcation

Magellan, 1519

Strait of Magellan, 1520

Magellan, 1520

Equator

Magellan, 1521

PACIFIC OCEAN

MILES
0   1000   2000
0   1000 2000
KILOMETERS

G. W. Ward

Duarte Coelho opened Thailand and southern Vietnam to Portuguese commerce, and the following year Fernão Peres de An-
drade reached trade agreements on the Chinese mainland with both
Peking and Canton.

Half a world away, Columbus had continued to make one
landing after another in the New World, sending back reports on
his increasing knowledge of the Orient. However, there was a
growing suspicion among the mariners who had followed in his
wake that they were not in Asia at all. By the late 1490s landings
had been made in Honduras, Venezuela, Newfoundland, and on
the North American mainland. In 1500 Gaspar Côrte-Real reached
Labrador, and that same year Pedro Cabral, storm-driven from a
course he had set for the Cape of Good Hope, stumbled upon
Brazil. Cabral hoisted Portugal's colors over Brazil; Vicente Yáñez
Pinzón claimed it for Spain.

With the discovery of Panama, Colombia, and the mouth of
the Amazon, a very long coastline had begun to take shape. It
remained for Amerigo Vespucci, a Florentine merchant in the
service of the Medicis, to define the emerging truth. In Spain on
business, Vespucci had caught the exploration fever and sailed
westward under the Portuguese flag. Later, in a letter to Italian
friends, he wrote that on June 16, 1497, during one of his four
expeditions to what he called the *novo mondo,* he had touched the
mainland of a new continent. Although doubt was later cast on
this claim, both Columbus and the Spanish government, which
awarded Vespucci a lifetime appointment as *piloto mayor* — chief
of Spain's pilots — believed him reliable. In April 1507 Martin
Waldseemüller, professor of cosmography at the University of
Saint-Dié, produced the first map showing the Western Hemisphere. He called it "America," and thirty years later Gerardus
Mercator followed Waldseemüller's precedent, though by then it
was clear that the New World comprised more than one continent.

By the second decade of the new century — the 1510s — Europe's developing image of the Americas resembled an enormous
jigsaw puzzle whose pieces were rapidly falling into place. Commissioned by the English crown, John Cabot had explored the St.
Lawrence River. Others were mapping the east coast of North
America from the Savannah River north to what is now Charles-

ton. On April 2, 1513, Juan Ponce de León, pursuing the medieval dream of eternal youth, landed four hundred miles to the south. Naming his discovery Florida (from *Pascua Florida,* Easter), he declared it to be Spanish territory. Other Spaniards claimed Argentina and explored the Gulf of Mexico, planting their flag in the Yucatán Peninsula. Toward the end of the decade, Montezuma II made the capital error of cordially welcoming Hernando Cortés, thereby sealing his fate as Mexico's last Aztec emperor.

Although patriotic ardor burned in all these adventurers, their overarching goal had not changed. They were still looking for the mysterious East. The unexpected appearance of the New World had merely whetted appetites. Columbus had been thoroughly discredited by now, but the riddle remained: If the Americas were where the Orient was supposed to be, where was the Orient? And what, exactly, lay beyond the newly found landmass? Their logs reveal that early in the century several of them had stumbled close to the answer. In 1501 Rodrigo de Bastidas had explored Panama's Atlantic coast. Late in the following year Columbus himself, making his final Atlantic voyage, had been blown ashore on Panama's isthmus. It was the worst storm in his experience; his men, he wrote in his journal, "were so worn out that they longed for death to end their dreadful suffering." Unaware that the Pacific Ocean lay only forty miles away, he and his exhausted crews celebrated Christmas and the New Year in a harbor near the eastern end of what later became the Panama Canal. Seven years later Spanish conquistadores actually founded a colony at Darién. But they, too, failed to cross the narrow strip of land.

Vasco Núñez de Balboa did it. On September 25, 1513, the thirty-eight-year-old Balboa, a member of a Spanish expedition led by Rodrigo de Bastidas, climbed his celebrated peak and beheld the vast Pacific below. Clambering down, he reached the shore of the ocean four days later, christened it the South Sea (*El Mar del Sur*), and claimed it "and all its shores" for his sovereign. This was both extravagant and, in a way, impious; it defied the Vatican policy set forth by Alexander VI after Columbus's first voyage. The Borgia pope was partial to Spain, being Spanish himself, but Portugal could not be denied her new empire; the Portuguese role in the explorations had been too great.

The pontiff therefore awarded the Portuguese all non-Christian lands east, and Spain all those west, of an imaginary north-south line drawn 100 leagues west of the Azores and the Cape Verde Islands. This had infuriated England's Henry VII, who, refusing to recognize papal jurisdiction, vowed to build his own empire and designated Cabot as its first builder. For various reasons Lisbon and Valladolid* had also been dissatisfied. War between them

*Or Aranda de Duero, also in Castile, or Barcelona, in Aragón. Since the marriage of Ferdinand and Isabella, uniting Castile and Aragón, the court had become a traveling circus. Madrid did not become the capital of Spain until 1561.

Balboa claims the Pacific, 1513

appeared imminent. Then they negotiated the Treaty of Torde-
sillas, redrawing the line 270 leagues farther west. The pope's
decision was accepted as valid for discoveries until then, but in the
future the Spaniards could claim whatever they could reach by
sailing westward and the Portuguese what *they* could find sailing
to the east. But this, too, was unsatisfactory. The negotiators had
overlooked the fact that the world was round. Eventually explorers
from the two countries would meet. Thus the Moluccas — the
Spice Islands — fell in a gray area. Portugal had occupied them
and claimed them, but Spain sulked. And everyone wanted them.
To Ferdinand Magellan, the dilemma represented opportunity.

DURING THESE YEARS of high excitement in the Americas, Magellan
was a Portuguese soldier on the other side of the world, where
Lisbon's trade was flourishing and men-at-arms like him were
fighting to expand King Manuel's colonial territories. Beginning
in 1505 he served there seven years, variously stationed in Africa,
India, Malacca, and Mozambique. This was when Portugal broke
Muslim power in the Indian Ocean. By all accounts, Magellan
repeatedly distinguished himself in combat and at sea.

In his idle hours, spent on the docks, he talked to Asian pilots
and navigators from as far away as Okinawa, asking about tides,
winds, magnetic compass readings — the kind of information
which, if they had kept records, would have been in their rutters.
Through this method he became as well informed about the Indonesian archipelago as any European seaman. But he was equally
interested in reports from the New World, particularly accounts
of Balboa's discovery. Like all European mariners, he believed
that the new sea west of Panama must be very small. The great
question was how it could be reached by water — where one could
find what the Portuguese called *o braço do mar* and Spaniards *el
paso* — a strait through which ships could pass from the Atlantic
to El Mar del Sur beyond.

Repeated testing of the hemispheric land barrier had proved
discouraging. The narrowness of the Panamanian isthmus was
unmatched elsewhere. From Labrador, at the sixtieth degree of
north latitude, to at least lower Brazil, at the thirtieth degree of
south latitude, the Americas presented a solid, intimidating front

of earth and stone. In the north the thousands of islands and inlets above what is now the Canadian mainland raised hopes for a northwest passage, and in some breasts these hopes endured for four centuries, until the Norwegian explorer Roald Amundsen threaded the countless straits between 1906 and 1909, only to find that the freezing of sea lanes and other arctic conditions made the route impractical. Most navigators had written off the north four centuries earlier, however. It was generally agreed that the break in the landmass, if there was one, must be in the south. Yet searchers there had also been frustrated. Some early cartographers showed the southern continent extending all the way to Antarctica.

That was more or less the situation on October 20, 1517, when the approximately forty-year-old Magellan, having renounced his Portuguese nationality, arrived in Seville accompanied by several pilots and his Malayan slave Enrique. He had come to offer his services to the Spanish crown. What befell him there resembles one of those Victorian morality tales in which Ragged Dick or Faithful Fred reaches the teeming city, is bewildered by its chaos, foils scheming rogues bent upon exploiting him, meets kind allies, survives a series of disappointments, and finally wins through by pluck and daring.

Magellan encountered no rogues then — they would come later — but Seville was certainly chaotic, especially within the Casa de Contratación, the royal house of trade. It was there that merchants who were prepared to finance expeditions met captains eager to lead them, there that the two bargained under supervision of the king's magistrates, and there that the Portuguese explorer headed. The hall was surrounded by taverns swarming with adventurers, pilots, and seasoned mariners, some of them men who had sailed with Columbus, Côrte-Real, or John and Sebastian Cabot, and all of them bearing maps and plans guaranteed to enrich their King Carlos, their sponsors, and, not incidentally, themselves. Magellan, in need of an ally, found one in Diego Barbosa, a fellow Portuguese expatriate well acquainted with the Magellan family. Diego had served the Spanish crown here for fourteen years. He took an instant liking to Magellan. So did his son Duarte, a mariner himself. Finally, Beatriz Barbosa, the daughter of the family, fell in love with Magellan, and, after a brief courtship, became his bride.

Backed by his new relatives, Magellan approached the Casa de Contratación and formally presented the proposition which he and Ruy Faleiro, a Portuguese astronomer, had drawn up in Lisbon. It envisaged a westward voyage halfway round the globe to the Moluccas, the expedition to be led by him and funded by the Spanish crown, whose possessions the islands would then become. A commission of three officials rejected the plan, but immediately after the hearing, one of the commissioners, Juan de Aranda, sent word that he wished to see the petitioner in private. Aranda — the Casa's *agente,* or factor — wanted to question Magellan further. Being a man of business, he was intrigued by the possibility of wresting the Spice Islands from Portugal. After hearing further details he offered to sponsor Magellan's application for royal support. In return he expected one-eighth of the enterprise's profits. That winter he carried on delicate negotiations with the chancellor of Castile and enlisted the help of the monarch's privy councillors. Meantime Magellan had written Faleiro, summoning him to Spain.

EARLY IN THE FOLLOWING YEAR King Carlos, with the approval of his privy council, received the partners at Valladolid. Magellan and Faleiro convinced him that the Moluccas, the remote Indo-Pacific archipelago then known as the Spice Islands, lay on Spain's side of the papal line of demarcation. They also said that the Portuguese route there — through the Indian Ocean and the Sunda Sea — was needlessly long. The islands, they explained, could be reached by a much shorter route from the west. To be sure, this meant penetrating the American barrier from the south, but that could be done by sailing through a South American paso whose location was known to them alone. Persuaded, Carlos pledged his support of the partners from Lisbon. He put it in writing; then, after knighting Magellan, he appointed him capitán-general of what he christened the Armada de Molucca.

Thus the enterprise was launched — or so the record reads. Common sense, however, insists that there must have been more to it than that. The new admiral had been only one of hundreds of supplicants in the Casa that day. He had succeeded where the others had been turned away, not because he had charmed the Barbosas, Aranda, the king's privy council, and the king himself — his charm, by all accounts, was slight — but because he had struck them as an exceptionally qualified Portuguese captain and navigator who knew precisely what he was doing.

His knowledge of the south seas was profound. Although he had never reached the Spice Islands, he had learned a great deal about them from a friend, one Francisco Serrão, a Portuguese skipper who had been so smitten with the islands that he had decided to spend the rest of his life there, fathering children and basking in the paradisaical climate. Serrão had written long, lyrical, detailed letters describing the archipelago; Magellan had showed them to the Spaniards in Valladolid. It was true, he conceded, that he had yet to sail in the waters of the Western Hemisphere. Yet he was knowledgeable about them. As a Portuguese of noble blood with service in Africa, Asia, and the islands beyond, he had had access to Lisbon's celebrated Tesouraria (Treasury). There, before defecting to Spain, he had pored over the rutters, logs, and sailing directions of fellow countrymen who had explored the Americas. Their accumulated knowledge was now his.

It was his certitude, however, which had impressed the Spanish court most. Other petitioners had speculated. Magellan said he *knew,* and his decisive manner confirmed him. He was absolutely positive that the Moluccas belonged to Spain, and Faleiro had brought a globe of his own design to back him up. Both men assured the court that they knew precisely where to find the paso, the legendary open sesame to Balboa's ocean. When the king had asked why it wasn't shown on the globe, Magellan had replied that the secret was too precious; they could not risk a leak.

His conviction was genuine, but it was built on quicksand. Faleiro's globe was flawed. Due to compensating errors, his calculations of longitude were only four degrees off, but that was enough to discredit them. The islands were on Portugal's side of the line, not Spain's, and the more men learned about that part of the world the stronger Lisbon's claim would become. And — far more important — the partners' assurance that Magellan could find the strait linking the Atlantic and the Pacific was equally false. After five centuries their error is clear, though their sources seemed plausible at the time. The first was a map drawn by Martin Behaim, the Nuremberg geographer who had been royal cartographer to the Portuguese court; the second a globe produced by Johannes Schöner in 1515; and the third a report from the western Atlantic which reached Magellan either shortly before, or soon after, his move from Lisbon to Seville. The map and the globe showed a southern passage between the oceans. In the light of later evidence it is clear that Behaim and Schöner had put it in the wrong place, but they appeared to have been confirmed in 1516, when Juan Díaz de Solís, who had been sailing along the coast of South America under the illusion that he was near the Malayan Peninsula, came upon the gigantic funnel-shaped estuary leading to what is now Buenos Aires.

Although Díaz de Solís was killed by Indians, members of his expedition found their way home, and to Magellan their description of the Río de la Plata, as Sebastian Cabot later named it, must have seemed to be the final piece of the puzzle. Indeed, even today it is hard to believe that the estuary — actually the outlet of two enormous rivers — is not open sea. Its mouth is 140 miles wide, and its western shore is 170 miles inland. To Europeans accustomed to the Guadiana River of Spain and Portugal, the Tiber, or the Rhine, it must have resembled the great straits they knew — the Dardanelles or Gibraltar. They were wrong, and so was Magellan, misled by them. But persuasive errors have played key roles in history before. So it was here. Had the capitán-general known the truth, his confidence would have been eroded. Carlos and his privy council would have rejected the uncertain applicant. Even if they hadn't, Magellan's iron will, which was to become vital to the voyage, would have been weakened, probably fatally.

How much Lisbon learned about the Valladolid audience is unknown. Probably very little. But it was enough: a seasoned Portuguese mariner, familiar with the Tesouraria's holiest secrets, had been commissioned by the Castilian monarch to pry the Spice Islands loose from Portugal. His fleet was already forming up. It is a measure of Manuel's alarm that he instructed his ambassador to Madrid, Álvaro da Costa, to sabotage the expedition. Fortunately for history, Costa was a fool. He attempted to coerce

Magellan, and when that failed he tried to intimidate the Spanish
king, first telling him that Portugal would regard continued support of the venture as an unfriendly act, then that Magellan and
Faleiro wanted to return home but had been denied permission to
leave Seville — a lie which, when exposed, resulted in the cold
dismissal of the bumbling envoy. Nevertheless, attempts to sand-
bag the undertaking continued, and some of them were a nuisance.
When Magellan began signing up crewmen, Sebastian Álvarez,
Portugal's consul on the spot, urged them to desert. He also spread
vicious rumors; cornering the flota's four Spanish captains, he
whispered to them that their capitán-general was a double agent
who planned to lower Spain's colors, raise Portugal's, and defect
with the entire armada.

This ugly seed fell on fertile ground. Only one of the four was
an experienced professional mariner; the other three were haughty
young dons, Castilian courtiers held in high favor by their sovereign, resentful of their subordination to a foreigner. Thus the
enterprise began to accumulate difficulties long before its five anchors were weighed. Because of Álvarez's dirty tricks — he fed
gossips tales that the mission was highly dangerous and the vessels
unseaworthy — the recruitment of seamen bogged down. Those
who finally signed on were the dregs of the waterfront: ragged,
filthy, diseased drifters who babbled to one another in broken
Spanish, Portuguese, Italian, German, English — even Arabic.
Meddlesome officials of the port of Seville tried to reject the Portuguese among them, including several who were Magellan relatives; Duarte Barbosa, his brother-in-law; and Estevão Gomes,
one of the ablest pilots in either Iberian country.

The capitán-general was thwarted again and again. He ordered
equipment; it failed to arrive. Funds which had been promised by
Carlos and his privy council miscarried. Magellan, his patience
endless, successfully appealed to the king and royal agents. Finally
he confronted the most intractable obstacle: his partner. Faleiro,
who had never been to sea, insisted that they share a joint command. It was an impossible demand; had it been met, the ships
would not have survived the first leg of their long journey. Precisely how the admiral deflected this challenge is unknown. Some
accounts say that Faleiro was declared insane; others tell of an

imperial edict appointing him commander of a second expedition, which never sailed. In any event, he turned his maps and astronomical tables over to Magellan, and the five bowsprits finally took the bone in their teeth on September 20, 1519, sailing westward before the wind, under taut sails bearing Spain's royal cross of St. James.

The capitán-general watched the mainland recede in the wake of *Trinidad* — his flagship, or *capitana*. Then he opened an unsettling, last-minute dispatch from his father-in-law, relaying reports of a conspiracy between three of the Spanish noblemen. The leader was Juan de Cartagena, commander of *San Antonio* and an intimate of the bishop of Burgos, thought by some to be the bishop's bastard. When the right moment arrived, Diego Barbosa had been told, Cartagena would give the signal for a mutiny.

BARBOSA was no alarmist. The hostility of the dons was real. One of them had precipitated a violent public row with Magellan before the fleet had even left Seville, and it is not unlikely that the

Magellan's Armada de Molucca sails from Spain

Castilians had decided to get rid of him after he had disclosed his planned route. He had no choice but to take the warning seriously, and it provided the voyage's first test of his leadership. His response was revealing, if not altogether reassuring. If patience and thoroughness were among his traits, so were an extraordinary passion for secrecy, insistence upon ruthless discipline, and determination to dominate his subordinates at any cost. To plot mutiny, if the report was true, was criminal, but the dons' feelings of resentment were not. Nor were they unreasonable. As holders of royal commissions the officers rightly expected that, once at sea, they would be taken into their admiral's confidence, provided with maps, informed of the course they would follow, and, most important, told the location of the all-important paso.

He told them nothing, gave them nothing. Resolving to force any revolt into the open but not to lose, he kept the Castilians at a safe distance. During the first, ten-week leg of the voyage, from Spain to Brazil, the other vessels were ordered to follow in the flagship's wake. Late each afternoon a lantern was hung from *Trinidad's* fantail. Under standing orders, they were required to keep it in sight, and when the lamp flashed a signal at sunset each day the four subordinate galleons — *San Antonio* (Cartagena), *Concepción* (Gaspar de Quesada), *Santiago* (Juan Serrano), and *Victoria* (Luis de Mendoza) — approached the flagship's stern to receive orders for the three night watches.

The dons fumed. Cartagena, as senior captain and skipper of the fleet's largest vessel, attempted to serve as their spokesman. He merely provoked a snub. The Spanish captains were baffled by their commander's sailing direction. They had assumed that he would take them directly to the New World. Instead, when they reached 27 degrees north latitude, he changed their course. Now they were paralleling the African coast. He had an excellent reason for this. Before leaving Spain a reliable informant had brought him ominous news: Manuel of Portugal had sent two flotillas to intercept him. They would be lying athwart the direct route to Brazil. Magellan had decided to evade them; he would skirt Africa and then cross the Atlantic Narrows. Had he told his skippers that, they would have understood at once. But he was

taciturn by nature and distrusted them anyway. So when Carta-
gena called out from his deck, asking where he was taking them,
Magellan replied: *"¡Que le siguiessen y no pidiessen más cuenta!"*
("Follow me and don't ask questions!")

Furious, the offended don answered this insult with one of his
own. For three successive days he absented himself from the sunset
ritual, remaining below and sending his quartermaster topside
with instructions to address the fleet commander, not as capitán-
general, which custom required, but merely as capitán. Magellan
ignored the slight, feigning indifference, then called a meeting of
all armada officers aboard the flagship. Again Cartagena tried to
question him; again the admiral disregarded him. He was deliberately inciting insubordination, and when he succeeded — when
the young nobleman lost his temper and shouted that he would
refuse to obey future orders — Magellan put him under arrest.
He seized him, snapped, *"Sed preso"* ("You are my prisoner"),
and turned him over to a nearby *alguacil,* or master-at-arms. Another Spanish officer, Antonio de Coca, replaced Cartagena on
San Antonio's quarterdeck. The other three Castilian officers stood
mute and the moment passed. For the present, at least, the admiral's authority as capitán-general had survived defiance.

On Tuesday, November 29, 1519, *Trinidad*'s lookout raised the
Brazilian coast, and two weeks later the five ships sailed into the
bay of Rio de Janeiro, discovered by the Portuguese eighteen years
earlier. Although Magellan never confided in anyone, in Rio he
held the first of his many talks with a member of the expedition,
a youth who, after the voyage, was to become his biographer.
Antonio Pigafetta was a member of the Venetian nobility who
had come aboard representing the signory of Venice. Don Antonio's mission was to observe and report home on the spice trade,
but soon his chief interest, and his idol, was the capitán-general.
In his diary he began entering copious descriptions of the admiral's
every move, noting, for example, that in Rio Magellan tasted
pineapple for the first time and converted all the natives on shore
to Christianity.

Delighted with the weather and the local women, the fleet's
crews would have preferred to linger in Rio indefinitely, but their

leader ordered them to hoist sail; according to Schöner's globe, the Río de Solís, as the Río de la Plata was then called, lay a thousand miles to the south, and he was impatient to find his priceless *paso*. After hugging the shore for two weeks, the flagship, with the other vessels streaming behind, passed the cape of Santa María and then, just beyond a low hill which they christened Montevidi — today Montevideo, Uruguay — lookouts sighted the great estuary. The men, seeing that it was impossible to glimpse a far shore, cheered lustily; without exception, Pigafetta wrote, they believed this to be the mouth of the legendary strait. Their leader was sure of it, convinced that here, where Juan Díaz de Solís had died less than four years earlier, lay the inlet which would lead him to Balboa's Mar del Sur and, six hundred leagues to the west, the coveted, disputed Spice Islands.

HIS DISCOVERY of his crushing error came gradually, like a man's realization that he has irrevocably lost his most prized possession. *It has to be here*, he tells himself, or, *I left it there; it must be somewhere*. The fact that it is forever gone is insupportable at first;

The Río de la Plata, from an early atlas

acceptance of the disaster comes slowly, accompanied by a sickening feeling of emptiness. So the bleak truth must have come to Magellan. Despite Faleiro's calculations, Schöner's globe, Behaim's map, and the fourteen-year-old Portuguese pilots' rutters in Lisbon's Tesouraria, the capitán-general had found, not a strait, but only an immense bay. He was nothing if not stubborn. For nearly a month he explored and reexplored the Plata, desperately trying to find an opening and always failing. Finally, on Thursday, February 2, 1520, he abandoned hope. Once that happened — once he grasped the implications of his defeat — the depth of his grief can only be imagined. It meant that his every Valladolid assurance, given in good faith to King Carlos and his privy council, had been false. He could share his disappointment with no one; if his Castilian captains knew the truth, they would clap him in irons, lock him up in the flagship's brig, and return him to Spain, a defrocked Knight Commander of Santiago charged with fraud, imposture, and extortion of royal funds. Abandoning his search was therefore out of the question. Like Cortés at Veracruz, he had burned his boats. A return to Portugal, where he was wanted for treason, was also out of the question. Either he found glory, or disgrace — and execution — would find him.

The strait, if it existed, could only lie to the southwest; thus his future, if he had one, also lay there. In the first week of February, without a word of explanation to his baffled officers and men, who knew only that their destination was the balmy south seas, he led them crawling through treacherous currents and surging tides, down the desolate, barren, and increasingly bitter Patagonian coast toward antarctic latitudes, praying that his dream would be redeemed by the reach around the next cape, or the next, or the one after that. Every harbor, every cove was scouted, with his leadsmen taking soundings, till shoals forced him to quit and move on to the next inlet. On February 24 his hopes rose in the Golfo San Matías. He sent parties of men in ship's boats to search thoroughly. They did, but returned weary and dejected, having found nothing. The Bahía de los Patos followed, then the Bahía de los Trabajos and the Golfo San Jorge. All ended in disappointment.

Each day the weather grew more depressing. No European had

ever been this close to the South Pole.* The days grew shorter, the nights longer, the winds fiercer, the seas grayer; the waves towered higher, and the southern winter lay ahead. To grasp the full horror of the deteriorating climate, it is necessary only to translate degrees of southern latitude into northern latitude. Rio de Janeiro, where they had first landed, is as far below the equator as Key West is above it. By the same reckoning the Río de la Plata is comparable to northern Florida, the Golfo San Matías to Boston, and Puerto San Julián, which they reached after thirty-seven days of struggling through shocking weather, to Nova Scotia. The sails of their five little ships were whitened by sleet and hail. Cyclones battered them twice a week or more. Both forecastles and after-castles had been repeatedly blown away on every vessel and replaced by ship's carpenters. Crews shrank as the corpses of men pried loose from frozen rigging slid to briny graves. Yet the paso remained as elusive as ever.

In dismal, chilly, miserable Puerto San Julián, having inched down 1,330 miles since leaving the Río de la Plata, Magellan decided to hole up in winter quarters. They had reached the forty-ninth parallel — the forty-ninth degree of south latitude. There, on Saturday, March 31, he told his royal captains that he meant to continue south until he had found the strait, even if it took them below seventy degrees. Some thought they heard him promise to turn back if their frustration continued as far down as seventy-five degrees south latitude, but if he said it, he cannot have known what it meant; at that parallel the fleet would have been frozen fast in what is now the Antarctic's Weddell Sea. Nevertheless his mood was undeniably implacable. Sunday morning — Palm Sunday — he reduced bread and wine rations for all hands. Almost certainly he intended to provoke revolt. He was aware that the tinder was there, awaiting a spark. There were Spaniards in the crews who were loyal to their Castilian officers. And the dons, he knew, were in an ugly mood. On Monday he summoned them to dine with him. Their refusal was curt. It was a *desafío*, a

---

*Vespucci claimed that he had sailed to fifty degrees south latitude in 1502, but he has never been taken seriously.

challenge; in effect they had thrown down the gauntlet. And that
evening, April 2, 1520, they mutinied.

THEY CAME AT NIGHT — thirty armed Spaniards in a longboat, led
by Juan de Cartagena, Antonio de Coca, and Gaspar de Quesada,
rowing with muffled oars toward *San Antonio,* the largest ship in
the fleet. King Carlos's privy council would have been surprised
to know that Cartagena no longer commanded the ship. In Valladolid the planners of the expedition had envisaged the capitán-
general on the quarterdeck of the flagship *Trinidad,* with the Castilians commanding the other four. But once at sea, Magellan,
exercising his supreme powers as admiral, had begun switching
skippers. Now, six and a half months after their departure, a
Portuguese officer, Álvaro de Mesquita, one of Magellan's cousins, conned *San Antonio.* Only *Concepción* and *Victoria* remained
in the hands of the dons. If Cartagena could regain his old command, however, the mutineers, controlling three vessels, could
bar the way to the open sea and hold their admiral at bay. And
aboard *San Antonio,* all hands were asleep. Why Magellan had not
alerted Mesquita and ordered him to post guards is puzzling. Ordinarily he was the most vigilant of leaders, and the omens of
trouble had been unmistakable. Perhaps he could not believe they
would actually rebel. They were, after all, well-bred aristocrats,
who had sworn holy oaths of obedience in Seville. And treachery
was not only a capital offense; it was also shameful. He may also
have doubted their resolve. In the coming days they were, in fact,
to prove irresolute, but at the outset they moved with confidence,
swarming up rope ladders and boarding the big ship, which
quickly became their prize. Mesquita awoke to find himself surrounded by men with drawn swords, and, moments later, man-
acled and confined to the purser's cabin. Until now the coup had
been bloodless. Then Mesquita's officers, wakened by the tumult,
demanded an explanation, and one of them, the ship's master,
Juan de Elorriaga, roughly challenged the mutineers. Quesada and
his servant knifed Elorriaga six times; the officer fell to the deck
mortally wounded. That ended the resistance. After clapping all
crewmen loyal to Magellan in irons, the mutineers broke into the

storeroom and issued wine to the rest of the men. Quesada remained aboard and brought Juan Sebastián del Cano over to serve
as master. The others quietly returned to their own ships.

Tuesday morning Magellan rose as usual, unaware of any
change in his command. He was soon to be enlightened. In winter
quarters the fleet's daily routine began with dispatching a ship's
boat ashore. Its mission there was to fetch water and wood for all
five vessels, each of which contributed men to the working party.
When the boat reached *San Antonio,* its bos'n was vexed to find
no rope ladder lowered and no crewmen ready to join him. He
angrily called for an explanation and was told that the ship was
now under the command of Capitán Gaspar de Quesada, who no
longer honored orders from the "*así llamado*" ("so-called") capitán-
general. The bos'n hastily returned to *Trinidad.* Magellan calmly
instructed him to tour the other vessels, demanding pledges of
loyalty. *Victoria* and *Concepción* refused. Only *Santiago*'s Serrano,
Spanish but loyal, swore that he would remain so.

Thus the lines of battle were drawn. In any fight *Santiago* —
at seventy-five tons the smallest of the five — would be quickly
sunk. The flagship could not continue round the world alone. The
admiral seemed checkmated, but his dilemma over the paso —
not to mention his temperament — meant that yielding was out
of the question. Now, as so often, patience was his sheet anchor.
He quietly awaited word from the rebels. When that word
arrived — in the form of a letter from Quesada, speaking for the
others — it revealed their pathetic weakness. Their noble birth
was to be their undoing after all. The letter expressed no wrath,
no piratical defiance; there was no ultimatum, nor even a list of
demands. Instead the dons were submitting a *suplica,* a petition.
On reflection they had decided to acknowledge his supreme authority, as conferred by their sovereign. In their subordinate role
they merely asked for better treatment at his hands, a little respect
for their high birth, and some information about his plans, particularly how he proposed to reach the Spice Islands. All this was
set forth in the most florid, most oleaginous Spanish prose.

Mutineers may command, but they cannot beg. Their strength
derives from force alone; if they disavow it, they are naked. Magellan now had their measure; with audacity, he could regain

control of his fleet. He knew the rebel captains expected him to lunge toward *San Antonio*. The ship's size argued for that; so did his cousin's imprisonment there; so did the presence on its quarterdeck of Quesada, now the chief conspirator. Therefore Magellan, knowing the value of the unexpected, decided to retake *Victoria*, whose Castilian commander was the less formidable Luis de Mendoza. The counterattack would be made by two longboats. The larger boat, with the wind at its back, would carry fifteen heavily armed men led by Duarte Barbosa. To lead the other, smaller craft the admiral picked Gonzalo Gómez de Espinosa, the fleet's master-at-arms and commander of its marine guard. Gómez's crew consisted of only five men, but its mission was crucial — to strike the first blow and thereby create a diversion.

Piloting his boat to within hailing distance of *Victoria*, Gómez called ahead that he bore a letter from the capitán-general. Mendoza, feeling unthreatened by the little boat — he had sixty Spaniards behind him — gave the master-at-arms permission to board. That closed the trap, for while Gómez had the undivided attention of the ship's crew, Barbosa and his men, unobserved in the bleak fog, slipped around the vessel's lee side.

Magellan's letter bluntly summoned Mendoza to the flagship. After reading it, the don, scornful of so obvious a trap, cried derisively, "You won't catch me going there!" — "*¡No me pillarás allá!*" His laugh was cut off; Gómez, with one violent slash, had slit his throat. That was a signal to Barbosa and his party; they sprang on deck and attacked the mutineers from behind. Within minutes *Victoria* was the admiral's prize and Barbosa was issuing orders to hoist sails. Before the other two rebel ships could grasp what had happened, *Trinidad, Santiago,* and *Victoria* had formed a rough line across the mouth of the bay, cutting off the only line of escape. Helpless, they capitulated. Mesquita, freed from his irons, chaired the subsequent court-martial. On Saturday his cousin the capitán-general passed sentence.

Knowing he would need as many hands as possible once he resumed the voyage, Magellan spared all but Quesada, Cartagena, and a Spanish priest who had fomented the rebellion. There was only one execution; Quesada, guilty of murder, had to die. Because he was an aristocrat, he was spared the garrote. But there was also

blood on the hands of his servant, Luis de Molino. Molino protested that he had only been obeying orders, and Magellan, giving
that weight, told him that he would be permitted to live provided
he swung the blade decapitating his master — a grisly choice,
though it cannot have taken Molino long to make it. As was
customary in that time, the bodies of both treacherous captains,
Mendoza and Quesada, were drawn and quartered, after which
the reeking, bleeding quarters were displayed on poles, the theory
being that the spectacle would intimidate any men too dull to have
learned the wages of mutiny.

That left Cartagena, who had held high office under the king,
and the priest, an anointed man of God. The capitán-general could
not bring himself to shed the blood of either. Yet carrying them
around the world in irons was impractical. Therefore they were
to be imprisoned until the fleet departed Puerto San Julián and
then left behind. As the five vessels sailed on August 24, the two
marooned men were abandoned on the frigid shore with a thin
ration of wine and food. Magellan had declared that he was leaving
their fate to a merciful God, but in the sixteenth century the quality
of divine mercy had proved to be strained and brackish. During
the wretched days that lay ahead for the castaways they may have
envied their drawn and quartered co-conspirators.

But at that point Magellan's prospects did not appear to be
much brighter. In quelling the mutiny he had, in a sense, increased
the odds against himself. If he reappeared in Seville discredited by
failure, it was doubtful that Spanish authorities would accept his
version of the violent interlude in San Julián. The gruesome deaths
of three Castilian noblemen and a priest would certainly be in-
vestigated, and it was by no means certain that the dons' mild
suplica would be seen as justification for execution. The capitán-
general might well find himself on trial for murder. Only if he
returned a conqueror could he expect amnesty, and as weeks
wore on conquest had seemed more elusive than ever. The armada
was down to four ships now; *Santiago,* sent on an exploring mission, had been lost in a storm. Mighty gales tossed them daily;
the weather was growing steadily worse. To the west, snow-
capped mountains were clearly visible. They began to see "sea-
wolves," or seals, and penguins, which they called "ducks without

wings" ("*patos sin alas*"). After anchoring below fifty degrees south latitude, Magellan decided to hibernate for another eight weeks, until he could be certain that winter was spent. By now he must have been close to total despair. Every hope had died glimmering. The possibility of redemption seemed very remote. During a year at sea he had covered nearly nine thousand miles, suppressed a bloody uprising, explored every indentation in what seemed to be an endless coast of rocks and sand, and found absolutely nothing.

His desolation was ironic, for during those eight fearful, brooding weeks, from August 26 to October 18, he was only 150 miles — two sailing days — from immortality.

ON SUNDAY, October 21, 1520, a day of high, harsh, howling winds, lookouts clinging to the fleet's topmasts sighted a steep eminence which, as they approached, was perceived as a wall of naked white cliffs. Closing, they saw that these formed a cape, beyond which lay an immense bay of black water. The day was St. Ursula's. In remembrance of her, Magellan christened the peninsula Cabo de los Vírgenes. But his officers, still dreaming of the south seas, were unimpressed. The sound, all four pilots agreed, was a fjord similar to those which had been observed in Norway. "We all believed," Don Antonio Pigafetta wrote afterward, "that it was a blind alley." Only their commander was curious. However, because he had wasted over three weeks investigating the Río de la Plata nine months earlier, he could spare little for this exploration. He told *San Antonio* and *Concepción* that he wanted them to see how far westward they could sail into the bay, but he wanted them back in five days at most.

As the fifth day waned with no sign of them, he grew anxious, and then was alarmed when the lookout in the masthead of his flagship reported a distant column of smoke — then the maritime signal sent by shipwrecked sailors. Magellan was issuing the order to lower boats when the sails of both missing vessels appeared off the port bow. They were gaily decorated with flags, all hands were shouting and waving, and as they hove to their cannons fired three thundering salvos. Clearly something extraordinary had happened.

Serrano boarded the flagship from *Concepción* to explain. They had been approaching the western end of the harbor, he reported, when a squall overtook them. As it cleared they saw that the bay did not end. Instead a channel — "first narrows," he called it — opened. Passing through this, they had entered a broad body of water, then "second narrows," followed by another widening in the channel. On the third day they had to turn about, to return in the five days allotted them. But they had found no end to the passage; every narrowing led to another opening. The width of the labyrinthine waterway varied from two to twenty miles. Seamen casting lead had found no bottom. They had not entered a river; the water was brine all the way, and on both sides the tides ebbed and flowed.

The stoical Magellan betrayed no excitement, but he called for a final salvo of bombards in honor of King Carlos — who, unknown to him, was now being crowned Emperor Charles V — and led his men in prayer. The following morning, Thursday, October 25, with his *Trinidad* leading the way, all four ships glided past the barren headlands, and entered the strange new watercourse, named Canal de Todos los Santos by the capitán-general but known to history as the Strait of Magellan. Off his starboard prow, although he did not know it, was the southernmost tip of what is now known as South America; to port, a large island and a maze of smaller islands beneath which lay Cape Horn, some 350 miles above the Antarctic Peninsula. So cold was the island maze that the shivering Indians who lived there warmed themselves over perpetual fires. The flames, visible to Magellan, prompted him to call the southern shore Tierra del Fuego — Land of Fire.

Negotiating the strait's tortuous turns later challenged sailors of all ages, but for the flota's helmsmen, dependent upon wooden tillers and clumsy, bellying sails, it was exhausting. The passage was a confused, tangled skein. At various points it led westward, northward, and southward. Again and again it halved and became *two* channels, forcing the admiral to pause and divide his command until he knew which one was the throughway. The bays assumed weird shapes. In the lateral channels rocks, appearing beneath sudden shoals, threatened to gouge holes in the ships' bottoms, and on the first day one wild squall followed another, sometimes threatening to capsize the lead ship, Magellan's *Trinidad*. Then the weather improved. In this they were singularly lucky; subsequent navigators found that foul weather was usually prevalent throughout the strait. Indeed, that became a major reason for their failure to get through it.

After a month in the seaway no one doubted that they had found the legendary paso. Three hundred miles of it lay behind them, and now unfamiliar birds flew overhead, a sure sign of another ocean ahead. Another fork confronted them. After ordering *San Antonio* and *Concepción* to spend a maximum of five days investigating the southeastern route — *Trinidad* and *Victoria* would wait here — Magellan called a meeting of his officers. He faced a decision — whether to sail home with news of their discovery or continue on to the Spice Islands — and he wanted their reports on the amount of provisions left. All told the same story: soon they would be running short. The holds contained three months of supplies, no more. Estevão Gomes, pilot of the *San Antonio,* argued vehemently that they should turn back. Stores were not the only consideration, he said; the ships were badly in need of refitting. Furthermore, no one knew the distance between them and the islands. If it was far, the entire fleet might perish on the merciless ocean, victims of thirst and starvation, their fate forever unknown.

It was good advice. Magellan chose to ignore it. They would push on, he said; no doubt there would be hardships, but even if they had to eat the leather on the ships' yards, he would keep his promise to King Carlos, trusting to God to help them and provide them with good fortune ("*de pasar adelante y descubrir lo que había prometido*"). The captains were enjoined, on pain of death, from telling their men of the supply shortage. Gomes was unconvinced, however; the prospect of sailing onward frightened him even more than Magellan's threat of death and mutilation for mutineers. He decided to quit the armada with his ship. During the scouting of the southeastern channel, *San Antonio,* with Mesquita in command, showed Serrano's *Concepción* its heels. Serrano did not know precisely what had happened, but since desertion by the capitán-general's cousin was impossible, he inferred that the pilot had led a successful revolt against the captain. Magellan had to face the hard fact that his biggest ship, with the bulk of his stores, was headed homeward. He was now down to three bottoms, and the supply situation, bad as it had been, was now worse. Yet he never considered altering his course. In an order issued "in the Channel of Todos los Santos, off the mouth of the Río del Isleo, on November 21, fifty-three degrees south of the equator," he declared that as "capitán-general of this armada" he had taken the "grave decision to continue the voyage."

His resolution was strengthened when another pinnace, sent ahead, reappeared on the third day with the electrifying news that Balboa's Mar del Sur had been found. Hurrying there, the admiral looked out on the prize Columbus, Cabot, Vespucci, and Pinzón had sought in vain: the mightiest of oceans, stretching to all horizons, deep and blue and vast with promise. Its peaceful, *pacífico* appearance inspired his name for it, though that came later. In that first rapturous moment he could not speak. Perhaps for the first time in his adult life, he was overcome by emotion, and his reserve broke. Don Antonio writes that *"il capitano-generale lacrimó per allegrezza"* — Magellan had burst into tears.

THE LITTLE armada's 12,600-mile crossing of the Pacific, the greatest physical unit on earth, is one of history's imperishable tales of the sea, and like so many of the others it is a story of extraordinary human suffering, of agony so excruciating that only those who have been pushed to the extremes of human endurance can even comprehend it. Lacking maps, adequate navigational instruments, or the remotest idea of where they were, they sailed onward for over three months, from November to March, moving northwestward under frayed rigging, rotting sails, and a pitiless sun.

Even for the age of discovery, Magellan's situation was unique. Previous explorers had known that if all else failed, they could always return to Europe. That option was closed to him. Ignorant of South America — having started from the mouth of a strait known only to him — he had no base to fall back upon. Once he had left the eastern horizon behind, he had to sail on — and on, and on.

He had no way of knowing the true width of the Pacific. All the information available to him vastly underestimated its extent.

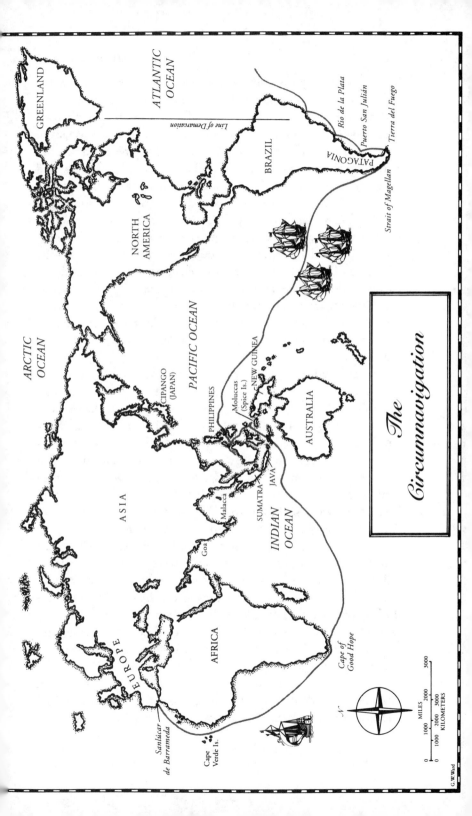

ATLANTIC OCEAN

GREENLAND

Line of Demarcation

Rio de la Plata

Puerto San Julián

Tierra del Fuego

PATAGONIA

BRAZIL

Strait of Magellan

NORTH AMERICA

ARCTIC OCEAN

PACIFIC OCEAN

CIPANGO (JAPAN)

PHILIPPINES

Moluccas (Spice Is.)

NEW GUINEA

AUSTRALIA

ASIA

Malacca

SUMATRA

JAVA

INDIAN OCEAN

Goa

EUROPE

AFRICA

Cape of Good Hope

Sanlúcar de Barrameda

Cape Verde Is.

The Circumnavigation

N

MILES
0   1000   2000   3000

KILOMETERS
0   1000   2000   3000

G. W. Ward

In Europe it was assumed that everything depended upon the location of Ptolemy's Terra Australis Incognita, a necessary balance for a spherical world, without which the entire planet would topple over. But some assumptions had been made, and Magellan was acting upon them. In fact they were all wrong. Had he been told the actual distance that lay ahead of his small boats, he would have been incredulous; no one in Europe had ever dreamed that so broad a sea even existed. It was as though all his sources of information — the cartographers, astronomers, and cosmographers of the time — had conspired to betray him. Schöner's globe, then thought reliable, put Japan only a few hundred leagues west of Mexico. Indeed, everything Magellan had read or heard had encouraged him to believe that after a short cruise he would raise Dai Nippon. Instead he was lost on the earth's greatest ocean, a trackless seascape so enormous that if all the earth's landmasses were dumped into it, thousands of miles of water would still remain.

The expedition had left Sanlúcar with 420 casks of wine. All were drained. One by one the other staples vanished — cheese, dried fish, salt pork, beans, peas, anchovies, cereals, onions, raisins, and lentils — until they were left with kegs of brackish, foul-smelling water and biscuits which, having first crumbled into a gray powder, were now slimy with rat droppings and alive with maggots. These, mixed with sawdust, formed a vile muck men could get down only by holding their noses. Rats, which could be roasted, were so prized that they sold for half a ducat each. The capitán-general had warned them that they might have to eat leather, and it came to that. Desperate to appease their stomach pangs, "the famine-stricken fellows," wrote Antonio Pigafetta, who was one of them, "were forced to gnaw the hides with which the mainyard was covered to prevent chafing." Because these leather strips had been hardened by "the sun and rain and wind," he explained, "we were obliged to soften them by putting them overboard four or five days, after which we cooked them on embers and ate them thus."

The serenity of the Pacific maddened the crews. Yet, as Don Antonio realized, it also saved them: "But for the grace of God and the Blessed Virgin in sending us such magnificent weather, we should all have perished in this gigantic ocean." Some died anyhow; nineteen succumbed to starvation and were heaved overboard. Those left were emaciated, hollow-cheeked wraiths, their flesh covered with ulcers and bellies distended by edema. Scurvy swelled their gums, teeth fell out, sores formed inside their mouths; swallowing became almost impossible, and then, for the doomed, completely impossible. Too weak to rise, some men sprawled on decks, cowering in patches of shade; those able to stand hobbled about on sticks, babbling to themselves, senile men in their early twenties.

No other vessels crossed their path; indeed, in the six months that passed after they left San Julián they did not encounter another soul. False hopes were raised twice, about halfway through their ordeal, when islands were sighted which proved to be uninhabited and with no bottom for anchoring. Finally, on March 6, 1521, when the life expectancy of the hardiest of them could have been measured in days, they made a genuine landfall. It was Guam in the Marianas, then a nameless isle which, they found, was inhabited by hostile Micronesians — natives who were alienated, perhaps, by the stench emanating from the very bowels of the three wretched ships. Nevertheless Guam provided them with a reprieve. After a warrior party had paddled out to the fleet and stolen a skiff, Magellan sent forty armed men ashore to recover it. They returned with the skiff, and, far more important, fresh water, fish, fruit, poultry, and meat.

Pressing on after three days of convalescence, *Trinidad, Concepción,* and *Victoria* sighted the large Philippine island of Samar on March 16, and then, south of it, tiny Suluan and its neighbor, Homonhon, in the entrance to what is now Leyte Gulf. According to Pigafetta, the capitán-general believed that he had found the Moluccas, but that is highly improbable; Magellan was too skillful a navigator, and knew Oceania too well, to have confused north and south latitude. The Spice Islands were over a thousand miles away. The likeliest explanation for Don Antonio's confusion is that the admiral, realizing there was no hope of wrenching the Moluccas away from Portugal, had decided to make amends by staking another claim in the name of the Spanish king. And that is precisely what he did, declaring the archipelago, together with all men and beasts therein, to be the property of His Christian Majesty, the sovereign of Castile and Aragon.*

He had chosen to go ashore on Homonhon because it appeared to be uninhabited; his men were too sick to cope with another unfriendly reception. But some natives, beaming with hospitality, crossed over from Suluan bringing quantities of oranges, palm wine, fowls, vegetables, and an abundance of two nutritious delicacies new to the Europeans: bananas and coconuts. When the admiral responded with gifts of bright kerchiefs, bells and bracelets of brass, gaudy red caps, and colored glass beads, they were delighted.

In their pleasure the capitán-general found a kind of retroactive exoneration. The port officials in Sanlúcar had laughed at his cargo manifests listing such gewgaws. Indeed, the privy council in Valladolid had at first balked when it found itself being billed for, among other trifles, a thousand mirrors, fifty dozen pairs of scissors, and twenty thousand noisemakers. He had explained that he anticipated possible difficulties in establishing rapport with strange natives, and his service in the Orient had convinced him that trinkets would smooth the way. After he had once more paraded his knowledge of islands — even exhibiting his Malayan slave Enrique — the privy council had deferred to his judgment, but the ridicule of the officious panjandrums on the docks had rankled him.

Enrique was still with him, and now, three years after he had been a privileged spectator at his master's royal audience, this retainer unexpectedly presented him with a gift beyond price. On March 25, during their second week in the Philippines, the expedition moved on to the neighboring island of Limasawa. They were in the Visayan Islands, a part of the enormous Philippine archipelago which is linked, culturally and linguistically, with Sumatra and Malaya. Shortly after they had landed on the new island Magellan heard a great cheering and, moving toward the noise, found his servant surrounded by merry natives. It took a while to sort things out. Born in the Visayans, Enrique had been sold

---

*He christened the islands San Lázaro. Twenty years later they were renamed for Philip II, "the most Catholic of kings."

into slavery in Sumatra and sent to Malacca, where Magellan had acquired him. Since leaving the Malayan Peninsula in 1512, he had accompanied his owner to India, Africa, Portugal, Spain, and, for the past eighteen months, on this voyage. An apt linguist, he was fluent in both Portuguese and Spanish, but here on Limasawa, for the first time since his childhood, he had overheard people speaking his native language. He had joined in, and they had welcomed him as one of their own.

The significance of this incident was enormous. Enrique was merely happy, chattering away in Malayan, but Magellan was ecstatic. Both were back on familiar ground, which meant that by sailing westward they had returned to the lands where they had first met. Obviously Enrique was the first circumnavigator of the world. By completing the circuit of the globe, the expedition had provided the first empirical proof that it was a sphere.

In Christendom it was Semana Santa, Holy Week. A full year had passed since the San Julián mutiny. The paso had been found and threaded, the great ocean crossed, and the earth circumnavigated. Magellan and his men were rejoicing, riding high on a cloud of euphoria, which was both understandable and ominous — ominous because they were celebrating in one way, he in another, and the two would become irreconcilable. They entered a collision course after April 7, when Magellan spent three days sailing his flota to the much larger island of Cebu, between Leyte and Negros. There the interplay between the commander and his crews took on overtones of dramatic conflict, which was to end tragically.

The seamen were expressing their jubilation in the immemorial manner of men who have cheated death. They were mostly young, and after two weeks of rest and a restorative diet they felt virile. None had known female companionship since leaving Brazil at the end of 1519, five seasons earlier. Even if the girls on Cebu had been sheathed in Mother Hubbards, the crews' discipline would have yielded to lust. As it was, by custom only married women wore clothing. The youths were surrounded by naked, nubile maidens who stirred uncontrollable desire in sailors who had been raised in a society which regarded nudity as prurient. The proximity of the sexes provided maximum temptation, the dense jungle offered maximum opportunity, and the predictable result was a saturnalia. The men ran wild. Afterward they said that the Filipino maidens preferred white lovers, finding them exotic and more vigorous than native boys. Of course, that was what they would say. Yet there has never been any suggestion that their advances were resisted. Apparently the apposition of the two cultures created a powerful sexual tension. The crewmen, being Christians, were afflicted with a sense of sin which increased their carnal appetites, while the guiltless, innocent girls enjoyed wanton tumbles beneath the banyans and, afterward, the gift of a mirror, a bracelet, a bangle, or a knife.

All this should have been anticipated. It had been, in the sense that Magellan's standing orders forbade it. But orders do not enforce themselves, particularly under such circumstances. A martinet was needed, and Magellan was exhibiting a strange passivity, wholly out of character and entirely inadequate to the crisis. He did attempt one corrective measure; on his orders the fleet chaplain, Pedro de Valderrama, denounced sexual intercourse with pagan women as a mortal sin. Unfortunately the only consequence of that was an irreverent farce; before mounting the girls, seamen baptized them, thus desecrating a holy rite and reducing the padre's threat to a joke. The Filipino men, of course, did not find it laughable. Their pride was deeply wounded. As the debauchery continued, fathers and brothers decided that their hospitality was being exploited, and for husbands the humiliation was even greater. The writhing women in the bush were not only sisters and daughters; many were also wives. Some of the seamen were running amok in harems, where gifts of mirrors and bracelets were also appreciated. The situation was volatile, deteriorating, and building dangerously.

Although venery was the most flagrant of the crews' offenses, it was not the only one. Other standing orders of the armada were being flouted, and by officers as well as men. Indeed, the worst offender was the capitán-general's brother-in-law. Since the fall Magellan's most trusted captains had been Duarte Barbosa, captain of *Victoria,* and the Castilian Juan Serrano, *Concepción*'s commander. Private trade with the natives was forbidden to all members of the armada, yet some officers, *Victoria*'s skipper among them, were surreptitiously bartering iron, new to the islands and obviously useful, for gold and pearls, which, to Philippine peasants who hadn't the remotest idea of their value on the other side of the world, were commonplace and useless. Barbosa was also guilty of drunkenness, absence without leave, and a record of prurience which was remarkable even in the midst of what had become, in effect, a festival of lechery. During this critical period Magellan's mind was on other things, but after marines brought his brother-in-law staggering back to his ship after a three-day binge, the capitán-general had to act. Barbosa was arrested, shackled, demoted, and deprived of his command.

Had the admiral hewed to that line, restoring order by brandishing the whip, he might have survived the voyage to enjoy the fruits of his great success. But in those heady days, carried away by his sense of exultation, he too had abandoned himself to excesses. As his men wallowed in indulgence, he was exploring another extreme. Since his arrival in the Philippines he had been gripped by a religious fever. It was not an immaculate piety; like the European missionaries who followed him to far lands over the next four centuries, he confused evangelical zeal with colonial imperialism. Even as he converted Filipinos to Christianity, he also expected them to accept Spanish sovereignty. He saw no divided loyalties in this, no dual objectives; to him it was one crusade, with crucifix and flag advancing together.

EASTER'S ARRIVAL on March 31, their first Sunday at Limasawa, had provided an opportunity which, the devout Magellan believed, was God-sent. He had seized it by entertaining his hosts on Limasawa with a theological version of bangles and beads — a flamboyant Mass. Padre Valderrama was asked to celebrate the services with flair, and the flota's officers were ordered to provide him with every possible assistance. Their commander wanted a show, and he got it. An altar having been brought ashore, a glittering cross was attached to it. The priest, wearing his vestments, performed Eastertide rituals, after which the capitán-general and his men approached in twos, kissed the crucifix, and received the host while gunners aboard the ships fired volleys and all hands cheered.

The armada's guests that morning had been Rajah Colambu, whose Mindanao jurisdiction included Suluan, and his brother Siaui. Already Magellan was singling out influential chieftains for attention — men who, once they had accepted Christ, could rule in the king's name until royal administrators arrived from Spain. The Easter spectacle had served its purpose admirably. After Valderrama's Mass the two guests of honor had knelt before the altar, imitated the movements of the supplicants who had preceded them, and then, according to one account, ordered native carpenters to build a cross so large that when it had been "set on the summit of the highest mountain in the neighborhood, all might see and adore it." Before their departure, Magellan had told the brothers that if they should find themselves at war with other, pagan, natives, his men and ships would be at their disposal. If that force did not prove adequate, he would return from Spain with one which was.

On Cebu he stalked a more powerful figure, his majesty the rajah Datu Humabon, ruler of the great island. The rajah's entourage included a Muslim trader who had just arrived from Siam on a junk and who, recognizing the cross of St. James on the sails of the arriving fleet, whispered that these visitors were the pillagers of India and Malaya. Humabon ignored the warning; warming to the capitán-general from their first meeting, the rajah immediately consented, through Enrique, to a perpetual treaty of peace with Spain. Pressed by Magellan, he also agreed to burn his pagan idols and worship Jesus Christ as his lord and savior. Once more Magellan played the role of stage manager; the rajah's initiation in his new faith, celebrated on the second Sunday after Easter, was even more liturgical and ostentatious than the earlier Mass on Limasawa. Humabon's subjects massed densely outdoors round a market square, in the midst of which an altar, decorated with palm branches, dominated a high platform. Behind the altar and beneath a sheltering canopy were two thrones wreathed in red and purple satin. Humabon occupied one throne; the other awaited the arrival of the capitán-general.

Magellan made a spectacular entrance. Wearing an immaculate white robe and preceded by forty men in gleaming armor, he advanced beneath the fluttering silken banner of Castile and

Aragon, unfurled here for the first time since it had been presented to him, twenty months earlier, in Seville's church of Santa María de la Victoria. As a band played stirring marches, the armada's officers paraded behind their leader. The Spaniards bowed their heads, a large cross was raised above the platform, and the fleet's cannons boomed across the harbor. That nearly ended the ceremony. The native congregation, hearing gunfire for the first time, panicked, began to scatter, and returned only when they saw that their ruler — who had been forewarned — remained composed and enthroned.

The rajah knelt and was baptized; Magellan, as his godfather, renamed him Don Carlos. His majesty's heir, his brother, and his nephew, the king of Limasawa, followed him to the font; so, unhappily, did the Muslim trader from Siam, who had been given no choice. They were christened Hernando, Juan, Miguel, and Cristóbal. All that was pro forma, in Spain if not in the Philippines, but the rituals which followed would have stunned Christians throughout Europe, Catholic and otherwise. Worshipers of the Lord Jesus were expected to be monogamous, or at least to pay monogamy lip service. Humabon, however, had drawn the line there. He wanted to save his soul but refused to abandon his harem. After protracted negotiations Magellan had succeeded where the emissaries of Henry VIII, in their appeals to Pope Clement, had failed. Padre Valderrama was persuaded to overlook the rajah's little quirk. Therefore the women, costumed and gaudy with lipstick and fingernail polish, were presented one by one (there were forty in all) and blessed with such Spanish names as Juana, Catarina, Juanita, and Isabella. Humabon's favorite — Doña Johanna, as she now was, the namesake, unknown to her, of Spain's demented queen mother — received special recognition. Because she outranked the others, Magellan presented her with a carved image of the Madonna and child. Then the spectators were invited to enjoy Christian rebirths themselves.

Only a few hundred came forward then, but by the end of the following week virtually every inhabitant of Cebu — a total of twenty-two hundred, according to one of the flota's crew — had chosen Christ. The surge in conversions was a personal triumph for Magellan. It was also a striking example of how a religious fanatic, which is what he had become, may be invested with psychic gifts. After the royal christenings at the outdoor Mass, Humabon, taking him aside, had told him that one member of the island's ruling family longed to be baptized but had been too ill to attend, and was, in fact, dying. Investigating, the capitán-general had found the man so sick that, in the words of Don Antonio, he "could neither speak nor move." Magellan discovered something else; the women nursing the afflicted man were also praying for him, but praying as heathens — thus seeking to propitiate the pagan idols their rajah had just repudiated. Shocked and indignant, the admiral-become-preacher denounced the infidel nurses, sent them away, and decided to try his hand at faith healing. With Humabon as his witness, he vowed to demonstrate how belief in Christ could cure the doomed. After baptizing the patient, the patient's wife, and their ten children, he asked the man how he felt. Miraculously reinvested with the power of speech, the invalid replied haltingly that he felt well. Magellan put him on a regimen of milk and herbs, and within five days the man who had been given up for lost was 'up and about.

THIS FEAT made a tremendous impression on both the Filipinos and the officers of the fleet, though the two saw it very differently. The natives became passionate converts, while the officers worried. Increasingly they had been troubled by their commander's state of religious exaltation. They considered themselves devout, but they were aware that God, in his wisdom, did not smile consistently upon those who sought to work miracles. All were familiar with, or had heard of, at least one religieux who had suffered a humiliating public disappointment, and they were chilled by the thought of what might have happened if their commander's patient had collapsed before his eyes and died. Furthermore, they regarded Magellan's altruistic, indulgent approach to the natives as folly, contrasting sharply with the Iberian school of colonial administration developed by earlier explorers. Had this expedition been led by Cortés, or the pitiless Da Gama, the Filipinos would now be unchristened slaves. Not all of Magellan's lieutenants felt that way, and none was prepared to reproach him

to his face, but all agreed that after three weeks on Cebu it was
time to resume the voyage.

At an officers' council, called by their commander, they proposed immediate departure. No mention was made of the growing
hostility of the native men, a consequence of the seamen's goatish
rampages. Instead they advanced their strongest arguments, and
chose their ablest spokesmen to advance them. Serrano, now the
armada's senior captain, pointed out that they had been sent, not
as colonizers or priests, but to find the western route to the Spice
Islands. That was their sole mission. In fact, their royal orders
specifically forbade deviation from it. Others spoke up. At their
last council, they recalled, the capitán-general had justified the call
at this port on the ground that, in reporting to the king, they
could more fully describe the archipelago's possibilities. They now
knew all they needed to know about Cebu. There was no reason
to remain any longer. It was time to go.

Once again Magellan disagreed. Having discovered the Philippines, he believed it his duty to assure their loyalty to Spain.
To him the Datu Humabon was no longer a native chieftain; he
was Don Carlos, a Christian king. Then, to the horror of the
council, he revealed that he had given this ruler certain assurances.
They were, in effect, a repetition of his guarantee to the brothers
Colambu and Siaui. The enemies of Humabon-Carlos, the rajah-
king, were also Spain's enemies. Any man who refused to acknowledge his sovereignty — or the divinity of Christ — would
be killed and his property confiscated.

Such an enemy, he told the astonished council, existed. His
name was Lapulapu, and he was the petty rajah of Mactan, a tiny
isle nearby. Traditionally Mactan had fallen within the dominion
of Cebu's rajah, but Lapulapu was an irascible insurgent. He was
also particularly hostile toward the men in the Spanish fleet; recently he had ignored a requisition for supplies to feed the visitors.
Magellan regarded this refusal as an excellent reason for a trial of
strength. He intended to form a punitive shore party, armed seamen who would teach the defiant pagan a lesson, and he had
decided to lead it himself.

His officers were appalled. The Spanish monarch had expressly ordered the capitán-general to remain with the fleet, aloof from all landing parties. Indeed, it was a basic principle of both the Spanish and Portuguese governments that the leaders of naval expeditions should never risk their lives in such hazardous adventures. Duarte Barbosa reminded his brother-in-law that the last man to ignore that rule, Juan Díaz de Solís, had been killed at the Río de la Plata. Magellan waved him off. Since his triumphant debut as a faith healer he had felt invincible. In the coming fight, he told the council, he would rely on the cross of Jesus and the support of his patroness, Our Lady of Victory. Armed as he was by them, he could not fail.

NOW IN LATE APRIL of 1521, on the eve of this wholly unnecessary battle, Magellan was everything he had never been. He had never before been reckless, imprudent, careless, or forgetful of the tactical lessons he had learned during Portuguese operations in East Africa, India, Morocco, and Malaya. But he had not been a soldier of Christ then. Here, shielded by divine intervention, he scorned the precautions observed by mortal men preparing for action. Professional fighting men value deception, secrecy, surprise. He announced to Spaniards and Filipinos alike that he would invade Mactan on Saturday, April 27 — he believed it was his lucky day — and he invited the people of Cebu to come watch. Before going into action professional fighters study the terrain, and, if the operation is to be amphibious, the tides. Because he disdained all he had learned, he was unaware of Mactan's encircling reef, which at low tide — at the hour he had chosen for his attack — would prevent his ships from providing covering fire. Professionals court allies. He loftily declined the rajah-king's offer of a thousand veteran warriors, rejected Crown Prince Lumai's suggestion that he take the enemy from the rear with a diversionary landing, and rebuffed the Cacique Zula, a Mactan rival of Lapu-lapu, who proposed that he attack the flank of the rebel chief as the Spaniards waded ashore. Magellan urged each of them to join the spectators, including all the converted chieftains, who would watch from a score of balangays — native canoes — offshore. He needed no help, he said; he and his men could, and would, do the job alone.

Magellan's strategy was not without precedent. Samuel Eliot Morison points out that "almost every group of European intruders into Africa and America felt that to cement an alliance with the nearest tribe of natives they must deploy fire power against next-door enemies." Champlain in Canada, Cortés in Mexico, the English in the Carolinas, the Portuguese in India and Africa — all had conquered by dividing. "But," Morison adds, "for Magellan to do it here, when he had the local situation well in hand, was utter folly."

He might have pulled it off, had he picked the right men, and enough of them, and then handled them properly. Estimates of the force which would oppose him range from 1,500 to 2,000 natives, but they were an undisciplined mob, a prey to panic, armed with only the most primitive weapons. The whole lot could have been easily routed by 150 properly equipped Spaniards trained in the use of crossbows and harquebuses and led by Gómez de Espinosa, the armada's alguacil, and his disciplined marines. Cortés and Francisco Pizarro, similarly outnumbered, vanquished the Mexicans and Peruvians. But Magellan spurned conventional approaches. He limited his landing party to 60 seamen because, he said, he intended to show the Filipinos a victory won by Christian soldiers against the greatest odds imaginable. And he wanted to lead only volunteers, 20 from each vessel. This meant that the party would include none of the tough marines, who, deeply offended, stayed on their ships. In the end, according to Don Antonio, Magellan wound up with a motley contingent of unseasoned, unblooded cooks, stewards, and cabin boys — crew temperamentally unsuited for the job ahead, unfamiliar with their weapons, and, as it turned out, inadequately protected by armor, which should have been one of their chief advantages in the fight; corselets and helmets were issued to them, but not — and this was to prove decisive — greaves or leg armor. Lastly, their capitán-general was to be their only officer. That, too, was his doing. Because the members of the council had disapproved of his plan, he had excluded them.

Since the humiliation of Lapulapu would serve as well as his defeat, Magellan decided to give him a final chance. Late Friday evening, as the inexperienced volunteers prepared to pile into three bateaux and row ashore at midnight — undrilled, unrehearsed, unaccompanied even by petty officers — their admiral sent an ultimatum ashore, choosing as couriers his slave Enrique and the Siamese Muslim trader, now known to his fellow Catholics as Cristóbal. The rebel chieftain would be spared, he was told, if he acknowledged the' local suzerainty of Cebu's "Christian king," accepted the Spanish sovereign as his overlord, and paid tribute to Magellan as commander of the armada. If, on the other hand, he persisted in his defiance, he would learn that Spanish lances could wound. Lapulapu scorned the terms. In a fractious reply he jeered that his troops were also armed with lances, fashioned from the finest bamboo, and with fire-hardened stakes. The Spaniards were amused by that, and laughed even harder at the naive post-script. He would be grateful, the petty rajah added, if the Spaniards would delay their attack until morning, when his opposing force would be greater. Here Magellan actually obliged him. Overes-timating his foe's intelligence, he decided that the request was an attempt to trick him into a night attack. He therefore postponed his operation. It hardly mattered. The landing party — sixty men — arrived in the dark anyway. After a brief pull at the oars the three craft ran aground three hours before daybreak.

THEY WERE NOT, however, ashore. When the Saturday sun rose on an ebb tide, they found themselves stranded on the reef, still far from the beach. Realizing that the boats could not negotiate the intervening coral, Magellan detailed eleven men to remain aboard and cover the landing with the bateaux bombards. Then he stepped out into thigh-deep water and ordered the remaining seamen to follow him and storm the shore. Several of the crew repeatedly implored him not to lead, writes Pigafetta, "but he, like a good shepherd, refused to abandon his flock."

As they stumbled forward, encumbered by their armor and waist deep in water, it dawned upon the more experienced of them that there would be no covering fire. The reef was too far out; the boats' small cannons could not reach the enemy. Broadsides from the more powerful guns of the fleet might have been feasible, but Barbosa and Serrano, having been excluded from the mission, were sulking in their bunks below decks, and there was no way their commander could reach them.

The attackers, wading in with all their equipment, were exhausted even before they reached the surf line. There they became confused. Facing them were three forces of naked warriors drawn up, not at the water's edge, as they had expected, but well inland. According to Pigafetta, Lapulapu, displaying an intuitive grasp of tactics, had deployed his troops behind a triple line of trenches, forming a crescent to envelop the advancing invaders. He had also stationed himself and his bodyguard behind the deepest part of the crescent, out of the Spaniards' range. If they wanted him, they would have to come after him. Magellan's experience dictated a prudent withdrawal, but after all his grandiloquence that would mean a shaming loss of face. Instead he issued the command to open fire. Those seamen trained in the use of harquebuses and crossbows responded as best they could, but their ragged volley accomplished nothing. None of the balls, bolts, and arrows reached the mini-rajah, and the rest of them rattled ineffectively off the wooden shields of his men. According to Pigafetta, who was to remain with his capitán-general until the end, the noise of the muskets at first frightened the defenders into backing away, but the respite was brief. Magellan, "wishing to reserve the ammunition for a later stage of the encounter," in Don Antonio's words, called out, "¡Alto el fuego!" — "Cease fire!" — "but," Pigafetta continues, "his order was disregarded in the confusion. When the islanders realized that our fire was doing them little or no harm, they ceased to retire. Shouting more and more loudly, and jumping from side to side to disconcert our aim, they advanced simultaneously, under cover of their shields, assailing us with arrows, javelins . . . stones, and even filth, so that we were scarcely able to defend ourselves. Some of them began to throw lances with brazen points against our captain."

The landing party advanced until Magellan realized that the natives were trying to draw them into a trap. In an attempt to panic the enemy, he sent a small party to fire a nearby village. "This," Don Antonio writes, "only increased their ferocity." Actually it was worse than that. The party was cut off, and despite

their armor all of them — including Serrano's son-in-law — were
speared to death. Alarmed at last, the capitán-general ordered a
withdrawal to the boats. He handled it skillfully, dividing his
vastly outnumbered party in half, one half to hold the spearmen
at bay while the others recrossed the ditches. All went well until,
negotiating the last trench, they struck a snag and were held up.
Lapulapu scented triumph. Splitting his own force, he sent men
racing around both Spanish flanks in a bold attempt to cut them
off before they could reach the bateaux.

It was at that point that Magellan paid the ultimate price for
having left his marines behind. Discipline in the landing force
disintegrated; nearly forty of his men broke for the sea. They
lurched across the coral, reached the boats, and cowered there,
leaving their embattled leader to fight his last, terrible fight with
a loyal remnant: Don Antonio and a handful of others. The uneven
struggle lasted over an hour and was fought out in full view of a
floating, mesmerized, horrified, but largely immobile audience:
the rajah-king of Cebu, Prince Lumai, the Cacique Zula, the other
baptized chieftains in the balangays, and the timorous men in the
bateaux. The newly converted Filipinos awaited divine intervention by the Madonna, the saints, Our Lady of Victory, or Jesus
Christ himself. It never came. Ferdinand Magellan, Knight Commander of the Order of Santiago and emissary of His Christian
Majesty of Spain, had no miracles left. Toward the end a small
band of his new Christians, Cebu warriors unable to endure the
awful spectacle, landed on Mactan to rescue their godfather, but
the moment they were ashore a Spanish gunner out in the armada,
where no one had stirred till now, fired a medieval culverin at the
beach. Castilian luck being what it was that Saturday, the wild
shot scored a direct hit on the rescuers, killing four instantly and
dispersing the others.

But it took a lot to kill the capitán-general. A poisoned arrow
struck his unarmored right foot; reaching down, he ripped it out
and fought on. He and his embattled band were knee deep in surf
now, showered by stones, sod, and spears — Pigafetta writes that
the natives would retrieve the spears and hurl the same one five
or six times. Twice Magellan's helmet was knocked off; twice his
men recovered and replaced it. Then he was speared in the face.

Half blinded by his own blood, he slew his attacker with his lance, but the weight of the falling spearman wrenched the lance from his grip. Empty-handed, he started to draw his sword and found he couldn't; an earlier wound had severed the muscles in his sword arm. Seeing him helpless, Lapulapu's warriors closed in. All but four of Magellan's men were dead. The survivors tried to cover him with their bucklers, but a native wielding a long *terzado* — a scimitar — slashed beneath the shields, laying Magellan's game leg open. As he fell face downward in the water, Pigafetta, bleeding himself from an arrow, saw a dozen warriors "rush upon him with iron and bamboo spears and with their cutlasses, until they killed our mirror, our light and comfort, and our true guide." Somehow Don Antonio, Enrique, and the two others fought free. "Beholding him dead," Don Antonio writes, "we, being wounded, retreated as best we could to the boats, which were already pulling off."

Nothing of Magellan's person survived. That afternoon the grieving rajah-king, hoping to recover his remains, offered Mactan's victorious chief a handsome ransom of copper and iron for them. Lapulapu was elated; he had not possessed so much wealth in his lifetime. However, he was unable to produce the body. He could not find it. He searched; accompanied by a delegation from

The death of Magellan

Cebu, he and his warriors carefully examined the shallow surf
where Magellan had thrashed his last. The corpses of the other
victims lay where they had fallen among the battlefield debris —
arrows, discarded spears, fragments of armor — but that was all.
None of the capitán-general's parts turned up; no shred of flesh
or tissue, no shard of bone. The only explanation, as inescapable
as it is gruesome, is that Mactan's defenders, in their murderous
fever, literally tore him apart, and the sea, which had brought him
so far, bore his blood away. Since his wife and child died in Seville
before any member of the expedition could return to Spain, it
seemed that every evidence of Ferdinand Magellan's existence had
vanished from the earth.

IT WAS ILLUSION. His life had ended, but his voyage had not. To
be sure, its next few days were shaky. The magic nimbus which
had clothed the Spaniards in glory was gone, as dead as their
commander. The disgraceful behavior of the men who had fled
to the boats, abandoning their leader, left an unpleasant aftertaste
among Filipinos, but there was another reason for their disen-
chantment. After the chaplain's memorial service for him, the
armada's prurient seamen, insensitive to their loss, continued to
wear out their welcome by impregnating Filipino females. Long
afterward one member of the armada's crews, a Genoese, was
asked why the Visayan people had turned against them. He replied:
"Violation of the women was the main trouble."

The revulsion was felt on all levels of native life. In a particularly
striking act of backsliding, Cebu's rajah reverted to paganism and
deceit. On the Thursday following the tragic and pointless battle,
Humabon, as he again called himself, sent a message to the fleet.
Twenty-nine Spaniards — the best officers and most skillful pilots — were invited to dine ashore with him. According to Don
Antonio, who declined to attend, two of the guests, growing
suspicious, slipped away from the feast and returned to their ships.
They had thereby saved their lives; the others, including Duarte
Barbosa and Serrano, were cruelly slain. Terrified, the crews
aboard *Trinidad, Victoria,* and *Concepción* fled with the tide, blindly
groping their way through the archipelago. Off the Philippine
island of Bohol, between Cebu and Mindanao, the three galleons

became two. *Concepción* was leaking badly, and since there weren't enough seamen to nurse her along — since its departure from Sanlúcar the flota had lost 150 men — she was set afire and sunk.

On November 6, 1521, after four months of wandering through the Indonesian islands, *Victoria* reached the Moluccas. There she was joined by *Trinidad* — Magellan's flagship. But *Trinidad* would never again see European waters. She was on her last legs. It was not for lack of seamanship. Her captain now was Gómez de Espinosa, who had been Magellan's point man in suppressing the San Julián mutiny nineteen months earlier. But Gómez was luckless now. After sailing northward to a point off Hokkaido — trying to reach Panama — the capitán-general's old flagship was first driven south by high winds, then pursued by a Portuguese fleet. António de Brito, the fleet's commander, had heard of Magellan's expedition but not his death. He wanted to arrest him and clap him in irons. Finally cornering *Trinidad* in Ternate, in the Moluccas, he impounded her papers and stripped her of sails and gear. During a squall she "broke up," Morison notes, "and became a total loss." Brito's report to Lisbon testifies to the cruelty of the age. He had beheaded one member of *Trinidad*'s crew — because the man was Portuguese, he declared, he was a deserter — and had considered putting all the ship's complement to the sword. Instead, he wrote, "I detained them in Maluco because it is an unhealthy country, with the intention of having them die there." Something like that happened; only four of *Trinidad*'s crewmen survived and eventually made it back to Europe.

Victoria, more fit, sailed homeward carrying twenty-six tons of spices in her hold. It was the expedition's penultimate irony that her captain was Juan Sebastián del Cano, who, a year and a half earlier, had been among the leaders of the San Julián mutiny. He and his pilot, Francisco Albo, completed the expedition's circling of the globe. They did it superbly. Unlike Magellan, they faced no unknown waters; the seas beyond their prow were familiar and charted. There was, however, a challenge of another sort. Because her sails bore the royal cross of Castile and Aragon, *Victoria* was a fair prize for the Portuguese, and Manuel's empire had become so huge that Cano and Albo, sailing halfway round the world, had to avoid all ports of call in Malacca, the Indies,

Africa, and Mozambique. The Cape Verde Islands — known as
Ilhas do Cabo Verde since becoming part of the Portuguese royal
domain in 1495 — should also be avoided if at all possible. All
hands, according to Pigafetta, took a vow to die rather than fall
into the hands of the Portuguese (*"Ma inanti determinamo tutti morir
che andar in mano dei Portoghesi"*).

For the pilot this meant plotting one long detour after another
in a shaky, battered, worm-eaten ship reeking of decay; a listing
wreck of groaning timbers taking in water from every seam,
manned by sickly figures as they crept across the Indian Ocean,
round the tip of Africa, and, in extremis, up Africa's west coast —
altogether, a voyage of 17,800 excruciating miles, the longest leg
of the 39,300 miles covered by the expedition.* During their eight
months of agony nineteen sailors perished. The crew was reduced
to eighteen skeletal phantoms, all that remained of the 265 men
who had left Spain three years earlier. After a hairbreadth escape
from the Iberian enemy at Santiago, in the Cape Verde Islands —
they pretended they were returning from America — lookouts
sighted Cape St. Vincent on September 4, 1522. *Victoria* reached
Sanlúcar four days later, and then ended the voyage in triumph,
sailing up the Guadalquivir to Seville.

Long ago the Andalusians had given up the Armada de Molucca
for lost. Now its survivors were hailed for achieving, in the words
of one of their countrymen, "the most wonderful and greatest
thing that has ever happened in the world since God created it."
Waterfront landsmen tried to fathom what the emaciated crewmen, calling down to them from *Victoria*'s decks, meant when
they said that their cannons, now saluting the white bell tower of
Seville's La Giralda, had also been fired to celebrate the discoveries
of Magellan's Strait, the Pacific Ocean, and the Philippines. News
of their return rapidly spread across the city, across Spain, across
Europe. And now came the expedition's final cruel irony. In Valladolid Charles V, having returned from the unpleasantness with
Luther at Worms, was pleased to receive, and honor, the last
commander of the voyage's last ship — a man who, had he had

---

*Comparable distances: Columbus's first crossing, 3,900 miles; Liverpool to New
York, 3,576 miles; San Francisco to Yokohama, 5,221 miles.

his way in Puerto San Julián on April 2, 1520, would have over-thrown Magellan even before the fleet had reached the strait.

The canonization of Juan Sebastián del Cano arose from no misunderstanding. Over a year earlier *San Antonio*, conned by the treacherous Estevão Gomes and his partners in crime, had returned to Seville, where the authorities had convened a royal commission of inquiry. The renegades, assuming that the armada's remaining vessels had sunk with the loss of all hands, had their tale ready. The gist of it was that they had sailed away from Magellan after discovering that he was planning to betray his command to the Portuguese. Believing it their duty to resist, they testified, they had saved *San Antonio* by overpowering its captain — Magellan's cousin Álvaro de Mesquita — and returning home. Magellan's discovery of the strait had been unmentioned. There was a vague reference to the expedition's entering a bay (*"entraron en una bahía"*), but they had then sworn that his search for a paso had been futile (*"inútil sin provecho"*).

Unconvinced, the commissioners had withheld final judgment pending further news of the flota — meanwhile imprisoning, of all people, Captain Mesquita. Now that the truth was available to them, they released Mesquita and awarded him reparations. The doom of the traitors seemed certain. Logically, the next step should have been an investigation of the earlier mutiny, in which Cano had been their accomplice. It was never taken. He shielded them, and his word was enough, for tarnishing his new image was un-thinkable. Castile's powerful dons had faced a choice between lionizing the capitán-general and honoring the man who had brought the armada's last ship home. They reached their decision swiftly. The leader of the expedition was now merely a dead Portuguese. Cano, on the other hand, was not only a Spaniard, and very much alive; he was also a member of a noble Basque family. Therefore it was his name, not Magellan's, which was heard everywhere, exalted and aggrandized.

The emperor, displaying the same ineptness which had distin-guished his imperial performance at Worms, directed the farce. Summoning Cano to his court, he knighted him, granted him an annual pension of five hundred gold ducats, and presented him with a meretricious coat of arms on which the inscription *Primus circumdedisti me* (Thou first circumnavigated me) encircled a globe — thereby giving him full credit for all the capitán-general's achievements. What made all this particularly shameless was that Francisco Albo, whose logs contained the truth, and without whom *Victoria* could not have found safe harbor, had accompanied Cano to Valladolid. Afterward Antonio Pigafetta had also been received at the court; as a Venetian of noble birth, he could not be ignored. During the audience he had unwisely presented Charles with the holograph original of his shipboard diary. He never saw it again. Fortunately he had made a copy.

Magellan's name, when it was mentioned at all, was spoken almost with disdain. Before sailing he had left a will, but none of its beneficiaries — the poor, prisoners, those in the care of monasteries and infirmaries — received a single Spanish maravedi. In Seville he was survived only by his father-in-law, Diego Barbosa, who, having lost two of his children and a grandson to Magellan, cursed the day he had met him. Cano's advertisers seemed triumphant. It seems never to have occurred to them that history could not be so easily manipulated — that eventually Don Antonio, the other survivors, and the extant logs and records of the voyage would expose them, as in time they did. Nevertheless the most barefaced lies die hard when influence and prejudice have a vested interest in them. Even after true accounts of those three years had appeared and been verified, skepticism flourished. In Castile the feats of the world's greatest explorer continued to be distorted. His accomplishments were belittled, attributed to others, or, as in the case of the evangelistic obsession which marked his last days, mocked. It was said of the Philippines that he had found them pagan, left them pagan, and by his blundering had assured that they would remain pagan. In Spain the memory of this cruel sally died long before the century ended. Priests in the islands, however, savor it as the culminating Magellan irony, for there the crude Madonna and child which he presented to Rajah Humabon's first wife may still be found, reverently preserved, and there 60 million Filipinos — 85 percent of the population — are Roman Catholics.

SOME TWENTY-FIVE degrees from the south celestial pole two luminous galaxies, easily visible to the naked eye, span the night sky. These companions of the Milky Way are the Magellanic Clouds, trails of glory which arouse awe, give the heavens grandeur, and testify to the immensity of the universe. So high are they that their distance can be grasped only by a mighty sweep of the imagination. A ray of starlight from there, traveling at its speed of over 186,291 miles per second — 6 trillion miles a year — cannot become visible on earth for 160,000 years. Thus the illumination which was leaving the Clouds when Magellan emerged from his strait and crossed the Pacific will not reach this planet for another 1,595 centuries, a cosmic perspective which would have pleased him, as, say, the Magellan Project of NASA's Jet Propulsion Laboratory would not. The capitán-general believed in divine mysteries. He would have had little patience with technologists who poach on territory sovereign to God.

He was not the wisest man of his time. Erasmus was. Neither was he the most gifted. That, surely, was Leonardo. But Magellan became what, as a child, he had yearned to be — the era's greatest hero. The reason is intricate, but important to understand. Heroism is often confused with physical courage. In fact the two are very different. There was nothing heroic about Magellan's death. He went into that last darkness a seasoned campaigner, accompanied by his own men, and he was completely fearless because as he drew his last breath he believed — indeed *knew* — that paradise was imminent. Similarly, the soldier who throws himself on a live grenade, surrendering his life to save his comrades, may be awarded the medal of honor. Nevertheless his deed, being impulsive, is actually unheroic. Such acts, no more reflective than the swift withdrawal of a blistered hand from a red-hot stove, are involuntary. Heroism is the exact opposite — always deliberate, never mindless.

Neither, if it is valor of the first water, may it be part of a group endeavor. All movements, including armies, provide their participants with such tremendous support that pursuit of common goals, despite great risk, is little more than ardent conformity. Indeed, the truly brave member is the man who repudiates the communal objective, challenging the rest of the group outright. Since no such discordant note was ever heard around the Round Table, young Magellan, in his enchantment with the tales of

Arthur, Lancelot du Lac, and Gawain, was being gulled. It follows that generals, presidents — all leaders backed by blind masses — are seldom valiant, though interesting exceptions occasionally emerge. Politicians who defy their constituents over matters of principle, knowing they will be driven from office, qualify as heroic. So, to cite a rare military instance, did General MacArthur when, protesting endless casualty lists with no prospect of an armistice, he sacrificed his career and courted disgrace.

The hero acts alone, without encouragement, relying solely on conviction and his own inner resources. Shame does not discourage him; neither does obloquy. Indifferent to approval, reputation, wealth, or love, he cherishes only his personal sense of honor, which he permits no one else to judge. La Rochefoucauld, not always a cynic, wrote of him that he does "without witnesses what we would be capable of doing before everyone." Guided by an inner gyroscope, he pursues his vision single-mindedly, undiscouraged by rejections, defeat, or even the prospect of imminent death. Few men can even comprehend such fortitude. Virtually all crave some external incentive: the appreciation of peers, the possibility of exculpation, the promise of retroactive affection, the hope of rewards, applause, decorations — of emotional reparations in some form. Because these longings are completely normal, only a man with towering strength of character can suppress them.

In the long lists of history it is difficult to find another figure whose heroism matches Magellan's. For most sixteenth-century Europeans his *Vorstellung* — to circle the globe — was unimaginable. To launch the pursuit of this vision, he had to turn his back on his own country, inviting charges of treason. His ships, when they were delivered to him, were unseaworthy. Before his departure Portuguese agents repeatedly tried, with some success, to sabotage his expedition. When he did sail, his hodgepodge crews couldn't even communicate in the same tongue, and the background of the captains assigned to him almost guaranteed mutiny and treachery, which indeed followed. Unable even to confide in anyone else after his crushing disappointment at the Río de la Plata, he stubbornly continued his search for the strait he alone believed in, and when he had at last found it, deserters fled with his largest ship and the bulk of the fleet's provisions. Of his other four vessels, three could not complete the voyage. During the armada's crossing of the Pacific, an epic of fortitude, it was its commander's inflexible will which fueled morale and stamina. His discovery of the Philippines dwarfed his original goal — the Moluccas — and he died trying to bring them into the modern age.

The shabby circumstances of his death are troubling, representing flagrant deviance from his code of conduct. They may be partly explained by his exhilaration after sailing around the world, and partly by the fact that, living in a God-ridden age, he was distorted by its imperatives. Yet the distortion in him was slight when measured against other chief figures of his time. The hands of contemporary popes, kings, and reformers were drenched with innocent blood. His were spotless. Granted that his misjudgments on Mactan were unworthy of him, the fact remains that few men have paid so high a price for their lapses. He lost not only his life, but, of even greater moment, the triumphant completion of his voyage and vindication in his time.

His character was, of course, imperfect. But heroes need not be admirable, and indeed most have not been. The web of driving traits behind their accomplishments almost assures that. Men who do the remarkable — heroic and otherwise — frequently fail in their personal relationships. This unpleasant reality is usually glossed over in burnishing the images of the great. So many eminent statesmen, writers, painters, and composers have been intolerable sons, husbands, fathers, and friends that they may fairly be said to have been the rule. Lincoln's marriage was a disaster. Franklin Roosevelt, to put it in the kindest possible way, was a dissembler.

They were achievers. Genuine paladins are even likelier to have been objectionable. Yet their flaws, though deplorable, are irrelevant; in the end their heroism shines through untarnished. Had Ferdinand Magellan met Jesus Christ, the Galilean might have felt a pang of disappointment — which the capitán-general might have shared — but Magellan, like Christ, was also a hero. He still is. He always will be. Of all the tributes to him, therefore, the

Magellanic Clouds are the most appropriate. Like them, his memory shines down upon the world his voyage opened, illuminating it from infinity to eternity.

THE STARS had always been there, grazing the firmament, living sapphires in the great overarching vault of heaven, assuring the faithful that miserable though their present existence might be, there was hope of salvation, for somewhere beyond the magical sky lay paradise, awaiting the chosen. Believers in this tripartite universe knew after passing through purgatory — a temporary abode, unmentioned in the Bible — all souls were destined to dwell either up there in everlasting glory or down below, burning in endless damnation.

All this was thought to be literally true. Public opinion did not exist, even as a concept, but people knew what they had been told, and they cherished the faith which, in most cases, had been their only legacy. Emperors, kings, and princes were entitled to make judgments; the weak endured what they must, humbly grateful to Christ, meek and mild, who had come down to save worthless sinners; to Jesus, who had walked on water, raised the dead, healed the sick, cast out demons, multiplied loaves and fishes, and turned water into wine at Cana; Jesus, their Saviour, their Redeemer, the only begotten son of God Almighty, who dwelt with Him and the Holy Ghost, into whose angelic company any soul, however dim, might be welcomed. Mercy was also the solace of Mary, the mother of Jesus, who could appear at any time among common people, and who was known to have done so on several occasions. Anyone who questioned the Madonna's virginity, or the certainty of postmortem existence, or the meekness and mildness of Christ, went to the stake next morning at dawn, his appeals for last rites denied.

The fear of hell was probably a more effective check to savagery than the prospect of salvation. The point is moot; the certainty of either or the other possessed men from childhood, when they reached the age of awareness, sheathing them in a holy discipline. If evil flourished from time to time on earth, that was merely proof of its existence, reaffirming the credibility of the fallen angel Mephistopheles, the Prince of Darkness, the eternal enemy of both divinity and humanity. And if wickedness was the work of men who wore crowns or miters, that was between them and their maker. God often moved in a mysterious way, his wonders to perform.

In those times the Almighty was not then the benign, remote, almost constitutional monarch He has since become. He was always near, always omnipotent, given to blinding rages and ready to strike in direct and punitive ways. If crops were bountiful, He was rewarding the blameless. If they failed, He was punishing peasants who, though innocent themselves, were children or grandchildren of backsliders. And the stars, His mystical jewels, were nightly evidence of His vigilance and ubiquitousness. It was a star in the east which had led the wise men to the manger where Mary's babe lay, stars which could foretell man's fate, stars which bore profound meanings, for those who could read and interpret changes in the firmament.

Johannes Kepler was one of the great Renaissance astronomers. The discoverer of the three principles of planetary motion, he provided the transition from ancient geometrical description of the skies to modern dynamic astronomy. Yet his first publication, after his appointment as Imperial Mathematician to the Holy Roman Emperor's court in Prague, was *De Fundamentis Astrologine Certioribus* — "The More Certain Basics of Astrology" — in which he endorsed the established view that the lives of men are determined celestially. His astrological forecasts were regarded with awe. He cast the personal horoscopes of Emperor Rudolf II. Even so, in a world ruled by superstition men of science were always suspect. In his early forties, when he was at the peak of his powers, Kepler learned that his mother had been indicted as a witch. He hurried to her side, not sparing his horses, inspired partly by filial duty, no doubt, but also to save his own skin. Indictment was usually followed by torture and the stake. Had his skillful intervention not saved her, he himself would have been a candidate for disgrace, the loss of office, and possibly even a trial before the Inquisition.

Like the monk Cosmas, Babylonian astronomers believed that the world was flat. Homer (*c.* 900–800 B.C.) thought it a convex dish surrounded by the Oceanus stream. Pythagoras (500 B.C.) is believed to have been the first to identify it as a sphere. Hipparchus and Aristotle agreed. Both considered the possibility of a heliocentric system, with the earth moving in orbit round the sun, but dismissed it; neither realized that the stars are suns, not planets. Ptolemy (A.D. 140), enlarging upon the observations of Hipparchus, introduced the revolutionary concert of geocentrism — of a stationary, immovable earth as the center of the universe, with the sun, stars, and planets revolving around it. He devised an elaborate model of the heavens consisting of large and small circles, each tracking a heavenly body. This geocentric view of the cosmos, together with Aristotle's postulate on the fixity of the earth, became entrenched in thought, virtually Christian dogma. Ptolemy was wrong, but he dominated astronomical thinking for over one thousand three hundred years, and his influence on geography lasted even longer.

Although Copernicus saw through the elegant Ptolemaic riddle, his genius was largely unrecognized during his lifetime. He seems to have been excessively cautious. His first scientific paper was published when he was twenty-four, and by his early forties the Vatican was aware of his colleagues' respect for him. However, when he was invited to speak before a Lateran Council on calendar reform, he declined on the ground that he was not ready. After years of mathematical calculations he was convinced that his view of the solar system was correct, yet he made no attempt to publish it. He continued to hesitate, even after the pope formally asked for his conclusions. It was his friends who advanced what came to be called the Copernican Revolution. On May 24, 1543, as he lay dying in Frauenburg, they brought him the first copy of his great work.

Historians, being intellectual themselves, take a profound interest in the reflections and conclusions of learned men in the past. But most men, in any age, are unimpressed by new ideas. Many actually distrust them. In time, compelling thoughts may be translated into action; then they may acquire tremendous force. Einstein's general theories of relativity were a joke to those who did not understand them, but they understood the atomic bomb, and their laughter died with Hiroshima. That time had not arrived for Copernicus in his lifetime. However, Magellan's voyage —

a-way-station on the same journey — had been common knowledge for over twenty years. As an event, not an idea, it had
commanded instant attention; couriers had galloped off to tell the
emperor and the pope.

The wonder came later. Every day during the armada's long
voyage Pigafetta had scrupulously dated each entry in his diary,
beginning with "Tuesday, September 20, 1519." Their return to
Spain, he noted, was on "Saturday, September 6," but the Spaniards ashore shook their heads, insisting that it was Sunday, September 7. Don Antonio checked with Albo, who, on Magellan's
instructions, had also kept a record in his ship's log. Albo agreed.
Clearly all Spain could not be wrong about so simple a fact, so
they were left with a dilemma: somehow the flota had dropped
twenty-four hours out of the calendar. They had just proved
that the world was a sphere, but they were not yet thinking
spherically.

Once they did — once Europe did — the questions began. An
idea had become a fact. Ideas could be explained away, or replaced
with other plausible ideas. Facts were less malleable. And every
answer raised new questions. The survivors of the circumnavigation had discovered people living on the other side of the world
and converted them, thus giving them hope of salvation. But
where was their paradise, and where was Europe's? And where
was the underworld? As explorations continued, other voyagers
returned with tales of distant lands where other men, who had
never heard of the Scriptures, nevertheless believed in different
heavens. Moslems were heathen yet passages in their Koran had
a familiar ring; after death, they believed, all souls passed though
a wretched state, essentially purgatorial, before achieving joy and
bliss. The Chinese had a heaven, too; the Budhists had Nirvana,
the Hindus a bewildering assortment of postmortem Edens, in all
of which fear, suffering, and darkness were unknown. Christianity, it appeared, had much in common with the strange alien
faiths; even the virgin birth was not unique.

Christendom's leaders, both Catholic and Protestant, were
slow to grasp the threat to them; meantime, as the sixteenth
century wore on and became the seventeenth, the menace of
science became a Hydra for them. New men, skilled in mathemat-

ics, were challenging the convictions of millenia. Professor Michael Mästlin at the University of Tübingen had been a student of Copernicus; Kepler, his student, provided mathematical proof that the earth was orbiting the sun while rolling eastward, completing a full cycle every day. Throughout time men had believed that the stars were fixed and changeless; Kepler observed a supernova whose explosions remained visible for seventeen months and then vanished. He also demonstrated that the orbit of Mars is an ellipse, a heresy even among astronomers, who had been taught that planets, being heavenly bodies and therefore perfect, could move only in circles or combinations of circles.

The belief that the sun orbited the earth coexisted with its opposite, even among scientists, until Galileo appeared with his telescope, revealing that geocentrism was dead, that the Aristotelian theory of motion was dead with it, that the earth was not the center of the cosmos, that the universe was boundless and had no center. It was somewhere in all this ferment, around the year 1576, someone realized that the sun itself was a star. Giordano Bruno and Thomas Digges implied it, but the name of the man who grasped it is unknown. The astronomer Arthur Upgren observes that "the recognition of the Sun as a star must be one of the greatest paradigm changes in all of science, and one of the most unappreciated."

Its discovery was inevitable, however, once reason had discredited the Ptolemaic universe. Colin A. Ronan of the Royal Astronomical Society writes: "The dethronement of the earth from the center of the universe caused profound shock. No longer could the earth be considered the epitome of creation . . . And a belief in a correspondence between man, the microcosm, as a mirror of the surrounding universe, the macrocosm, was no longer valid. The successful challenge to the entire system of ancient authority required a complete change in man's philosophical conception of the universe."

It was in fact the crowning triumph of the age, the final, decisive blow to the past. Those with the most to lose denied the discoveries, both terrestrial and ideological, and denounced those who recognized them as heretical. And the pope led the reaction. He would have been extraordinary if it he had not, for that would have been a betrayal of his two hundred and fifty-six predecessors in Saint Peter's chair. The Church had always held that whenever observed experience conflicted with Holy Scripture, observation had to yield. And the authority of the Bible, historically interpreted, denied the possibility of a heliocentric system.

Accordingly, the Holy Office in Rome declared that the notion of a moving earth circling the sun was "philosophically foolish and absurd and formally heretical, inasmuch as it expressly contradicts the doctrines of Holy Scripture in many places, both according to their literal meaning and according to the common exposition and interpretation of the Holy Fathers and learned theologians." Twenty-eight successive pontiffs agreed. It took the Church three hundred years to change its mind. Copernicus's *De revolutionibus* was removed from the Catholic Index in 1758. The ban on Galileo's *Dialogue* continued until 1822, exactly three centuries after Albo's log and Don Antonio's diary had become available to the Holy See.

Nevertheless, patristic obduracy could not resurrect a discredited myth. The power of the medieval mind had been irrevocably broken. Its dogmatism, its infallibility, its absolute lack of ambiguity, were lost. They had already been deeply troubled. The Renaissance, nationalism, humanism, rising literacy, and the new horizons of trade — all these had challenged blind, ritualistic allegiance to the assumptions of a thousand years. But Europe was no longer the world, and the world was no longer the center of the universe. Since the earth was revolving daily, heaven and hell could not be located where they had been thought to be, and in rational minds there was a growing skepticism that either of them existed. Satan without hell was implausible. God without heaven was inconceivable, at least the medieval God was, but here reason ended. Christendom found the prospect of a godless world intolerable. Because faith in a higher power was needed, it would be necessary to find, or even to invent, another Creator, a new King of Kings and Lord of Lords — "*Si Dieu n'existait pas, il faudrait l'inventer,*" (If God did not exist, it would be necessary to invent him"), Voltaire would write in 1770.

He insisted that it was unnecessary. He scorned *l'infâme*, as he called the Church, but not God's existence — "*toute la nature crie qu'il existe.''* Yet he protested too much. Doubt plagued Voltaire. Strong, ardent, and devout men have been struggling with that challenge for nearly five centuries. They have met with varying degrees of success. Worldwide there are now a billion Christians alive. Confidence in an afterlife, however, is another matter. The specter of doubt haunts shrines and altars. Worshippers want to believe, and most of the time they persuade themselves that they do. But suppressing doubt is hard. Secular society makes it harder. Hardest of all is the sense of loss, the knowledge that the serenity of medieval faith, and the certitude of everlasting glory, are forever gone.

ACKNOWLEDGMENTS AND
SOURCES

BIBLIOGRAPHIES are useful guides for readers who want to learn more, but they can be deceptive. Traditional bibliographical structure is sometimes misleading; the order of the works which are cited is determined by the alphabetical order of the first letter in scholars' last names. Furthermore, every entry appears as the equal of every other, which is an affront to common sense. A writer of history may have used only a single anecdote from one source, while another source served as the underpinning of his entire book.

Let me set down those works which have been the underpinning of this volume. First — for their scope and rich detail — are three volumes from Will Durant's eleven-volume *Story of Civilization:* volume 4, *The Age of Faith;* volume 5, *The Renaissance;* and volume 6, *The Reformation.* The events of those twelve centuries, from the sack of Rome in A.D. 410 to the beheading of Anne Boleyn in 1536, emerge from Durant's pages in splendid array.

Another towering monument of historicism is the eight-volumed *The New Cambridge Medieval History,* particularly volume 1, *The Christian Roman Empire and the Foundation of the Teutonic Kingdoms;* volume 5, *Contest of Empire and Papacy;* volume 6, *Victory of the Papacy;* volume 7, *Decline of Empire and Papacy;* and volume 8, *The Close of the Middle Ages.* This great work leads to the equally comprehensive *The New Cambridge Modern History,* fourteen volumes, especially volume 1, *The Renaissance: 1493–1520,* and volume 2, *The Reformation, 1520–1559.* Other general works which I found useful were the three volumes of Sidney Painter's *A History of the Middle Ages, 284–1500,* James Westfall Thompson's two-volume *The Middle Ages, 300–1500,* R.H.C. Davis's popular *A History of Medieval Europe, from Constantine to*

Saint Louis, and *The Dictionary of National Biography, From the Earliest Times to 1900* in twenty-two volumes.

Those who audit the past rarely agree in their interpretations of it. But all writers, though they view history through discrepant prisms, deal with the same facts. In searching for them, the work to which I turned most often is recent: *The New Encyclopaedia Britannica,* the fifteenth edition of the greatest of encyclopedias. As the editors observe in their foreword, the excellence of such a work "rests on the authority of the scholars who wrote the articles." Therefore they recruited the best. The major articles in the *New Britannica* often run to thirty thousand words or more, and their authors are celebrated. Among those whose contributions were of great value to me were Georges Paul Gusdorf of the University of Strasbourg on the history of humanistic scholarship, Roland H. Bainton of Yale on the Reformation, Martin Brett of the University of Auckland on the Middle Ages, the Reverend Ernest Gordon Rupp of Cambridge on Martin Luther and Desiderius Erasmus, his Cambridge colleague Geoffrey R. Elton on King Henry VIII, Colin Alistair Ronan of the Royal Astronomical Society on Copernicus, Robert M. Kingdon of the University of Wisconsin on John Calvin; Michael de Ferdinandy of the University of Puerto Rico on Emperor Charles V, the Reverend Francis Xavier Murphy of Rome on Pope Alexander VI, and Ludwig Heinrich Heydenreich of the University of Munich on Leonardo da Vinci.

Life on a Medieval Barony, which appeared in 1924, was the work of William Stearns Davis, then a professor of history at the University of Wisconsin. Davis was writing about the thirteenth century, but his picture of a medieval community is valid in depicting the fifteenth and sixteenth centuries. I couldn't have recreated medieval Europe without it. It has been a favorite of mine for fifty years.

Two handy reference books — provided they are used with caution — recount the historical past, day by day. They are *The Timetables of History,* by Bernard Grun, and *The People's Chronology,* by James Trager.

MY ASSISTANT, Gloria Cone, has been tireless and loyal, and once more I am grateful for the assistance and support provided by the staff of Wesleyan University's Olin Memorial Library, led by J. Robert Adams, Caleb T. Winchester Librarian. Joan Jurale, the head reference librarian — who stands at the very top of her demanding profession — was especially helpful. So were Edmund A. Rubacha, reference librarian; Susanne Javorski, art librarian; Erhard F. Konerding, documents librarian; and Steven Lebergott, head of interlibrary loans. Others on the Olin staff who were particularly helpful to me were Alan Nathanson, bibliographer, and Ann Frances Wakefield.

Finally, I again express my gratitude to Don Congdon, my literary agent and cherished friend for forty-three years; Roger Donald, my charming, indefatigable editor for seventeen years; and my superb copy editor, Peggy Leith Anderson, who in my long experience is truly without peer.

W.M.

Abram, A. *English Life and Manners in the Later Middle Ages*. London, 1913.
Allen, J. W. *History of Political Thought in the Sixteenth Century*. London, 1951.
Ammianus Marcellinus. *Works*. 2 vols. Trans. John C. Rolfe. Cambridge, Mass., 1935–36.
Armstrong, Edward. *The Emperor Charles V*. 2 vols. London, 1910.
Atkinson, J. *Martin Luther and the Birth of Protestantism*. Baltimore, 1968.
Bainton, R. H. *Erasmus of Christendom*. New York, 1969.
———. *Here I Stand: A Life of Martin Luther*. New York, 1950.
———. *Hunted Heretic: The Life of Michael Servetus*. Boston, 1953.
———. *The Reformation of the Sixteenth Century*. Boston, 1953.
———. *The Travail of Religious Liberty*. Philadelphia, 1951.
Bax, Belfort. *German Society at the Close of the Middle Ages*. London, 1894.
Beard, Charles. *Martin Luther and the Reformation*. London, 1896.
———. *The Reformation of the Sixteenth Century in Relation to Modern Thought and Knowledge*. London, 1885.
Beazley, C. Raymond. *Prince Henry the Navigator: The Hero of Portugal and of Modern Discovery, 1394–1460 A.D.* London, 1901.
Bedoyére, Michel de la. *The Meddlesome Friar and the Wayward Pope: The Story of the Conflict Between Savonarola and Alexander VI*. London, 1958.
Beer, Max. *Social Struggles in the Middle Ages*. London, 1924.
Belloc, Hilaire. *How the Reformation Happened*. London, 1950.
Benesch, Otto. *The Art of the Renaissance in Northern Europe*. Rev. ed. London, 1965.

Benzing, Josef, and Helmut Claus. *Lutherbibliographie. Verzeichnis der gedruckten Schriften Martin Luthers bis zu dessen Tod.* Baden-Baden, 1989.

Berence, Fred. *Lucrèce Borgia.* Paris, 1951.

Beuf, Carlo. *Cesare Borgia, the Machiavellian Prince.* Toronto, 1942.

Boissonnade, Prosper. *Life and Work in Medieval Europe.* New York, 1927.

Bornkamm, Heinrich. *Luthers geistige Welt.* Gütersloh, Germany, 1953.

Brandi, Karl. *The Emperor Charles V: The Growth and Destiny of a Man and a World Empire.* New York, 1939.

Brion, Marcel. *The Medici: A Great Florentine Family.* New York, 1969.

Brown, Norman O. *Life Against Death: The Psychoanalytical Meaning of History.* Middletown, Conn., 1959.

Bruce, Marie Louise. *Anne Boleyn.* New York, 1972.

Bryce, James. *The Holy Roman Empire.* New York, 1921.

Burchard, John. *"Pope Alexander VI and His Court." Extracts from the Latin Diary of the Papal Master of Ceremonies, 1484–1506.* Ed. F. L. Glaser. New York, 1921.

Burckhardt, Jacob. *The Civilization of the Renaissance in Italy.* New York, 1952.

Burnet, Gilbert. *History of the Reformation of the Church of England.* 2 vols. London, 1841.

Burtt, E. A. *A Critical and Comparative Analysis of Copernicus, Kepler, and Descartes.* London, 1924, 1987.

Bury, J. B. *History of the Later Roman Empire.* 2 vols. London, 1923.

Calvesi, Maurizio. *Treasures of the Vatican.* Trans. J. Emmons. Geneva, 1962.

Cambridge Medieval History. 8 vols. New York, 1924–36.

Carlyle, Thomas. *Heroes and Hero Worship.* New York, 1901.

Catholic Encyclopedia, 1907–12, and *New Catholic Encyclopedia,* 1967. New York.

Cellini, Benvenuto. *Autobiography.* New York, 1948.

Chadwick, Owen. *The Reformation.* London, 1964.

Chamberlin, E. R. *The Bad Popes.* New York, 1969.

Chambers, David Sanderson. "The Economic Predicament of Renaissance Cardinals." In W. M. Bowsky, ed., *Studies in Medieval and Renaissance History,* vol. 3. Lincoln, Nebr., 1966.

Clément, H. *Les Borgia. Histoire du pape Alexandre VI, de César et de Lucrèce Borgia.* Paris, 1882.

Cloulas, Ivan. *The Borgias.* Trans. Gilda Roberts. New York, 1989.

Comines, Philippe de. *Memoirs.* 2 vols. London, 1900.

Coughlan, Robert. *The World of Michelangelo: 1475–1564.* New York, 1966.

Coulton, G. G. *The Black Death.* New York, 1930.

———. *Chaucer and His England.* London, 1921.

———. *Inquisition and Liberty.* London, 1938.

———. *Life in the Middle Ages.* 4 vols. Cambridge, England, 1930.

———. *The Medieval Scene.* Cambridge, England, 1930.

———. *The Medieval Village.* Cambridge, England, 1925.

———. *Social Life in Britain from the Conquest to the Reformation.* Cambridge, England, 1938.

Creighton, Mandell. *Cardinal Wolsey.* London, 1888.

———. *History of the Papacy During the Reformation.* 5 vols. London, 1882–94.

Crump, C. G., and Jacob, E. F. *The Legacy of the Middle Ages.* Oxford, 1926.

David, Maurice. *Who Was Columbus?* New York, 1933.

Davis, William Stearns. *Life on a Medieval Barony: A Picture of a Typical Feudal Community in the Thirteenth Century.* New York, 1923.

DeRoo, Peter. *Material for a History of Pope Alexander VI.* 5 vols. Bruges, Belgium, 1924.

DeWulf, Maurice. *History of Medieval Philosophy.* 2 vols. London, 1925.

Dickens, A. G. *The English Reformation.* New York, 1964.

———. *Reformation and Society in Sixteenth-Century Europe.* New York, 1966.

The Dictionary of National Biography, From the Earliest Times to 1900. 22 vols. London, 1967–68.

Dictionnaire de Biographie Française. Paris, 1967.

Dill, John. *Roman Society in the Last Century of the Western Empire.* London, 1905.

Dillenberger, John. *Martin Luther: Selections from His Writings.* New York, 1961.

Dillenberger, John, and Claude Welch. *Protestant Christianity Interpreted Through Its Development.* New York, 1954.

Dizionario Biografico degli Italiani. Rome, 1962.

Dodge, Bertha S. *Quests for Spices and New Worlds.* Hamden, Conn., 1988.

D'Orliac, Jehanne. *The Moon Mistress: Diane de Poitiers.* Philadelphia, 1930.

Duby, Georges. *L'Économie rurale et la vie des campagnes dans l'occident médiéval.* 2 vols. Paris, 1962.

Duhem, Pierre. *Études sur Leonardo de Vinci.* 3 vols. Paris, 1906 f.

Durant, Will. *The Age of Faith.* New York, 1950.

———. *The Reformation.* New York, 1957.

———. *The Renaissance.* New York, 1953.

Ebeling, G. *Luther: An Introduction to His Thought.* Philadelphia, 1970.

Ehrenberg, Richard. *Das Zeitalter der Fugger.* 2 vols. Jena, Germany, 1896.

Enciclopedia Italiana. Rome, 1962.

Erasmus, Desiderius. *Colloquies.* 2 vols. London, 1878.

———. *Education of a Christian Prince.* New York, 1936.

———. *Epistles.* 3 vols. London, 1901.

———. *The Praise of Folly.* Trans. with an introduction and commentary by Clarence H. Miller. New Haven, 1979.

Erikson, E. H. *Young Man Luther: A Study in Psychoanalysis and History.* New York, 1958.

Erlanger, Rachel. *Lucrezia Borgia: A Biography.* New York, 1978.

Farner, O. *Zwingli the Reformer: His Life and Work.* Hamden, Conn., 1964.

Febvre, Lucien, and Henri-Jean Martin. *The Coming of the Book: The Impact of Printing, 1450–1800.* London, 1976.

Ferguson, Wallace. *The Renaissance in Historical Thought.* Boston, 1948.

Ferrara, Oreste. *The Borgia Pope.* Trans. from Spanish. London, 1942.

Flick, A. C. *The Decline of the Medieval Church.* New York, 1930.

Fosdick, H. E. *Great Voices of the Reformation.* New York, 1952.

France, Anatole. *Rabelais.* New York, 1928.

Freeman-Grenville, G.S.P. *Chronology of World History: A Calendar of Principal Events from 3000 B.C. to A.D. 1973.* London, 1975.

Froissart, Sir John. *Chronicles.* 2 vols. London, 1848.

Froude, J. A. *The Divorce of Catherine of Aragon.* New York, 1891.

———. *Life and Letters of Erasmus.* New York, 1894.

———. *Reign of Mary Tudor.* New York, 1910.

Funck-Brentano, Frantz. *Lucrèce Borgia.* Paris, 1932.

———. *The Renaissance.* Trans. New York, 1936.

Fusero, Clemente. *The Borgias*. Trans. Peter Green. New York, 1972.

Gallier, Anatole de. "César Borgia. Documents sur son séjour en France." *Bulletin de la Société d'Archéologie de la Drôme* (Valence, France), vol. 29 (1895).

Gasquet, Francis Cardinal. *Eve of the Reformation*. London, 1927.

————. *Henry VIII and the English Monasteries*. 2 vols. London, 1888.

Gastine, Louis. *César Borgia*. Paris, 1911.

Gibbon, Edward. *Decline and Fall of the Roman Empire*. 6 vols. London, 1900.

Gilbert, W. *Lucrezia Borgia, Duchess of Ferrara*. London, 1869.

Gilmore, Myron P. *The World of Humanism, 1453–1517*. New York, 1958.

Gilson, Étienne. *History of Christian Philosophy in the Middle Ages*. New York, 1955.

————. *Reason and Revelations in the Middle Ages*. New York, 1938.

Glück, Gustav. *Die Kunst der Renaissance in Deutschland*. Berlin, 1928.

Gordon, A. *The Lives of Pope Alexander VI and His Son Cesare Borgia*. Philadelphia, 1844.

Graff, Harvey J., ed. *Literacy and Social Development in the West: A Reader*. Cambridge, England, 1981.

Graves, F. P. *Peter Ramus*. New York, 1912.

Green, Mrs. J. R. *Town Life in the Fifteenth Century*. 2 vols. New York, 1907.

Grun, Bernhard. *The Timetables of History*. New York, 1975.

Guicciardini, Francesco. *The History of Italy*. Trans. S. Alexander. New York, 1969.

Guillemard, Francis Henry Hill. *The Life of Ferdinand Magellan and the First Circumnavigation of the Globe*. London, 1890.

Hackett, Francis. *Francis I*. New York, 1935.

Hale, J. R. *Machiavelli and Renaissance Italy*. New York, 1960.

————. *Renaissance Europe: 1480–1520*. Berkeley, 1971.

Haller, Johannes. *Die Epochen der deutschen Geschichte*. Stuttgart, 1928.

Hanson, Earl P., ed. *South from the Spanish Main: South America Seen Through the Eyes of Its Discoverers*. New York, 1967.

Hearnshaw, F. J., ed. *Medieval Contributions to Modern Civilization*. New York, 1922.

Henderson, E. F. *History of Germany in the Middle Ages*. London, 1894.

Heydenreich, L. H. *Leonardo da Vinci*. 2 vols. New York, 1954.

Hildebrand, Arthur Sturges. *Magellan*. New York, 1924.

Hillerbrand, Hans J. *The World of the Reformation*. New York, 1973.

Hughes, Philip. *A History of the Church*. Vol. 3. New York, 1947.

————. *The Reformation in England*. 2 vols. London, 1950–54.

Huizinga, Johan. *Erasmus*. Trans., 3rd ed. New York, 1952.

————. *Erasmus and the Age of the Reformation*. Trans. New York, 1957.

————. *Men and Ideas*. New York, 1959.

————. *The Waning of the Middle Ages*. New York, 1954.

James, William. *Varieties of Religious Experience*. New York, 1935.

Janelle, Pierre. *La crise religieuse du XVIe siècle*. Paris, 1950.

Janssen, Johannes. *History of the German People at the Close of the Middle Ages*. 16 vols. St. Louis, n.d.

Jordanes. *Gothic History of Jordanes in English Version* [De origine actibus Getarum, sixth century]. Princeton, 1915.

Joyner, Timothy. *Magellan*. Camden, Maine, 1992.

Jusserand, J. J. *English Wayfaring Life in the Middle Ages*. London, 1891.

Kamen, H. *The Spanish Inquisition.* London, 1965.

Kern, Fritz. *Kingship and Law in the Middle Ages.* Oxford, 1939.

Kesten, Hermann. *Copernicus and His World.* New York, 1945.

Knowles, David. *The Christian Centuries.* Vol. 2 in *The Middle Ages.* New York, 1968.

———. *The Monastic Order in England.* 2nd ed. Cambridge, England, 1963.

Lacroix, Paul. *Histoire de la prostitution . . . .* 4 vols. Brussels, 1861.

———. *Manners, Customs, and Dress During the Middle Ages.* New York, 1876.

Landes, David. *Revolution in Time.* Cambridge, Mass., 1983.

La Sizeranne, R. de. *César Borgia et le duc d'Urbino.* Paris, 1924.

Lea, Henry C. *History of the Inquisition of the Middle Ages.* 3 vols. New York, 1888.

———. *Studies in Church History.* Philadelphia, 1883.

Ledderhose, C. F. *Life of Philip Melanchthon.* Philadelphia, 1855.

Lehmann-Haupt, Hellmut. *Gutenberg und der Meister der Spielkarten.* New Haven, Conn., 1962.

Lester, Charles Edwards. *The Life and Voyages of Americus Vespucius.* New York, 1846.

Levy, R. *César Borgia.* Paris, 1930.

Lortz, J. *Die Reformation in Deutschland.* 2 vols. Friebert im Breisgan, 1965.

———. *How the Reformation Came.* Trans. New York, 1964.

Louis, Paul. *Ancient Rome at Work.* New York, 1927.

Luther, Martin. *An den christlichen Adel deutscher Nation von des christlichen standes besserung.* Halle, Germany, 1847.

———. *Works of Martin Luther.* The Philadelphia Edition, with an introduction and notes. Philadelphia, 1930.

McCabe, Joseph. *Crises in the History of the Papacy.* New York, 1916.

McCurdy, Edward, ed. *The Notebooks of Leonardo da Vinci.* 2 vols. New York, 1938.

Machiavelli, Niccolò. *Il principe.* Trans. with an introduction by Harvey C. Mansfield, Jr. Chicago, 1985.

McNally, Robert E., S.J. *Reform of the Church.* New York, 1963.

Madariaga, Salvador de. *Christopher Columbus.* London, 1949.

Maitland, S. R. *Essays on the Reformation.* London, 1849.

Mallett, Michael. *The Borgias: The Rise and Fall of a Renaissance Dynasty.* New York, 1969.

Malory, Sir Thomas. *Le morte d'Arthur.* London, 1927.

Manschreck, C. L. *Melanchthon: The Quiet Reformer.* New York, 1958.

Mattingly, Garret. *Catherine of Aragon.* London, 1942.

Maulde La Clavière, R. De. *The Women of the Renaissance.* New York, 1905.

Meyer, Conrad F. *Huttens letzte Tage.* Vol. 8. Bern, Switzerland, 1871.

Michelet, Jules. *History of France.* 2 vols. New York, 1880.

Monter, E. William. *Calvin's Geneva.* New York, 1967.

Morison, Samuel Eliot. *Admiral of the Ocean Sea: A Life of Christopher Columbus.* 2 vols. Boston, 1942.

———. *The European Discovery of America: The Northern Voyages.* New York, 1971.

———. *The European Discovery of America: The Southern Voyages.* New York, 1974.

Müntz, Eugène. *Leonardo da Vinci.* 2 vols. London, 1898.

Murray, Robert H. *Erasmus and Luther*. London, 1920.

The New Cambridge Medieval History. 8 vols. Cambridge, England, 1924–36.

The New Cambridge Modern History. 14 vols. Cambridge, England, 1957–79.

Nichols, J. H. *Primer for Protestants*. New York, 1947.

Oberman, Heiko Augustinus. *The Harvest of Medieval Theology: Gabriel Biel and Late Medieval Nominalism*. Cambridge, Mass., 1967.

Olin, John C. *The Catholic Reformation: Savonarola to Ignatius Loyola, 1495–1540*. New York, 1969.

Ollivier, M.I.H. *Le Pape Alexander VI et les Borgia*. Paris, 1870.

O'Malley, John. *Praise and Blame in Rome: Renaissance Rhetoric, Doctrine and Reform in the Sacred Orators of the Papal Court, 1450–1521*. Durham, N.C., 1972.

Painter, Sidney. *A History of the Middle Ages, 284–1500*. New York, 1953.

Panofsky, Erwin. *Albrecht Dürer*. 2 vols. Princeton, 1948.

Parr, Charles McKew. *So Noble a Captain: The Life and Times of Ferdinand Magellan*. New York, 1953.

Parry, J. H. *The Age of Reconnaissance*. London, 1963.

Partner, Peter. "The Budget of the Roman Church in the Renaissance Period." In E. F. Jacob, ed., *Italian Renaissance Studies*. London, 1960.

Pastor, Ludwig von. *The History of the Popes, from the Close of the Middle Ages*. 2nd ed., vols. 5–9. Ed. by F. I. Antrobus and R. F. Kerr. Trans. from German. St. Louis, 1902–10.

Penrose, Boies. *Travel and Discovery in the Renaissance, 1420–1620*. Cambridge, Mass., 1963.

Philips, J.R.S. *The Medieval Expansion of Europe*. New York, 1988.

Pigafetta, Antonio. *Le voyage et navigation faict par les Espaignols*. Trans. Paula Spurlin Paige. Ann Arbor, Mich., 1969.

Pirenne, Henri. *Medieval Cities*. Princeton, 1925.

Pollard, A. F. *Henry VIII*. London, 1925.

Polnitz, Gotz von. *Die Fugger*. 3d ed. Frankfurt am Main, Germany, 1970.

Poole, R. L. *Illustrations of the History of Medieval Thought and Learning*. New York, 1920.

Portigliatti, Giuseppe. *The Borgias. Alexander VI, Cesare and Lucrezia*. Trans. from Italian. London, 1928.

Post, Regnerus Richardus. *The Modern Devotion: Confrontation with Reformation and Humanism*. Leiden, Holland, 1968.

Prescott, W. H. *History of the Reign of Ferdinand and Isabella, the Catholic*. 2 vols. Philadelphia, 1890.

Prezzolini, Giuseppe. *Machiavelli*. New York, 1967.

Rabelais, François. *Gargantua; Pantagruel*. Paris, 1939.

Ranke, Leopold von. *History of the Popes . . . in the Sixteenth and Seventeenth Centuries*. 3 vols. Trans. London, 1847.

———. *History of the Reformation in Germany*. London, 1905.

Rashdall, Hastings. *Universities of Europe in the Middle Ages*. 3 vols. Oxford, 1936.

Reynolds, E. E. *The Field Is Won: The Life and Death of Saint Thomas More*. London and New York, 1968.

Richard, Ernst. *History of German Civilization*. New York, 1911.

Richepin, Jean. *Les debuts de César Borgia*. Paris, 1891.

Richter, Jean P. *The Literary Works of Leonardo da Vinci*. 2 vols. London, 1970.

Robertson, Sir Charles G. *Caesar Borgia*. Oxford, 1891.

Robertson, J. M. *Short History of Freethought*. 2 vols. London, 1914.

Robertson, William. *History of the Reign of Charles V*. 2 vols. London, 1878.

Roper, William. *Life of Sir Thomas More.* In More, *Utopia.* New York, n.d.

Roscoe, William. *The Life and Pontificate of Leo X.* 2 vols. London, 1853.

Rosen, Edward, ed. *Three Copernican Treatises.* New York, 1939.

Rostovtzeff, M. *History of the Ancient World.* Vol. 2 in *Social and Economic History of the Roman Empire.* Oxford, 1926.

Routh, C.R.N., ed. *They Saw It Happen in Europe, 1450–1600.* Oxford, 1965.

Rupp, E. G., and B. Drewery, eds. *Martin Luther.* London, 1970.

Rupp, E. G., and P. S. Watson, eds. *Luther and Erasmus.* Philadelphia, 1969.

Ruppel, Aloys Leonhard. *Johannes Gutenberg: Sein Leben und sein Werk.* Nieuwkoop, Netherlands, 1967.

Russell, Josiah Cox. *The Control of Late Ancient and Medieval Population.* Philadelphia, 1985.

Sabatini, Rafael. *The Life of Cesare Borgia.* London, 1912.

Scarisbrick, J. J. *Henry VIII.* London, 1968.

Schaff, David S. *History of the Christian Church.* Vol. 6. Grand Rapids, Mich., 1910.

Schoenhof, Jacob. *History of Money and Prices.* New York, 1896.

Scholderer, Victor. *Johann Gutenberg.* London, 1963.

Scott, William B. *Albert Dürer.* London, 1869.

Smith, Preserved. *The Age of the Reformation.* New York, 1920.

———. *Erasmus: A Study of His Life, Ideals and Place in History.* New York, 1923.

———. *The Life and Letters of Martin Luther.* Boston and New York, 1911.

Southern, Richard W. *The Making of the Middle Ages.* London and New York, 1953.

———. *Western Society and the Church in the Middle Ages.* England, 1970.

Spinka, Matthew. *John Hus: A Biography.* Princeton, 1968.

Stanley, Henry Edway John of Alderley, Lord, ed. *The First Voyage Around the World by Magellan.* London, 1874.

———. *The Three Voyages of Vasco da Gama.* New York, 1963.

Stephen, Sir Leslie, and Sir Sidney Lee. *The Dictionary of National Biography.* Oxford, 1917–.

Strauss, D. F. *Ulrich von Hutten.* London, 1874.

Symonds, J. A. *The Catholic Reaction.* 2 vols. London, 1914.

Taylor, Henry Osborne. *The Mediaeval Mind: A History of the Development of Thought and Emotion in the Middle Ages.* 2 vols. 4th ed. Cambridge, Mass., 1959.

Todd, John M. *The Reformation.* New York, 1971.

Trager, James, ed. *The People's Chronology.* New York, 1979.

Trevelyan, George M. *English Social History.* London, 1947.

Truc, G. *Rome et les Borgias.* Paris, 1939.

Tuchman, Barbara W. *The March of Folly: From Troy to Vietnam.* New York, 1984.

Turner, E. S. *History of Courting.* New York, 1955.

Tyler, Royall. *The Emperor Charles V.* Princeton, 1956.

Ullman, Walter. *The Growth of Papal Government in the Middle Ages.* London, 1965.

———. *A Short History of the Papacy in the Middle Ages.* London, 1972.

Usher, Abbot P. *History of Mechanical Inventions.* New York, 1929.

Vacandard, Elphège. *The Inquisition.* New York, 1908.

Vanderlinden, H. "Alexander VI and the Demarcation of the Maritime and

Colonial Domains of Spain and Portugal." *American Historical Review*, vol. 22 (1917).

Villari, Pasquale. *Life and Times of Niccolò Machiavelli.* 2 vols. New York, n.d.

Waas, Glenn E. *The Legendary Character of Kaiser Maximilian.* New York, 1941.

Waliszewski, Kazimierz. *Ivan the Terrible.* Philadelphia, 1904.

Walker, Williston. *John Calvin.* New York, 1906.

———. *John Calvin: The Organizer of Reformed Protestantism, 1509–1564.* New York, 1969.

Weber, Max. *The Protestant Ethic and the Spirit of Capitalism.* London, 1948.

Wendel, François. *Calvin: The Origin and Development of His Religious Thought.* London and New York, 1963.

Williams, G. H. *The Radical Reformation.* Philadelphia, 1962.

Winchester, Simon. "The Strait — and Dire Straits — of Magellan." *Smithsonian*, vol. 22, no. 1 (April 1991).

Woltmann, Alfred. *Holbein and His Times.* London, 1872.

Woodward, W. H. *Cesare Borgia.* London, 1913.

Wright, Thomas. *History of Domestic Manners and Sentiments in England During the Middle Ages.* London, 1862.

Yriarte, Charles. *César Borgia.* Paris, 1889.

Zeeden, E. W. *Luther und die Reformation.* 2 vols. Freiburg, Germany, 1950–52.

Zweig, Stefan. *Conqueror of the Seas: The Story of Magellan.* Trans. Eden and Cedar Paul. New York, 1938.

INDEX